CAPITALISM, CULTURE, AND DECLINE IN BRITAIN
1750–1990

CAPITALISM, CULTURE, AND DECLINE IN BRITAIN
1750–1990

W. D. Rubinstein

London and New York

First published in 1993
by Routledge
11 New Fetter Lane, London EC4P 4EE

Simultaneously published in the USA and Canada
by Routledge
29 West 35th Street, New York, NY 10001

Reprinted 1993 (twice)

Typeset in 10/12 Palatino by Witwell Ltd, Southport

Printed in Great Britain by
Antony Rowe Ltd, Chippenham, Wiltshire

British Library Cataloguing in Publication Data
Rubinstein, W. D. Capitalism, Culture and Decline in Britain, 1750-1990
I. Title 330.941

Library of Congress Cataloging in Publication Data
Rubinstein, W. D.
Capitalism, culture, and decline in Britain, 1750-1990 / W. D. Rubinstein.
p. cm.
Includes bibliographical references and index.
1. Great Britain—Economic conditions—1945-. 2. Elite (Social
sciences)—Great Britain—History. 3. Great Britain—Social
conditions—1945-. 4. Great Britain—Politics and government—1945-
I. Title.
HC256.R83 1993
330.941—dc20 92-24481

ISBN 0 415 03718 2 (hbk)

CONTENTS

TABLES

PREFACE

I would like to thank Claire L'Enfant of Routledge for her patience in waiting for this long-delayed book. I must also thank the secretarial staff at the Faculty of Social Sciences, Deakin University, Frances Baensch, Toni Board and Loretta Jurecek, for their unfailing efficiency in word-processing the manuscript.

Some of the arguments made in this book were first presented in a paper on this topic presented at a symposium on 'British Culture vs. British Industry?' at Glasgow University in May 1986 and later appeared in a collection of essays emerging in part from this symposium: Bruce Collins and Keith Robbins (eds), *British Culture and Economic Decline* (Weidenfeld & Nicolson, London, 1990).

W. D. Rubinstein, 1992

In
memory of
W. G. D. Manns

1

The British economy since industrialisation and the 'cultural critique'

The aim of this book is to analyse and dispute a widely-held theory of Britain's 'economic decline' since the mid-nineteenth century, and to offer an alternative view which has important implications for our understanding of British society and culture in the modern period. The most common view of modern British economic history may be put concisely, but not inaccurately, as follows: Britain was the first nation to experience an industrial revolution, which began around 1760 and, by 1850, had transformed Britain into the 'workshop of the world', the pre-eminent industrial and manufacturing power of the time. After Britain's short-lived mid-Victorian economic zenith (1850-70) Britain experienced a relentless period of economic decline, now lasting for over 120 years, wherein it not merely lost its industrial hegemony but was surpassed by virtually every other western nation and, recently, by many on the rim of east Asia. Moreover, this unrelieved period of relative economic contraction became steadily more severe, with each generational era witnessing, roughly speaking, a less impressive performance in relative international terms than the one before.

According to its proponents, this continuing decline has had many causes, some more acceptable and justifiable than others. It was probably inherently impossible for a comparatively small island-nation to maintain such a lead in the long run, especially after larger and more populous states like the United States and Germany industrialised. The existence of rival industrial centres almost automatically meant that Britain could no longer enjoy the same unchallenged superiority at manufacturing and exporting that it could when it was the only industrialised nation. Britain's world-wide Empire and its involvement in two costly world wars and the Cold War virtually bankrupted her. Many fundamental institutions of the British economy, from the banking system to the trade unions, inhibited rational economic development, especially in industry and manufacturing.

Possibly the most commonly heard explanation for Britain's economic decline is that which we will term the 'cultural critique'. According to this argument, a key to understanding the reasons for Britain's decline lies in the effects of British culture upon Britain's entrepreneurship. British culture in its various manifestations and institutions was (and is) anti-industrial and anti-business. The chief mechanism for the intergenerational transmission of anti-business values is the British educational system, especially the fee-paying public schools and the universities where the sons of businessmen have, since the early Victorian period, chiefly been educated. The traditional and central aim of the public schools and the older universities – especially the former – was to produce the 'English gentleman', a well-rounded amateur who was ill-equipped for the rough and tumble of business life and who, in any case, regarded business life and the pursuit of profit as vulgar and distasteful activities, unsuitable for the well-bred. Many, perhaps most such gentlemanly products of the public schools joined the landed gentry, either by land purchase or marriage into older established families; most of the others spent their lives as the backbone of the governing class of the Empire and the military. More broadly, too, British culture was anti-business and anti-industrial in other important ways. It was pervasively anti-urban, both in the views presented by its central cultural figures and its governing elites who looked backward to the pre-industrial landed aristocracy and to the landed gentry as the ideal, and to rural life as inherently better than urban life. Britain's traditions were, in many cases, hopelessly unmodernised and often bordered on feudal survivals. Although Britain was the first country to industrialise, it was among the last to retain institutions like the House of Lords and an established Church, while its legal system and educational institutions were serious obstacles to rapid economic growth. Its class structure was and is unusually rigid and wasteful of human resources. Unlike America or contemporary Japan, British culture was, generally speaking, anti-capitalist, regarding free market economics as unfair, its chief beneficiaries the despicable factory-owners and plutocrats of the age of *laissez-faire*, its chief victims the working class. This viewpoint was not only held by the British left – where it was and is universal – but by many British conservatives from Burke, Coleridge, and Disraeli onwards to Baldwin and Harold Macmillan. Capitalism in its *laissez-faire* form at any rate was also unethical and unchristian, as generations of British clergymen and secularised moralists like William Morris and R. H. Tawney have urged. This ethical critique of British capitalism has often been applied, too, to British power generally, especially in the acquisition and preservation of the Empire and Britain's participation in many wars.

The 'cultural critique' thus asserts a number of central historical contentions which it would be useful to enumerate specifically. First and foremost, Britain was both the earliest country to industrialise and was a primarily industrial and manufacturing economy. Britain's industrial decline is the most salient feature of its economic evolution since 1850, the industrial and manufacturing hegemony it enjoyed in the mid-Victorian period passing successively to Germany, the United States, and, most recently, Japan. More broadly too, Britain clearly *has* experienced a relative economic decline over the past 120 years and certainly in the past forty. Probably the most important reason for this decline, and certainly a very important one, is Britain's pervasively anti-industrial and anti-business culture, especially via the education typically offered to the middle classes. The end product of this is a society rooted in the past, pre-modern and anti-modern in most respects, and ill-equipped to deal with the modern world. It is as well that we have enumerated these central contentions as specifically as possible, for the aim of this book is to demonstrate that each of them, however familiar, is wrong – and not merely wrong, but arguably the very opposite of the truth.

On the face of it, there would appear to be abundant empirical and anecdotal evidence for the seemingly unarguable proposition of Britain's economic decline since 1870 and for cultural factors as a main cause of this decay. Of the fundamental importance of the industrial revolution most economic historians, until recently, were in complete agreement.[1] For instance, Carlo Cipolla, an eminent Italian economic historian, termed the industrial revolution the most important event in history since the neolithic revolution of *c.* 8000 BC (which introduced agriculture, the domestication of animals, and settled communities).[2] Professor Harold Perkin's widely known interpretation of British history from 1780 to 1880, *The Origins of Modern English Society* (1969), has termed the industrial revolution

> a revolution in men's access to the means of life, in control over their ecological environment, in their capacity to escape from the tyranny and niggardliness of nature. At the material level it can be described as a rise in human productivity, agricultural and demographic, on such a scale that it raised, as it were, the logarithmic index of society. . . .

> [T]he Industrial Revolution was – and is – a unique phase of historical development: the one-way road which, if travelled successfully, leads from the undeveloped society's comparative poverty, insecurity, and dependence on the bounty of nature to the comparative wealth, security and freedom of choice of the developed society. It is an irreversible revolution, in that any return to lower levels of productiveness would involve a catastrophe of such magnitude as almost certainly to bring down civilisation with it, if not totally to destroy human life itself,

and one compared with which the hydrogen bomb would be but a preliminary disaster.[3]

This fundamental explosion of productiveness unleashed by Britain's initial discovery and exploitation of the steam-engine, railways, steamships, mass-produced textiles, and engineering equipment between about 1770 and 1850 showed unmistakable signs of losing energy in the last decades of the nineteenth century; these disturbing signs became chronic, and perhaps irremedial, in the inter-war period. According to most economic historians who subscribe to this view of Britain's laggard development, one can point to many major reasons for the decline which began just over a century ago. The first and perhaps most important was the failure by British businesses and entrepreneurs to invest heavily in the new technology associated with what is sometimes known as the 'second industrial revolution' (in the period c. 1880–1914), in electricity, chemicals and new sources of motive power like the internal combustion engine, on anything like the scale which occurred in Britain's major rivals, especially Germany and the United States. Britain remained stubbornly attached to antiquated and increasingly uncompetitive industrial techniques. A second major reason for British decline is the other side of this coin: instead of being directed to new, productive industries and innovations, British investment increasingly went overseas, especially into developing the primary industries – minerals, rubber, jute, gold and diamonds – of the tropical Empire, or the infrastructure – railways, docks, public works, construction – in the temperate regions of the Empire settled by emigré Britons and of other countries, especially the United States and Argentina. Increasingly, wealthy Britons whose savings should more usefully have brought Britain into the modern age became *rentiers* and 'coupon-clippers' living off the profits readily available through the growth of other economies, including those which became rivals to British industry. Behind this lay a near-total failure by British finance and banking to invest in British manufacturing industry until the inter-war period at the earliest.

There was also a chronic failure to adopt the new corporate structure so successful in Germany and the United States, and a reliance on relatively small family businesses, even in those areas of manufacturing industry where economies of scale were obviously the only way for a firm to prosper in the new climate; an equally chronic conservatism in the choice of industries in which business activity did continue unabated in this period, with the old staple industries of the industrial revolution – cotton and woollen manufacturing, coal mining, shipbuilding – remaining the centre-piece of British enterprise until 1914; and notoriously poor salesmanship and marketing of British exports abroad. To compound a felony, Britain's managerial structure was also antiquated, with nepotism and the 'old boy network' rampant in choosing managerial appointments and with little or no promotion to senior levels of scientifically trained products of technological education, especially those lacking the right social background. Britain perversely maintained a dogmatic adherence to mid-Victorian *laissez-faire* long after it had become outmoded and inappropriate, with a concomitant refusal to protect British industry by national tariff barriers until the Great Depression of the 1930s, generations after Germany and the United States had achieved dynamic economic growth behind high tariff walls. There was also an equal or greater failure to create a nexus between the instrumentalities of the state, including the spheres of secondary education, the universities and research bodies, and British industry, again in contrast to more successful economies.[4]

The standard critique by economic historians of British economic performance during this period also links the failings of British entrepreneurship to an equally unfortunate series of consequences. The rate of economic growth in Britain – the level of increase of the total value of its goods and services – was consistently lower than that of its chief rivals, to the extent that while the British economy was roughly the same size as the American economy in 1870, by 1914 it had, remarkably, shrunk to only 37 per cent of the United States total (of course in the context of the fact that America's population was over twice as great as Britain's by this date).[5] Rates of economic growth of the per capita gross national product, surprisingly low even during the zenith of industrialisation, fell to less than one per cent per annum on average during the years 1873–1913.[6] Britain's share of world manufacturing, not unexpectedly, showed a continual downward trend across virtually all indices devised by economic historians to measure trends in this area, declining on one such index from 31.8 per cent of the world's total in 1870 to only 14.0 per cent in 1913; as a percentage of the world's manufacturing *exports* Britain's share probably declined from 37.1 per cent in 1883 to 25.4 per cent in 1913, while Germany's rose from 17.2 to 23.0 per cent and the share of the United States from only 3.4 per cent in 1883 to 11.0 per cent in 1913.[7] The post-Second World War era has seen an additional and, indeed, ever-speedier continuation of these historical trends. By the mid-1970s the chronic underperformance of the British economy was the subject of countless books, articles, and editorials, as well as the centre-piece of most political debate. Diagnoses of the reasons for Britain's economic malaise ranged from the frequently heard analyses of unusually low investment rates, poor management techniques, perpetually bad employer–trade union relations, shoddy workmanship and the unavailability of servicing, leading to a terrible British reputation in the export market, and the effects of an outmoded class structure, to the baneful effects of too few producers, a narrow-minded and counter-productive civil service structure, too frequent change of government and governmental policies, too great an expenditure on defence in view of the decline of British political power, and the continuing separation of the City and the banks from manufacturing industry. The 'cultural critique' is also a most prominent component of this agenda of failure. The explanations for decline were legion, almost always focusing on the decline of British manufacturing industry and on the apparent failure of any post-war government, prior to the mid-1980s, successfully to reverse or even halt this deterioration.[8] A number of international political considerations made Britain's economic decline seem even more galling than it was. Britain's former enemies, West Germany, Italy, and Japan, bombed to rubble in 1945, had clearly overtaken the 'victorious power' Britain in virtually every indicator of economic performance: Britain's per capita income and living standards had been matched, or soon would be, by countries like Portugal, Spain, and Greece which were minor states, 'backward' and virtually primitive only forty years before; the world's economic powerhouse was, increasingly, to be found in the rim of east Asia among non-European cultures. Of all the major economic powers of the world, perhaps only Britain failed (through the mid-1980s) to achieve a post-war 'economic miracle', a period of dramatic economic growth and evident to all observers.

Although no one denies the accuracy of these facts – though their relevance to the overall picture is more problematical, as we shall see – in fairness it must be pointed out that there has also existed, for almost as long, a tradition of scholarship among economic historians which minimises this alleged decline and argues that Britain's manufacturing industries, especially during the key period of 1870–1914, by no means performed as badly as their critics maintain. Individual heavy industries in Britain have been examined in detail by many scholars; their verdicts about the performance of these industries in this period have often been surprisingly sanguine.[9] Furthermore, the international context of Britain's performance must be considered: it was simply unreasonable to expect Britain to have maintained the same lead in manufacturing in 1910, where there were half a dozen countries which had industrialised, as in 1851, when it was the only country to have 'taken off'. The relatively optimistic view of Britain's performance in the 1870–1914 period also emphasises the unevenness of the areas of British decline – in 1914 Britain was substantially ahead of its rivals in several areas.

Elements favourable both to the pessimistic view of Britain's performance in this period and to the optimists' rejoinder may be seen

6

in Table 1.1, which compares the rate of growth of overall industrial production in six major European countries and the United States between 1815 and 1913, and then the output of coal and pig-iron, raw cotton consumption, merchant ships registered, and length of railway lines opened – all basic determinants of nineteenth-century industrial development – among these major states.

Most of these statistics point in the same direction, and two central points emerge from examining them. Table 1.1 (i) indicates the rate of growth of overall industrial production: it should be emphasised that what is measured here are *rates* of growth, not absolute industrial strength (that is, not how much *more* Britain produced than Italy, but how fast they grew). With these statistics the greater the numerical gap between the indices of industrial production, the higher the growth rate. Comparing 1870 with 1913, it will be seen that Britain, France, and Italy had almost identical growth rates, but Germany, Austria-Hungary, and Russia grew considerably more rapidly. Comparing 1900 with 1913 *every* country grew more rapidly than did Britain.

The tables which measure the volume of particular commodities also show a distinct pattern, or, rather, two patterns. In 1850, coincident with Britain's industrial zenith, with virtually every item considered here it is a case of England first and the rest nowhere: no country in history with the conceivable exception of the United States for the first ten years after the end of the Second World War ever enjoyed so near-hegemonic an industrial dominance as did mid-Victorian Britain. In most of these yardsticks of industrial predominance, indeed, Britain produced more than all the other major European powers combined.

By 1870, and unarguably by 1913, a very different picture had emerged. Among European states, in pig-iron output, a crucial measurement of industrial power, Germany now exceeded Britain's level of production by 60 per cent; similarly Germany very nearly caught up with Britain in coal output. If production in chemicals – not given here – is taken into account, Germany had probably surpassed Britain as the leading European power in many indices of economic development. Yet, as will be seen, it is simply wrong to see this picture as unrelievedly dark. Britain's raw cotton consumption – the basis for the oldest of staple industries – still exceeded the combined total of its two closest European rivals, while in merchant shipping tonnage Britain unquestionably remained supreme down to the First World War; her European rivals had hardly made a dent in the British lead. Consideration of the growth of railway mileage in Europe, too, indicates another inherent and unavoidable circumstance constraining Britain's economic development, its small size. Even though railways had been constructed more intensively and comprehensively in Britain than anywhere else, once Britain's rivals undertook a serious programme of railway building

Table 1.1 Comparative national statistics of economic development, 1815–1913

(i) Index of overall industrial production

	1815	1850	1870	1900	1913
UK	9.0	28.0	40.2	80.1	100
France	19.2	33.5	40.0	67.9	100
Austria (-Hungary)	–	–	28.6 (*1880*)	34.9	100
Germany	–	9.5	19.0	61.0	100
Italy	–	32.0 (*1861*)	40.0	61.0	100
Russia	–	8.8 (*1860*)	11.0	63.0	100
USA	–	–	13.7	55.0	100

(ii) Output of coal ('000 metric tons)

	1815	1850	1870	1913
UK	16,200	50,200	112,203	292,042
France	822	4,434	13,330	40,844
Austria (-Hungary)	95 (*1819*)	877	7,217	43,838
Germany	1,300 (*1817*)	6,900	34,003	277,342
Italy	–	34 (*1861*)	59	701
Russia	–	300 (*1860*)	690	36,050
Belgium	–	5,821	13,697	24,050
USA	–	–	18,543	433,465

(iii) Output of pig-iron ('000 metric tons)

	1815	1850	1870	1913
UK	330 (*1818*)	2,285	6,059	10,425
France	113 (*1819*)	406	1,178	5,207
Austria (-Hungary)	73 (*1828*)	155	279	1,758
Germany	85 (*1823*)	210	1,261	16,761
Italy	–	13	20	427
Russia	132 (*1817*)	228	359	4,641
Belgium	90 (*1831*)	145	565	2,485
USA	–	–	1,689	30,830

(iv) Raw cotton consumption ('000 metric tons)

	1815	1850	1870	1913
UK	37.0	267	489	988
France	*c.*8.0	59	94 (*1869*)	271
Austria (-Hungary)	4.7 (*1828*)	29	45	210
Germany	–	*c.*26	112 (*1871*)	478
Italy	–	12.4 (*1861*)	15	202
Russia	0.8	20	46	424
USA	–	–	181	1,312

(v) Length of railway lines opened (kilometres)

	1840	1860	1880	1913
UK	2,390	16,802	24,759	38,114
France	410	9,167	23,089	40,770
Austria (-Hungary)	144	2,927	11,429	22,981
Germany	469	11,089	18,876	63,378
Italy	20	2,404	6,429	18,873
Russia	27	1,626	10,731	70,156
USA	1,751	19,031	57,952	235,822

(vi) Merchant ships registered ('000 tons)

	1815	1850	1870	1913
UK	2,414	3,658	5,691	12,120
France	–	688	1,072	1,582
Austria (-Hungary)	–	260	457	616
Germany	–	513	939	3,320
Italy	–	654 (*1862*)	1,112	1,233
Russia		173 (*1859*)	260 (*1872*)	783
USA	803	3,535	4,247	7,896

Sources: B. R. Mitchell (ed.), *European Historical Statistics 1750–1975* (2nd edn, London, 1980), pp. 355–8, for Europe; Department of Commerce, Bureau of the Census, *Historical Statistics of the United States, Colonial Times to 1970*, 'Non-Farm Business Gross Domestic Product at Constant (1929) Prices', for USA. USA figures are for annual averages for 1869–78, 1897–1901, and 1912–16.

of their own, they were bound, in due course, to have larger systems, simply because there was more mileage to be constructed in these countries, with their larger areas.

The second major point to emerge from these tables is the extraordinary, indeed incredible, economic growth of the United States between 1870 and 1913. By 1913, the United States was already and beyond cavil the world's economic superpower to an extent that is not now often fully appreciated. In pig-iron production, to take one indicator, the United States in 1913 out-produced both Britain and Germany – combined. America led the world, by an awesome distance, in coal production and cotton consumption: in railway mileage the American total very nearly exceeded that of all the major European countries combined. Of course America was larger in area than all of Europe combined, but railway mileage was, at the time, an excellent guide to the sophistication of transport and communication in a particular country, as well as, in itself, a potent source of demand for many manufactured goods and spur to further growth. The uncanny position which the United States had achieved even before the First

World War indicates, as well, that the American economy, with the standard of living it was capable of generating, differed markedly from that of Europe *as a whole*, including Britain, while Britain's level of economic development was in many respects much more like that of the other major European powers than like that of the United States.

The catastrophe of the First World War, it is usually urged, made Britain's economic situation, previously disturbing if tolerable, vastly worse. Most animadversions on Britain's dismal economic performance in the inter-war period have regularly focused on a number of major elements in the overall picture. First, the inter-war economy witnessed a calamitous decline in Britain's old staple industries, especially cotton and woollen textiles, shipbuilding, many sections of engineering, and, perhaps less definitively, coalmining. Cotton yarn produced in Britain totalled 1,983 million pounds in 1912: by 1924 this figure had decreased by 30 per cent, to 1,395 million, and still further, to 1,048 million, in 1930.[10] Although there was some growth (as there was in nearly all sectors of the British economy) during the later 1930s, to 1,357 million pounds in 1937, it is absolutely clear that a disaster had overtaken the cotton textile industry in Britain, the very centre-piece of the world's first industrial revolution. Nor was this all: two facets of this industry-wide depression added immeasurably to its woes. The decline in cotton exports was even more traumatic than the overall fall in production, British cotton yarn and piece goods exports declining from 1,291 million pounds in 1913 to 756 million (on average) between 1920 and 1924, and to only 402 million (on average) in 1930–4; second, employment in the industry declined just as precipitously as did output, from 622,000 in 1912 to only 389,000 in 1930.[11] What was true in cotton was also the case in the other staples: the tonnage of ships launched in Britain declined from 2.1 million gross tons in 1920 to only 100,000 tons in 1932 at the bottom of the Depression.[12] Output of iron ore declined from about 16 million tons in 1913 to only 7.3 million in 1932; in only two years between 1921 and 1938 did iron ore output exceed 12 million tons.[13]

The inter-war period is, of course, virtually synonymous with mass unemployment, depicted unforgettably in a thousand newsreels and in works like *The Road to Wigan Pier*. The facts here are so familiar as hardly to need restatement: in the whole inter-war period, when the British labour force totalled around 20 million, unemployment never declined below 1,127,000 and remained over 2 million between mid-1930 and mid-1936, reaching a peak of 2,880,000 unemployed in September 1931.[14] This persistent level of high unemployment was something new in Britain's industrial history; it was, moreover, disproportionately confined to the Depressed Areas of the industrial revolution's homeland, to the north of England and the Celtic fringe, while London and the West Midlands experienced a considerable boom.

Critics of the British economy in the inter-war period have also returned again and again to Britain's declining position in international trade, and to the wrong-headed decision by Chancellor of the Exchequer Winston Churchill to return to the Gold Standard in 1926, thereby over-valuing the pound and making British exports more expensive at the very moment when a surge of exports was most required to alleviate the ills of the British economy. This allegedly tragic decision in turn greatly aggravated what many would see as the fourth element in Britain's difficult economic picture in the inter-war years, unprecedented labour unrest and militancy, with the General Strike beginning only five days after the decision to return to the Gold Standard. There had been considerable labour unrest before the First World War – nearly 41 million working days were lost through industrial disputes in 1912 – but the inter-war years, especially the 1920s, saw far more, with peaks of nearly 86 million working days lost through strike action in 1921 and 162 million in 1926, the year of the General Strike.[15]

Yet it is also agreed by all economic historians that the inter-war period was not unrelievedly black – not by any means. The latter part of the 1930s witnessed the perceptible growth of new industries, especially domestic consumer-good manufacturing based largely in West London – such modern consumer durables as radio sets, vacuum cleaners, and washing machines – considerable automobile manufacturing in the West Midlands and Oxford, and record home-building and construction. The world of 'semi-detached London', the new middle- and lower-middle-class commuter belts of north and north-west London, emerged during the inter-war years.[16] Chemicals, artificial fibres, steel production, and aircraft all grew significantly after the trough of the Depression. The cinema and other forms of popular amusement also boomed at this time. In the six years from 1933/4 to 1938/9, a total of 1,584,000 new homes were built in Great Britain, far more than in any other six-year period in history.[17] The *relative* conditions of boom and prosperity which had appeared in the later 1930s were probably a powerful economic argument in favour of Appeasement and against foreign entanglements, although rearmament after 1937 was itself a factor in increasing economic demand.

It is also a fact that the Great Depression of the early 1930s was probably less severe in Britain than in any other advanced capitalist country. One reason for this was thoroughly perverse: since 1921 there had already been an army of unemployed in the staple industries and older industrial areas, far greater in relative terms than in other industrial nations when the Depression struck. The situation could hardly get much worse than it had already been for eight years. Nor was the relative lack of severity for what was, by any standards, a disaster possibly without precedent any comfort for the millions caught up, through no fault of their own, in the 'Devil's Decade'. Nevertheless, compared with such analogous countries as the United States, Canada, Germany, Australia, and France, unemployment in Britain rose less sharply, and gross national product declined markedly less – indeed, hardly at all – while the recovery after 1933 was better than in most other industrial nations, with the new manufacturing industries of the Midlands and London leading the way.[18]

Even if the overall economic picture for Britain in this period was less grim than is widely supposed, and even if, indeed, Britain's economy was stronger and more productive in 1938 than in 1918 (or 1913), the fact remains that the other powers were also growing rapidly and at a rate that, in many cases, outstripped Britain's. Table 1.2, building on Table 1.1 above for the 1815–1914 era, illustrates the rather paradoxical situation faced by Britain in the inter-war period.

Two conclusions are immediate and striking from Table 1.2. First, once again the lead of the USA over the leading European powers was extraordinary and was already, by the 1920s, at least as great as – if not greater than – the lead enjoyed by America in the decade following the Second World War. The lead enjoyed by the United States following the First World War already entitled it to be termed the world's only true economic superpower. Second, Britain's position *vis-à-vis* other advanced industrial powers was hallmarked by two distinctive features: relatively slow but steady growth, along with a similar *relative* immunity to the worst ravages of the Great Depression. Compared with the catastrophic downturn suffered by, say, Germany or the USA in steel production between 1929 and 1932, Britain's level of decline was relatively low; in motor vehicles – where America saw a 75 per cent decline in production – Britain actually witnessed an increased output between 1929 and 1932.[19]

Nevertheless, the overall impression made by these statistics for Britain is that of lost opportunities and a lack of entrepreneurial vigour compared with her main rivals. Coal production declined over the whole period; steel output was only marginally higher in 1938 than in 1920. Electricity and motor vehicle production indeed saw impressive increases, but no more so than for most of the other countries. Nor do these figures indicate the losses suffered by the British economy in the old staple industries (except coal), where the devastation of the inter-war period was most severe.

Under Winston Churchill, Britain rose to its supreme international test during the Second World War. Despite enormous material devastation caused by the war and the astronomical financial indebtedness

Table 1.2 Comparative economic statistics of production, 1920–38

(i) Coal: Metric tons produced ('000 metric tons)[1]

	1920	1929	1932	1938
France	25,261	54,977	47,279	47,562
Germany	107,528	163,437	104,741	186,186
Russia	6,730	36,589	57,471	114,728
USA	515,564	484,153	280,789	315,997
UK	233,215	262,046	212,083	230,636

[1] France: Hard coal and lignite; Germany: Brown coal; Russia: Hard coal; USA: Bituminous coal.

(ii) Motor vehicles (commercial and private, '000)

	1920	1929	1932	1938
France	40	254	164	227
Germany	n/a (1925=49)	128	51	338
Russia	n/a	1	24	211
USA	2,227	5,337	1,332	2,508[2]
UK	n/a	212	232	445

[2] In 1937 the USA produced 4,820,000 motor vehicles; 1938 was a year of sharp recession.

(iii) Crude steel ('000 metric tons)

	1920	1929	1932	1938
France	2,706	9,716	5,616	6,137
Germany	9,278	16,245	5,771	22,656
Russia	194	4,854	5,927	18,057
USA	41,870	55,976	13,711	28,787[3]
UK	9,212	9,719	5,345	10,565

[3] The USA produced 51,348,000 metric tons in 1937.

(iv) Electricity (giga-watt hours)

	1920	1929	1932	1938
France	3.50	15.60	14.05	20.80
Germany	15.00	30.66	23.46	55.33
Russia	0.5	6.22	13.54	39.37
USA [4]	56.56	116.75	99.36	141.96
UK	5.4	16.98	19.46	33.77

[4] USA statistics are for electricity produced 'by electric utility and industrial generating plant'.

Sources: European statistics from B. R. Mitchell (ed.), *European Historical Statistics, 1750–1975* (2nd edn, London, 1980). USA statistics from US Department of Commerce, Bureau of the Census, *Historical Statistics of the United States, Colonial Times to 1970* (Washington, DC, 1975).

directly occasioned by that conflict, Britain emerged from the war still unquestionably a great power, its Prime Ministers Churchill and Attlee considered the equals, in negotiations for the post-war settlement, of America's Presidents Roosevelt and Truman and Soviet dictator Stalin at the Yalta and Potsdam Conferences of 1945; even a decade later, at the first Summit Conference in ten years, at Geneva in 1955, the 'Big Four' consisted of the USA, the USSR, Britain and France. Yet it became increasingly self-evident that if Britain had won the war, in every sense but the military it had lost the peace, and from the 1950s onward there began the steady stream of persistent criticism of virtually every aspect of Britain's economic performance, noted previously, which by the 1960s had become torrential and by the 1970s ubiquitous. The essential failings of the British economy in the years between about 1960 and the mid-1980s were discussed and rehearsed, it is safe to say, by all organs of opinion, by every leading politician, and by literally hundreds of economists and writers on public affairs. Most election campaigns between 1964 and the present have been fought almost exclusively between competing plans for righting Britain's chronic economic woes. Self-flagellation over Britain's economic failings became a national obsession to the extent that virtually everyone in Britain surely believes that the British economy suffered a catastrophic decline in the post-war years.

Critics of British economic performance normally highlight the pace of Britain's decline once again in terms of manufacturing output (and export performance) compared with its chief rivals. Some of the more recent and apparently devastating comparative statistics might be illustrated by Table 1.3.

Britain's overall share of world manufacturing output consistently diminished, declining from 20.5 per cent of the world total of manufactured goods in 1951–5 to 9.1 per cent in 1973–7 to perhaps only 5 per cent during the 1980s.[20]

Apart from the seemingly irrefutable factual evidence for Britain's economic decline, and the research of academic economic historians, chiefly concerned with purely economic factors, there has been the search for wider and more fundamental explanations of Britain's decline, and it is here that the historians, commentators, and journalists who have voiced what we term the 'cultural critique' have entered the debate, seeking to situate these economic facts in a deeper cultural and societal context. Of all the explanations which have been offered of Britain's apparently relentless economic decline, perhaps none is as often heard as those revolving around the allegedly injurious effects of British culture upon British capitalism, especially the deleterious effects British culture had on the quality of Britain's entrepreneurs. Although this causal connection has been heard with

Table 1.3 Comparative economic statistics of production, 1950-86

(i) Steel production ('000 metric tons)

	1950	1960	1970	1975
France	8,652	17,281	23,773	21,530
W. Germany	12,121	34,100	45,040	40,415
USSR	27,329	65,294	115,889	141,325
USA	87,793	90,011	119,233	
UK	16,554	24,695	28,316	20,098

(ii) Motor vehicles produced (commercial and passenger) ('000)

	1950	1960	1970	1975
France	354	1,370	2,712	3,306
W. Germany	301	2,047	3,825	3,153
USSR	359	640	1,159	1,966
USA	8,003	7,868	8,239	
UK	784	1,811	2,099	1,649

(iii) Electricity (giga-watts)

	1950	1960	1970	1975
France	33.03	72.12	140.71	178.51
W. Germany	46.10	116.42	242.61	301.80
USSR	91.23	292.27	740.93	1,038.63
USA	396.35	848.72	1,641.73	
UK	63.30	129.07	230.30	252.67

(iv) World electric energy production (billions of kilowatt hours)

	1980	1986
France	246.4	343.0
W. Germany	368.8	406.4
USSR	1,294.0	1,599.0
USA	2,354.0	2,583.0
UK	284.9	298.2
Japan	577.5	671.8
World	8,247.0	9,962.0

Sources: European statistics from B. R. Mitchell (ed), European Historical Statistics, 1750-1975 (2nd edn, London, 1980). USA statistics from US Department of Commerce, Bureau of the Census, Historical Statistics of the United States, Colonial Times to 1970 (Washington, DC, 1975). Department of International Economic and Social Affairs, Statistical Office, United Nations, 1987 Statistical Yearbook (New York, 1990), pp. 547-615.

the regularity of clockwork over the past quarter century it is, paradoxically, a rather new argument, at least in the extreme form which it has taken in recent years. It is, indeed, not easy to find a full-blown presentation of the 'cultural' thesis prior to the period of Harold Macmillan's premiership, when the antiquated nature of Britain's educational system was linked to its post-Suez decay by critics of the 'angry young men' school, for instance in a collection of essays edited by Arthur Koestler, *Suicide of a Nation?* (1963). To be sure, many late Victorians and Edwardians were fully aware of the formidable rivalry increasingly presented to Britain's industrial supremacy by the new powers of Germany and the United States, and there is a stratum of critical writings on Britain's challenge, of far-reaching political import-ance, dating from the 1890-1914 period. Yet it is very difficult to identify a work which specifically links Britain's distinctive culture, and its roots in Britain's peculiar class structure, to its economic decline before the 1960s. Few, seemingly, made such a connection before the present generation, either because far-reaching sociological and cultural argu-ments of this type were extraordinarily rare in Britain before the post-war development of sophisticated social analysis of a type now familiar to us, or because it was simply implausible to argue convincingly that Britain *had* declined; so long as Britain was regarded as indubitably a great power – as it was perhaps until Suez – there was nothing to explain.

Over the past twenty-five years, however, have come a flood of incisive critiques of the British economy, linking its lamentable performance to more fundamental cultural and class factors. It is both interesting and highly significant to note that the best known of these critiques have not come from academic economic historians, but from more mainstream historians and journalists. Of course, specific criticism of the poor performance of Britain's entrepreneurs – as opposed to other factors in Britain's economic decline – have frequently been voiced by economic historians, but they have seldom gone beyond an examination of the careers of entrepreneurs to look at wider and more underlying factors in British culture.[21] In the past twenty-five years or so, and especially in the last decade, however, it seems fair to say that the 'cultural critique' has gained unprecedented publicity through eloquent and persuasive popularisation. Probably the three most important of the popular advocates of this view have been Professor Martin J. Wiener, Anthony Sampson, and Corelli Barnett. Wiener is a senior American historian of modern Britain who holds an important university chair at Rice University in Texas and Barnett is a University Lecturer in Defence Studies at Cambridge, while Sampson is a renowned journalist, and all write from a non-specialist, non-technical viewpoint which has made their works both persuasive and popular. Anthony Sampson's *Anatomy of Britain* (1962) and its subsequent revised editions (appearing in 1965, 1971, and 1982) possibly did more than any other works to give currency to the notion of the British 'Establishment' as hopelessly reactionary, atavistic, class-ridden, and thoroughly inadequate, consistently ill at ease with the contemporary world of high technology and rational innovation, however delightful such survivals as the House of Lords and the Anglican bench of bishops might theoretically seem. Sampson's *metier* was a singularly skilful and cogent depiction of the 'anatomy' of Britain's ruling elite in remarkable detail, emphasising the background of privilege and the undoubted commonalities – especially attendance at a handful of the public schools and Oxbridge – of many leading members of the elite; in the earlier editions, complex genealogical tables set out the interrelationships of many of the Conservative party's leading members in the days of Harold Macmillan, a web of connections which took in significant leaders of the City, diplomacy, the senior civil service, and other components of the Establishment. Such depictions have appeared before – one thinks, for example, of Simon Haxey's *Tory M. P.* (1938), a work presenting very similar data on the personal and economic background of the Conservative party in the era of Stanley Baldwin and Neville Chamberlain. But, while Haxey's work was frankly written from a left-wing and socialist adversarial perspective (it was published by the Left Book Club), and could thus be readily dismissed as inherently biased and tendentious, Sampson's *Anatomy* has been the more convincing for its sedulous fairness and empathy with the elite figures it anatomised, the product of a high journalistic talent. Unlike Haxey, Sampson did not confine himself to highlighting the Conservative party and its links to big business, but described in equal detail the leadership of the Labour party, the trade unions, the universities, key scientific bodies, and other 'progressive' elements within the broader British elite. The first appearance of Sampson's *Anatomy* in 1962, too, came at a critical juncture for popular perceptions of the British Establishment. Although the Suez debacle and the pace of decolonisation seemed to spell the end of the old-style Tory imperialism and of the old certainty of Britain's superior place in the world, Harold Macmillan had, since becoming Prime Minister in 1957, proven remarkably adept at giving the traditional ruling elite a new lease of life. Macmillan's government, especially in its earlier stages, appeared in social and sociological terms to be a throwback to Lord Salisbury's golden days, with many leading ministers born or married into the traditional landed aristocracy and virtually all sprung from impeccable Establishment backgrounds. Certainly by the standards of a Conservative government a generation later, Macmillan's administration contained an extraordinary number of old Etonians, former guardsmen, and scions of families noticed in *Burke's Peerage and Baronetage*. The few prominent Conservatives who could be seen as having risen by their own merits, like Iain Macleod and Edward Heath, were normally depicted as 'thrusting', efficient 'new men' (favourite phrases of Sampson's), in stark contrast to the hopeless and preposterous incompetence of those born to a place in the hereditary elite. According to Sampson's depiction, Britain had the opportunity to enter the new, post-Sputnik, post-EEC world of high technology via a radical programme of 'modernisation', entailing the reform, above all, of its tired pre-industrial institutions like the House of Lords and the old universities. Confidence was almost always placed in the 'new men', the new knowledge, the new technology, and the new institutions to right Britain's deteriorating position; Britain's atavistic institutions were gorgeous, but always inherently outmoded and regressive. Sampson's striking talent for memorable depiction has guided a generation through the putative British Establishment – rather in the same way as Virgil guided Dante through Hell, one is tempted to add.

It is thus an important and notable feature of the more recent revisions of Sampson's *Anatomy*, especially the most recent edition (*The Changing Anatomy of Britain*, published in paperback in 1983), that they have become both more innured to the apparent ills of British society and less certain that their cure lies in radical and rational reform. In the 1983 edition of the *Anatomy*, Sampson notes that while he 'give[s] more attention to the special characteristics of British institutions, their self-deception and resistance to change', he also 'takes note of Howard's law (every change achieves the opposite of what was intended)', and that, since the first edition of the *Anatomy* appeared in 1962, 'Twenty years older, it is doubtless harder to maintain indignation about mistakes in high places. . . . The game of toppling father-figures loses some of its attractions in middle age.'[22] Although Sampson gave no reason for this new detachment apart from the ageing process, it seems likely that the unhappy experiences of the Wilson and Heath governments – committed, at least on paper, to just that kind of radical modernisation programme previously favoured by Sampson (and many others) – played a role in this evolution. When radical change did come, it was from an entirely unexpected source, Mrs Thatcher and her policies of *laissez-faire*.

The second of the intellectual trio whose views have done so much to establish the view of the British Establishment as hopelessly pre-modern and anti-intellectual is Corelli Barnett, author of works like *The Audit of War* (1987) and *The Collapse of British Power* (1972). Barnett is, primarily, a military historian whose critique of British decline has (unlike Wiener's and Sampson's) included a central lament for the diminution in Britain's military power and the loss of Empire. Even more than Wiener, Barnett is an academic historian whose books contain hundreds of footnote references and much original research. *The Audit of War*, perhaps Barnett's best book, is a telling and, within its limits, persuasive indictment of the alleged incompetence and backwardness of Britain's economy during and just after the Second World War, especially the 'lost victory' – the failure to use the destruction of the war to move into a genuinely modern late-industrial economy – a failure chiefly the responsibility of the controllers of Britain's Establishment. Almost all were traditional humanities-trained products of the older universities. Most shared the vision of a 'New Jerusalem' after the war, which, assisted by the rising tide of Labour and socialism, placed abstract social justice over economic reform and efficiency which alone, in the long run, could achieve that goal. *The Audit of War* is also a terrible indictment of British industrial inefficiency and fossilisation during the war itself, a fossilisation painfully evident to American industrialists visiting Britain, as well as to the British policy-makers observing America's mighty war machine after Pearl Harbour. Barnett includes, for instance, a vivid depiction of two missions by Sir Alexander Dunbar and Sir Roy Fedden to American war-production facilities in 1942-3:

> Both missions wrote of American aircraft factories with something of the wonder of men transported from a nineteenth-century red-brick industrial town to the world of 'Things to Come'. Here were vast structures permanently blacked out and brilliantly lit by fluorescent tubing; air-conditioned, spacious, clean, even elegant.[23]

The villains in Barnett's story are the old familiar ones – Britain's public school and university system, its civil service establishment, its backward-looking Conservative elite and their doctrinaire, irresponsible Labour challengers. Soft-hearted, addle-pated Christian socialists appear to have been especially calamitous to Britain's economic development; so, too, were the unwordly striped-trousered civil servants cloistered in Whitehall. Once again we learn that:

> The new romantic ideal of Christian education went on from Rugby and other freshly reformed public schools to capture the universities of Oxford and Cambridge. .... It was in this same period that exponents of what Newman called 'liberal knowledge', i. e. knowledge unrelated to what is 'particular and practical' and enshrined in such disciplines as the classics or mathematics, won a particular success which was to determine the character of the British state bureaucracy for the next century. ... Thus in the early 1850s was born the Whitehall mandarin, able at a touch to transmute life into paper and turn action into stone ...

essay-writers rather than problem solvers . . . an elite aloof from the ferocious struggle for survival going on in the world's market place.[24]

Yet, whatever its undoubted insights and important research, *The Audit of War* is a book which is problematical and questionable, especially as a general indictment. A Rip Van Winkle who fell asleep in 1912 and awoke today, being given *The Audit of War* to read prior to anything else, would assuredly conclude from it that Britain must have *lost* two world wars: there is nothing in Barnett's book from which the fact that Britain *won* both wars, over the powerful German industrial behemoth, can possibly be inferred. Of course, with a little help from its friends, but Britain had powerful friends: Germany had none, apart from like-minded dictatorships.

As well, some of the arguments about Britain's poor economic performance in *The Audit of War* can perhaps be challenged. To take one example, although Britain's military production began in 1938–9 at a much lower level than Germany's, most careful studies would now agree that the increase in Britain's military output between 1939 and 1945 was significantly greater than Germany's, demonstrating just that flexibility and dynamism under extreme pressure which Barnett argues it lacked.[25] Again, Barnett claims, regarding the decaying industrial areas of the north of England that

> As all the detailed evidence makes abundantly plain, the problem of the areas of high unemployment in the 1930s stemmed from their own obsoleteness as an industrial system, a problem not to be cured only temporarily masked, by turning up the Keynesian burner under the economy as a whole. Such indiscriminate stimulation of purchasing power could not in the long term induce the customer to buy old-fashioned, ill-designed, ill-made and over-priced products in preference to foreign goods which were none of these things.[26]

But the primary cause of failure of the north's traditional export industries, surely, was a long-term decline in foreign demand for the goods they produced *per se* – for coal, for ships, for cotton textiles. The most modern ship in the world, produced by the most efficient dockyard in the world, would simply not have been saleable to anyone, domestic or foreign, during much of the Depression. Much as with Wiener's book, *The Audit of War* and many of Barnett's other works with a similar message have received an unusual degree of publicity from sources which would not normally have noticed a less argumentative work on Britain's industrial effort during the Second World War. One reviewer claimed that Barnett's work 'will make your blood boil', another described it as 'unbearably painful', still another as 'a required-reading catalogue of bloody-mindedness and fat-headedness and cack-handedness [sic]'.

The last of the trio we are examining here, and in many respects the most influential, is Martin J. Wiener, the American historian whose *English Culture and the Decline of the Industrial Spirit, 1850–1980*, first appeared in 1981. Like Anthony Sampson, Wiener had considerable luck in the timing of his work; it appeared when Margaret Thatcher had been in power for two years but was at perhaps the nadir of her administration in terms of the impact made upon Britain's economic status. A persuasive general explanation for the valley into which Britain had descended was overdue, and Wiener's book, combining wide reading with a pleasant and intelligent style, quickly became one of the most influential works of history published since the war, as well as one of the few books by a university academic to be debated and discussed by government leaders and influential newspapers; it had, as well, the highly unusual distinction of being taken up by both the ideological right and left in British politics, at a time of sharp cleavage between the two, the left as a further stick with which to beat the English class system and its baneful effects, by the Thatcherite right in order to laud dynamic, thrusting *laissez-faire* capitalism untrammelled by the state control and semi-socialism traditionally associated with the post-Disraelian Conservative party, Tory 'wets', the civil service, muddle-headed clergymen, leftist intellectuals, and others who would be described in William James's term as 'tender-minded' rather than 'tough minded', all of which Thatcherism existed to sweep away.

Wiener's book opens with the pertinent observation that 'the leading problem of modern British history is the explanation of its economic decline. Until the later nineteen-sixties the generally accepted frame for the history of Britain over the previous century was that of a series of success stories.'[27] Wiener dismisses purely economic factors as insufficient by themselves to account for this decline, and places the blame, instead, squarely upon 'the values' of the directing strata 'which were always anti-industrial and normally anti-urban'.[28] 'The English nation adopt[ed] a conception of Englishness that virtually excluded industrialism.'[29] Granting that Britain did, indeed, have the world's first industrial revolution, Wiener echoes Marxist historians such as Perry Anderson and Tom Nairn in claiming that full-fledged institutionalisation of the values of the industrial bourgeoisie never occurred in the nineteenth century: the pre-existing landed aristocracy remained too strong while it was too easy for rising and ambitious industrialists to join in a country where upward social mobility into the gentry and even the aristocracy was far easier than on the continent and the social, economic, and political gap between the two groups far smaller. The product of this 'accommodation and absorption' during the Victorian period, according to Wiener, was 'the consolidation of a "gentrified" bourgeois culture, particularly the rooting of pseudo-aristocratic attitudes and values in upper-middle-class educated opinion'.[30] The grandsons of the thrusting, self-made business leaders of the industrial period – and of course this notion is not original to Wiener – were reshaped and remoulded by Britain's public schools, universities, and other institutions of the Establishment like the military officer corps, into 'English gentlemen', a group totally unfitted for business life, let alone for the innovative, profit-driven, ruthless, cunning entrepreneurship that had given Britain the world's first 'take off' into industrialisation. A central role in this derailing of talent, it is clear in this and most other critiques, was played by the reformed and expanded system of elite education which emerged in nineteenth-century Britain, especially the public schools. Wiener suggests that

> The public schools gradually relaxed their entrance barriers. Boys from commercial and industrial families, however, were admitted only if they disavowed their backgrounds and their class. However many businessmen's sons entered, few future businessmen emerged from these schools, and those who did were 'civilised'; that is, detached from the single-minded pursuit of production and profit.[31]

From the mid-Victorian period onwards, the 'anti-industrial spirit' permeated every sphere of British life, from the world of high culture, where a 'counter-revolution of values' animated virtually every significant writer, artist, and thinker into a thoroughgoing detestation of industrialism, mass capitalism, and city life, to middle-class popular culture, with its emphasis on rural and suburban domesticity, garden suburb living, and fiction and popular entertainment which denied or disguised Britain's industrial past, to the political sphere, where the twentieth-century left and right united in opposing *laissez-faire* capitalistic materialism and devoted much of their energies to an attempt to modify or destroy unbridled free enterprise. Even within the business world itself, the 'gentrification of the industrialist' produced a continuing bias against dynamic entrepreneurship as well as a 'conservative managerial culture' which 'braked growth'. Wiener concludes this section of his book by claiming that:

> Over the past century, then, high among the internal checks upon British economic growth has been a pattern of industrial behaviour suspicious of change, reluctant to innovate, energetic only in maintaining the status quo. The pattern of behaviour traces back in large measure to the culture absorption of the middle classes

into a quasi-aristocratic elite, which nurtured both the rustic and nostalgic myth of an 'English way of life' and the transfer of interest and energy away from the creation of wealth.[32]

Professor Wiener, who is primarily a historian of ideas and of intellectual movements, provides evidence for his thesis from an extraordinarily wide variety of sources, ranging from an obscure poem by Wilfred Scawen Blunt to an equally forgotten essay by Stanley Baldwin on the manifold virtues of rural England; more than twenty business histories are cited. It seems clear that Wiener's presentation is as seductive as his argument is appealing, and was pitched at just the right level between the popular and the erudite to win wide influence.

The cumulative effects of all of these works, at the heart of the post-Suez scholarly and high journalistic traditions of identifying British entrepreneurship, and the class and educational systems which provided its foundations, as being instrumental in causing Britain's post-1870 decline, have been to stamp upon informed opinion, especially informed non-academic opinion, the notion that Britain's post-1870 economic decline was rooted in the declining quality of its entrepreneurs, whose inadequacy was in turn occasioned by much deeper factors in modern British society. However much the proponents of this viewpoint might differ among themselves, they would seem to be in broad agreement over the underlying contentions of this argument, especially and most fundamentally the crucial contention that Britain's was, essentially, an industrial and manufacturing economy – the first in history – which declined after 1870 largely because of the effects of the anti-industrial cultural spirit endemic in the British economy, manifested especially through such middle- and upper-class institutions as the public schools and the universities, upon the progeny of the early generations of industrialists, as well as upon influential opinion-makers and other powerful men in British society.

This critique has, to be sure, been subjected to a variety of counter-argument, and the point should again be made that academic economic historians probably accept the accuracy of this viewpoint much less readily than politicians, newspaper editors, journalists, and informed public opinion. Professor Wiener's book in particular has attracted a very considerable body of adverse criticism, especially regarding his methodology. Many critics have pointed out that the mere massing of quotations by British writers who sang the praises of rural life in no way addresses the significance of writers with a very different viewpoint or of the real influence of such writers on behaviour and attitudes. Clergymen, for example, have constantly preached against 'sin', especially sexual immorality, but no one has ever demonstrated that as a result of their preaching, sinful behaviour has decreased.

Other commentators on Wiener's book have noted that the alleged tendency by British entrepreneurs to purchase land, become landed gentry, and see their children intermarry with the older aristocracy and gentry was hardly a product of the Victorian period but was by repute at least, a time-honoured feature of Britain's relatively open social structure back to medieval times or before. Still others have seen Britain's economic decline as primarily the product of other causes essentially unrelated to the quality of Britain's entrepreneurs or the underlying nature of its culture – to the fact that down to 1870 or so, Britain had no real economic rivals but then had many, several like the United States, Russia, and Germany larger and more richly endowed in resources; to the endogenous effects of the world wars on Britain's trade routes and established markets; to the trade unions or the Labour party.

While these points raised against the accuracy of the 'cultural critique' may each have considerable merit, they form no part of the contention made here. The argument which is made here, and which is the central argument of the book, is fundamentally very different. Our argument is that the most fundamental assumption made by advocates of the 'cultural critique' is wrong, namely that Britain's was centrally an *industrial* economy whose industrial and manufacturing lead vanished through qualitative decline after 1870. The view which will be advanced here is that Britain's was *never* fundamentally an industrial and manufacturing economy; rather, it was *always*, even at the height of the industrial revolution, essentially a commercial, financial, and ser-vice-based economy whose comparative advantage always lay with commerce and finance. Britain's apparent industrial decline was simply a working out of this process, a working out which became increasingly evident from about 1890, and which was, manifestly, coincidental with a continuing rise in the average standard of living in Britain rather than with a decline. What is so often seen as Britain's industrial decline or collapse can be seen, with greater accuracy, as a transfer of resources and entrepreneurial energies into other forms of business life. For this reason, the 'cultural critique' is radically misconceived indeed; in moving from industry to commerce, Britain's entrepreneurs were responding intelligently to realistically perceived opportunities. This movement, therefore, had little or nothing to do with any factor in Britain's underlying culture, elite educational system, or fundamental system of values, but was, again, an entirely rational economic response. On the contrary, a detailed and clear-headed analysis of Britain's culture, elite educational system, and fundamental system of values reveals that Britain was always unusually positivistic in its culture, and rational, moderate, and pro-capitalistic in its values. Similarly, while the public school system assisted in a rational adaption to the facts of Britain's true economic position, rather than a pre-modern obstacle to economic development, which had few or none of the deleterious effects (such as the 'haemorrhage of talent' of the scions of business families away from business life) which its many critics constantly suggest. The 'cultural critique' is, thus, not merely misconceived but a *non sequitur*, offering explanations for something which did not actually occur.

That Britain's economy was *always, even during the period 1815-70*, primarily a commercial/financial-oriented economy whose comparative advantage always lay in these areas and did so increasingly after 1870 will be a contention that is highly surprising to many readers, though probably less so to economic historians. Indeed, over the past twenty years or so it is probably fair to say that a great deal of the original research on post-1760 economic history has emphasised the relative unimportance of industrialisation in Britain, its slowness and haphazardness, as well as the now-enhanced perceptions of London and provincial entrepôts.[33] Increased importance is also now widely attached to the earlier phases of imperialism and to the 'gentlemanly capitalism' which emerged from Britain's old colonial system from 1688, which, in the words of Cain and Hopkins, 'preceded the industrial revolution, interacted with it, and retained [its] vitality after the onset of [Britain's] industrial decline'[34] – a summary which accords almost precisely with the thesis advanced here. Understood in this light, Britain's economic performance appears fundamentally different in many significant respects from the (as yet) far more familiar and reiterated lamentation over its industrial decline which has produced the 'cultural critique'. Indeed, it is no exaggeration to suggest that the whole evolution of modern Britain will appear significantly different if viewed from the perspective suggested here.

Several separate types of evidence can be advanced for the proposition that Britain's economy has always been, essentially, a commercial/ financial one which became more oriented toward commerce and finance still from the late nineteenth century onward: evidence from the distribution of the middle classes, in terms of numbers, geography, and incomes; from the occupational distribution of the employed population as a whole; and from the success of the City, and other commercial and financial businesses, *vis-à-vis* manufacturing industry. Let us consider each in turn.

We know a considerable amount about the geographical distribution of the British middle classes in modern times, and everything we know about this matter demonstrates, over and over again, the key importance of London and other commercial centres, and of the commercial and financial trades, for both the numbers and incomes of the British middle classes.

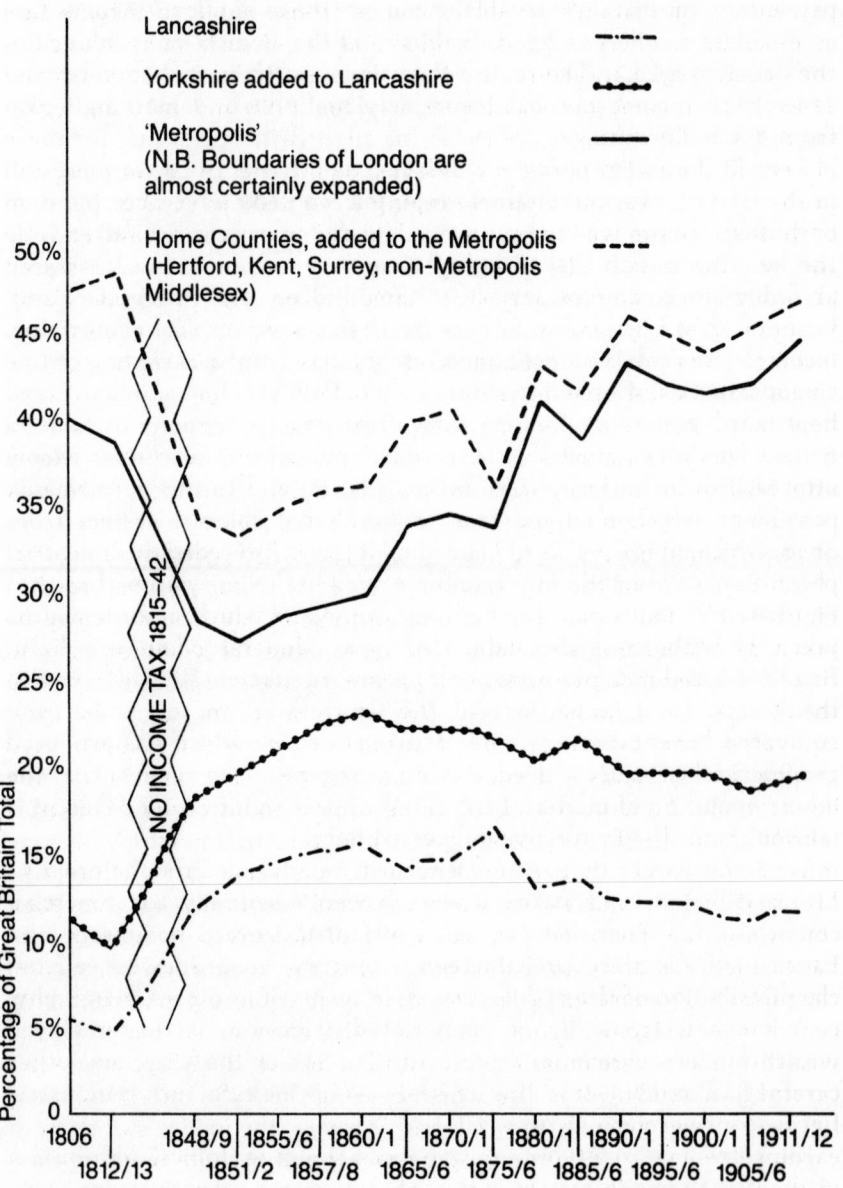

Figure 1.1: Percentage of Business and Professional Incomes (Schedules D and E, and Business Portions of A) of £100–£150 or more, by London and Leading Industrial Counties, 1806-1911/12.

Perhaps the most significant piece of evidence which can be adduced to support this contention is contained in Figure 1.1 which details the percentage of Britain's taxable incomes (those liable to income tax) assessed in, on the one hand, London and the Home Counties and, on the other hand, Lancashire and Yorkshire, in the period 1806–15 and 1848–1911. Income tax was levied between 1798 and 1815 and again from 1842. (Percentages are those for all of Britain, not just for these places.) In the earlier period it was levied on incomes of £60 or more and in the latter on various figures ranging from £100 to £160 or more: in both cases its aim was to tax the middle and upper classes and exclude the working class.[35] The nineteenth-century income tax was assessed according to a complex series of Schedules on *types* of income (land, farmers' rent, incomes derived from business or the professions, incomes from professional bodies, etc.) and, with the exception of one single statistical source (to be discussed below), it is impossible to know how many individual persons paid income tax in nineteenth-century Britain or how much, *in toto*, they owned. Nevertheless, from unpublished manuscript sources at the Public Record Office it is possible to ascertain where these persons lived, where their businesses or professional offices were located, and the broad patterns of geographical residence in the key economic areas of Britain are recorded in Figure 1.1.[36] The totals for London and the Home Counties may be taken as convenient shorthands or metaphors for commercial- and financial-based incomes generated by the British middle classes, while the totals for Lancashire and Yorkshire may be taken as their equivalent for industrial and manufacturing incomes. Both geographical shorthands – it goes without saying – are extremely crude descriptions: London contained significant manufacturing industries (although not the factory capitalism of the industrial north), while one must never forget that many cities in Lancashire and Yorkshire, like Liverpool, Hull, and Leeds were essentially commercial entrepôts, containing few factories. On balance, a dichotomy between London/ Lancashire-Yorkshire probably overstates the proportion of middle-class incomes generated by *manufacturing*: even in a great manufacturing centre like Glasgow, from 1870 to 1914 commercial and financial wealth-holders were more significant than industrialists, according to a careful local study.[37] It is also worth bearing closely in mind that these figures refer exclusively to *middle-class* incomes, the incomes of persons earning (generally) £100 or £150 or more, and exclude working-class incomes. It seems reasonable – though not certain – that the geographical distribution of the working classes and their incomes would increase the relative weight of the north of England and other industrial areas, although London contained by far the largest working class of any city in Britain (by several orders of magnitude), while inclusion of the rural working class would presumably advantage the south. It should also be kept in mind that Figure 1.1 records only business and professional incomes, not the rental income of landowners, which would add most significantly to the importance of 'old money' in the British economy.[38]

The overarching pattern suggested by Figure 1.1 is absolutely crucial to understanding the evolution of the British middle classes in modern times, and is, perhaps, the central argument made in this book. It will be seen that the income generated by London-based middle classes totalled nearly 50 per cent of the national middle-class income in the Napoleonic period (*after* thirty-five years of industrialisation), but declined in *relative* percentage terms until the 1850s, and then began a steady rise in the late Victorian and Edwardian periods, such that by the last years of peace prior to 1914 London's percentage of the national total was virtually as high as it had been a century before. In contrast, the share of Lancashire and Yorkshire rose dramatically until the 1860s, and then declined, slowly but perceptively. *At no time* did its share of Britain's middle-class income overtake that of London, and *at no time* was there a 'breakthrough' whereby the *essentially* commercial and financial (and professional) nature of the British middle classes gave up its lead to the industrial and manufacturing segment. From the Napoleonic era until the 1860s there was an extremely rapid rise in the share of middle-class incomes generated in Lancashire and Yorkshire, from just under 10 per cent of the national total in 1812–13 to just over 22 per cent in 1865–6, but these incomes, even at their peak, were still in a small minority of all incomes. From about 1870 onwards, however, the Lancashire/ Yorkshire percentage declined to about 19 per cent of the national total in 1911–12. What is now known of the very rich in nineteenth-century Britain shows exactly the same pattern, the predominance of London and of finance and commerce *vis-à-vis* industry.[39]

There are no directly comparable statistics of this kind for the post-1914 era, so far as I am aware, but it seems self-evident that the position of the former northern manufacturing middle classes has declined catastrophically, especially during the 1920s and since the mid-1960s, being routed, according to all accounts, in the 1980s. Not only have the traditional types of manufacturing industry staples all but disappeared (or literally disappeared, in the case of shipbuilding), but growth in manufacturing industries, such as in cars in the 1930–70 period or more recently in aerospace and computers, has been physically located away from the former heartland of the industrial revolution, while such growth as has occurred in the north has been chiefly in service industries like tourism. It seems virtually inconceivable on any reasonable assessment that a geographical breakdown of middle-class incomes (however defined) at regular intervals since 1914 would not show an even greater lead for London and the south than at the beginning of the century (and greater than average growth in regions like East Anglia and the West country), but with no place north of the Humber–Wash dividing line likely to show any relative growth apart from the West Midlands in the half century between 1920 and 1970, and places bordering on the North Sea which have been affected by the oil boom.

The figures presented above are for the amount of income assessed for taxation rather than the number of individual taxpayers or the number of individuals who may be said, by whatever definition is employed, to be a part of the middle class. As noted, there is, with one exception, apparently no source, either published or in manuscript form, which gives the actual number of persons in the middle class, or their geographical or occupational distribution. There is, however, one exception to this gap, a Return in the Parliamentary Papers in 1861 which lists the number of male persons charged to any of the Assessed Taxes or the Income Tax under Schedules B and D in 1859–60 in every parliamentary borough in England and Wales.[40] Despite its limitations, it is possible to work from this document and other contemporary material to ascertain the number of male persons with an income of £100 or more, and hence liable to pay income tax in 1859–60, from business or professional sources, who lived or had business premises in any parliamentary borough in England and Wales, together with the percentage of adult males in each such borough who were liable to income tax. The statistics here relate to the period when, relatively speaking, middle-class incomes generated in Britain's industrial north were very nearly at their peak, and just before the 'swing back' to London, which makes them especially significant. In Table 1.4 the total population in 1861, adult male population in 1861, number of income tax payers liable to tax under Schedules D and E (the schedules under which business and professional incomes were taxed), and the percentage of such taxpayers to all adult males, are given for 1859–60 for the eight London parliamentary boroughs of the time, and for all parliamentary boroughs in Lancashire and Yorkshire.

These returns may exaggerate the position of London *vis-à-vis* the north, since the Westminster returns include taxpayers under Schedule E (those employed by a public body or corporation) resident elsewhere; for this reason, a second, lower figure is given for the London boroughs, making the assumption that there were 50,000 fewer London taxpayers than are indicated here. On the other hand, these statistics include only parliamentary boroughs. Neither Chelsea nor most of Surrey (including Dulwich and Clapham), home to tens of thousands of middle-class families, were legally located in borough seats but in the adjacent county figures, and are hence excluded from these figures. So are women taxpayers, chiefly well-to-do widows and

Table 1.4 Number and percentage of income tax payers in London, Lancashire, and Yorkshire parliamentary boroughs in 1859–60

	Total population 1861	Adult males 1861	D&E taxpayers	Percentage D&E taxpayers to adult males
LONDON BOROUGHS				
London, City of	112,063	31,142	29,403	94.42
Finsbury	367,278	101,544	30,703	30.27
Marylebone	436,252	110,415	31,170	28.22
Tower Hamlets	317,900	80,333	27,449	34.17
Westminster	254,623	65,896	75,115	(113.99)
Lambeth	294,883	72,276	20,036	27.72
Southwark	193,593	52,231	8,782	16.81
Greenwich	139,436	40,102	4,848	12.09
London totals	2,116,028	553,939	227,506	41.07
Revised totals			(202,506)	(36.56)
LANCASHIRE BOROUGHS				
Ashton-under-Lyne	33,917	8,673	982	11.32
Blackburn	63,126	15,706	1,230	7.83
Bolton	70,395	17,638	1,379	7.82
Bury	37,563	9,860	651	6.60
Clitheroe	10,864	2,996	249	8.31
Lancaster	16,005	3,997	620	15.51
Liverpool	445,938	118,890	20,606	17.33
Manchester	357,979	91,607	14,031	15.32
Oldham	94,344	25,052	2,122	8.47
Preston	82,985	19,703	1,590	8.07
Rochdale	38,184	10,039	1,413	14.08
Salford	102,449	26,217	2,672	10.19
Warrington	26,947	7,012	665	9.48
Wigan	37,658	9,817	882	8.98
Lancashire totals	1,418,354	367,207	49,092	13.37
YORKSHIRE (W. R.) BOROUGHS				
Bradford	106,218	26,608	2,949	11.08
Halifax	37,014	9,596	1,257	13.10
Huddersfield	34,877	8,928	1,292	14.47
Knaresborough	5,402	1,504	310	20.61
Leeds	207,165	54,336	5,615	10.33
Pontefract	11,736	2,986	523	17.52
Ripon	6,172	1,634	282	17.26
Sheffield	185,172	48,889	4,613	9.44
Wakefield	23,150	6,454	756	11.71
Yorkshire totals	616,906	160,935	17,597	10.93

spinsters and disproportionately resident in London and the fashionable watering-places. So, too, are landowners (whose landed incomes are assessed under Schedule A, not included in this table), among them the great landed aristocrats who were certainly still the richest men in the country.

Whatever the case, however, the importance of London as the home *par excellence* of the Victorian middle classes emerges from these statistics with undeniable clarity. Although the total population of these London boroughs exceeded those of Lancashire and the West Riding by less than 4 per cent, London's taxpaying middle classes were three times as numerous as in the northern counties, a figure which may well understate rather than exaggerate the true position of London in the comparison. By 1860, a century of industrialisation may have transformed Britain into the 'workshop of the world', but the combined effects of urbanisation, the commercial revolution, and the industrial revolution upon Britain's middle classes were, in effect, systematically to advantage the most conservative elements within the middle and upper classes – bankers, merchants, and financiers within the entrepreneurial middle classes, professional men like lawyers and physicians, and Britain's landed aristocrats – rather than the newest and allegedly most 'dynamic' businessmen among factory capitalists who pioneered the use of the steam-engine, mechanised spinning and weaving, and modern engineering, which customarily form our mental image of the industrial revolution.

The great gap in size between the middle classes of London and those of the north we have discerned is, moreover, for the year 1860, when the growth rate of middle-class incomes in the north was nearly at its peak; after the 1860s, there was, as noted, a steady swing back to London, such that the differentials observed here were likely to have been much greater during the Edwardian period (although no comparable statistics to those given in Table 1.4 exist for any other date). Why was this? Was this the result of massive and chronic entrepreneurial failure which affected industrialists but not merchants and bankers – although (as discussed in Chapter 3) far more bankers, merchants, and middle-class Londoners generally were educated at public school and a university, so often cited as the *loci* of entrepreneurial failure, and were socially closer to the aristocracy? Surely such an argument – whose intrinsic merits will be discussed in detail in Chapter 3 – is less plausible than a far simpler one, that the comparative advantage of the British economy as a whole lay increasingly with commerce and finance rather than with industry, the partial and equivocal upsurge of industry and manufacturing from 1770 to 1860 being insufficient to transform this underlying secular trend?

The same striking trends we have seen among the middle classes are confirmed by national income and occupational statistics; indeed, it is probably confirmed by the very macroeconomic statistics which are apparently so unfavourable to Britain's economic performance over the past century.

While Britain was proverbially known as the 'workshop of the world', it was – rather surprisingly – never the case that the majority of its work force was employed in manufacturing and related industries, so far as the existing statistics – which are, admittedly, fairly patchy prior to the mid-nineteenth century – are able to show. This fact is significant, because a considerably higher portion of jobs in manufacturing and other heavy industries represent unskilled, semi-skilled, or skilled employment among the working classes, the bulk of the enormous increase in Britain's population which occurred after 1760 and coincidentally with the 'industrial revolution' as it is normally understood. There were a great many working-class jobs, of course, technically classified as part of the service sector, from postmen to train drivers and firemen, but by and large the middle- and lower-middle-class sections of society – what we now term the 'white collar' sector – are to be found in the services, while it is the manufacturing sector which contains the great labour-intensive industries and (as we have just seen) disproportionately smaller middle classes.

Given all the rough edges and inexactitudes in such historical figures, it seems perfectly clear from the available data that total employment in manufacturing industry never, at any time, amounted to one-half of the employed population, although it was, until recently, the largest single sector, as Table 1.5 makes clear.

Even these figures, however, certainly exaggerate the working-class share of employment in industry/manufacturing, for these categories comprise not merely ordinary factory operatives and miners, but the capitalists and managers in these occupations as well. It will also be seen, strikingly, that despite the strong swing back to London in the late nineteenth century as the chief venue of middle- and upper-class income earners, the British economy continued, to at least the 1960s, to generate enough investment in manufacturing industry to create employment in manufacturing and industry which actually saw a slight increase in the percentage of persons employed in this sector of the economy, compared even with the mid-Victorian zenith, although the services continued relentlessly to grow strongly and without a break.

As we have just noted, these statistics do not highlight class or status differences within the occupational distributions. Dr Guy Routh, Reader in Economics at the University of Sussex, has provided comparative statistics, from 1911, of the changing distribution of social class, by occupational status. The results here are extremely interesting, they strongly suggest a continuous 'levelling up' throughout this century

Table 1.5: Employment in industry/manufacturing, the services, and other components of the British economy, by percentages, 1861-1987

	1861	1881	1901	1921	1961	1981	1987
Industry/ Manufacturing	40.9	43.0	43.9	44.4	47.8	37.5	30.6
Services	20.7	23.6	30.2	41.3	41.2	see below	
Other (of which	38.4	33.4	25.9	14.3	5.0		
agricultural)	(26.5)	(18.5)	(12.6)	(9.0)	(3.9)		

	1981	1987
Commerce	25.4	35.5
Public and other services	34.8	32.5
Agriculture	2.3	1.4

Sources: 1861-1961: C. H. Feinstein, National Income, Expenditure, and Output of the United Kingdom, 1855-1965 (Cambridge, 1972), Tables 60 (T. 131) and 59 (T. 129); 1981-7: from Michael Ball, Fred Gray, and Linda McDowell, The Transformation of Britain (London, 1989), Table 3.1, p. 50. 'Industry/Manufacturing' includes the Orders of the Standard Industrial Classification of mining and quarrying; manufacturing; building and contracting; and gas, water, and electricity.

from manual 'blue collar' to non-manual 'white collar' employment, highly consistent with Britain's evolution toward an increasingly service-based economy, one whose ever-growing non-manual sector is hallmarked by comparatively larger incomes, more generous fringe benefits, and far less physically taxing work than in industry and manufacturing. Among males, from 1911 to 1979 the percentage in each occupational class group has been as shown in Table 1.6.

Prior to the period surveyed here, where the evidence, largely derived from the Census returns, is less precise, it also seems clear that, certainly from the later nineteenth century onwards, the middle-class professions and other non-manual male occupations were growing in number more rapidly than the general population. According to statistics amassed by Professor Harold Perkin, who has studied these trends in detail, employment in eight leading professions increased by 50.3 per cent between 1881 and 1911, compared with 47.7 per cent for all male occupations. (These eight professions included the old-established fields of clergymen and lawyers, whose numbers increased by only (respectively) 19.8 and 23.0 per cent in this period.) The non-manual branches of the civil service and local government increased no less than 183.9 per cent and all non-manual male occupations by 71.9 per cent between 1881 and 1911.[41]

All of these statistics appear to confirm what the economist Colin Clark termed 'Petty's Law' – after the seventeenth-century

Table 1.6 Occupational class and industrial status of occupied males in Great Britain, 1911–79, by percentage

	1911	1921	1931	1951	1971	1979
I Professional:						
A. Higher	1.34	1.36	1.50	2.56	4.87	15.7
B. Lower	1.61	2.02	2.03	3.16	5.95	
II Employers, administrative, managers:						
A. Employers and proprietors	7.74	7.69	7.65	5.74	5.07	16.4
B. Managers and administrators	3.91	4.28	4.54	6.78	10.91	
III Clerical workers	5.48	5.40	5.53	6.35	6.38	5.9
IV Foremen, inspectors, supervisors	1.75	1.91	2.00	3.28	5.04	6.9
V Skilled manual	32.99	32.30	29.96	30.36	29.08	19.2
VI Semi-skilled	33.63	28.30	28.85	27.92	20.82	19.1
VII Unskilled	11.55	16.72	17.92	13.84	11.89	4.7
	100.00	100.00	100.00	100.00	100.00	100.00

Source: Guy Routh, Occupation and Pay in Great Britain, 1906–79 (London 1980), Tables 1.1 (pp. 6–7) and 1.20 (p. 45). The 1979 data is taken from the New Earnings Survey (NES), not from the Census (as is the data from 1911 to 1971). The 1979 figure includes a further 14.6 per cent of 'Manual, Unclassified'. The 1971 total for all manual workers is 61.79 per cent; the 1979 total is 57.6 per cent.

mathematician and scholar Sir William Petty, who in the 1670s observed that economies seem inevitably to move from those with primary production as their base to manufacturing to 'merchandise' – what we totally term the tertiary or service section since – in Petty's blunt words – 'there is much more to be gained' in each new phase of the progression.[42] The accuracy of this remarkable insight is fundamental, in my view, to understanding the evolution of the British economy and the inferences we ought to draw from its growth and change. Nevertheless, the British economy did exhibit some sui generis features. It clearly did not progress from largely agricultural to a manufacturing to a service economy in any simple or straightforward sense. Britain probably ceased to be a chiefly agricultural economy as early as the eighteenth century. By the mid-eighteenth century it was essentially a highly prosperous commercial economy, with an equally efficient (and unique) agricultural sector based upon primogeniture and the 'triple division' of land tenure, and totally lacking a peasantry in the continental sense. It had already acquired a world-wide Empire whose importance for Britain's economy was probably far greater than the importance of its second Empire during the late Victorian and Edwardian era. Its standard of living and per capita income were already then uniquely high for a European society and already as high as that enjoyed by a stable developing country experiencing industrialisation.[43] Into this relatively satisfactory situation there appeared the twin hurricanes of industrialisation and unprecedented population growth, such that Britain's rate of economic expansion would be obliged to rise continuously and strongly merely to keep pace with its demographic explosion. But as we have seen, at no time did heavy industry and manufacturing actually become the predominant sectors of the economy: taking the very long-term view, Britain appears to have passed (very early) from an agricultural economy to a commercial one without as pronounced an industrial interval as many believe, although the evidence suggests that from the early nineteenth century until about 1860 manufacturing was certainly rising in importance at a disproportionate rate. For some, and certainly for many new men and families who entered the new manufacturing industries and processes, there was indeed 'much more to be gained' from them, although at no time was this the case *collectively* for the economy as a whole; similarly, for the vast new population produced by Britain's unprecedented demographic growth, there was more to be gained by working in a factory or a coal mine than by the alternatives – declining pre-industrial trades, emigration, or the workhouse.

Nevertheless, the most sophisticated and relevant recent research appears to show clearly that Britain's was never an industrial economy, but, since the early modern period, was always essentially a commercial or commercial/financial economy with a brief interruption of factory capitalism in the first half of the nineteenth century, whose importance has probably been exaggerated by the fact that it had the world's first modern factories, by the fact that it is highly visible, obvious, and unpleasant, and by the importance given to it by Marxism.

The third general point which might usefully be made about the divisions within British capitalism is the more qualitative one about the continuing prosperity and importance of the City and commercial/financial capitalism *vis-à-vis* manufacturing industry. Unlike British manufacturing industry – whose decline, at least before the 1970s, is in any case arguable – Britain's role as a financial centre experienced no equivalent decline, or one which was evidently due solely to the rise of rival centres. 'Since World War Two, the City has been able to overcome the decline of the British economy', as Youssef Cassis, one of the leading historians of the City's banking elite, has put it.[44] In 1860, Lancashire and the West Riding together constituted the pre-eminent industrial and manufacturing region in the world. By 1910, Lancashire and the West Riding (together with Glasgow and the West Midlands) clearly and unarguably had to share this distinction with the industrialised areas of the United States, centring on the Great Lakes, and with the Ruhr region in Germany. By 1990, manufacturing industry centred, in descending order of prominence, on the rim of east Asia, second in the industrial heartland of the continental EC, especially in Germany, and third in the older and newer manufacturing centres of the United States. Britain in general and Lancashire in particular were far back in the pack, although perhaps not so far back as some have suggested. In direct contrast to this progressive decline, while in 1860 the City of London was the pre-eminent financial centre of the world, and while in 1910 New York and, conceivably but not certainly, Berlin were second-running rivals to London's continuing pre-eminence, in 1990 London was still unarguably one of the three great financial centres of the world, along with New York and Tokyo. This role reflected both the failure of Britain's manufacturing and political declines to shake London's pre-eminence in a fundamental way and the successful entrepreneurial response, by the City, to the openings provided by European unity and the failure by New York to build on the lead it perhaps might have enjoyed following the Second World War. By 1981 it was estimated by one study that financial institutions situated in the City of London had 'at their disposal, the massive treasury of some £562 billion', over which 'they exercise the power to dispose of as they please'.[45] Banks accounted for £332 billion of this sum; insurance companies, building societies, pension funds, and trusts for the rest.[46] After 1981, at least until the effects of the New York Stock Market crash of 1987 made themselves felt, the City continued to attract foreign banks, financial institutions, and currency dealers in ever greater numbers.

It is frequently claimed by political historians and radical critics of British economic policy in this century that government policy has consistently favoured the City and finance at the expense of manufacturing industry. The failure of Britain to adopt Joseph Chamberlain's tariff proposals at the turn of the century, and, more notoriously, the decision to return to the Gold Standard in 1925, are the most frequently cited examples of this bias, together with a generalised and chronic failure to compel British finance to invest more heavily in manufacturing industry.[47] Nevertheless, despite these often-heard accounts, most governments (of all persuasions) since the 1930s *have* repeatedly enacted major schemes to direct greater investment in the high unemployment areas of the north. It is fair to say that these schemes often met with much success, especially Douglas Jay's area policies in the post-war Labour government, although in the context of full employment and a labour shortage.[48] What is perhaps most striking about the continuing and chronic gap between the prosperous south and the impoverished north is that, *despite* the best efforts of most modern British governments, the geographical divide continues to appear and reappear with the regularity of clockwork. The inference is that this divide is extremely deeply founded in both economic and social realities, and that attempts to alter this state of affairs are unlikely to succeed.

A closer examination of British commerce and finance also reveals many features of continuing and, internationally, possibly unique strength, which have given to these sectors of the economy their long-term vigour in the face of frequently alleged relative decline in other sectors. For instance the London Stock Exchange, was, historically, probably far better organised than its New York counterpart. R. C. Michie, in a careful and imaginative recent study of both exchanges in the period 1850–1914, has highlighted the clear superiority of London in this period; his study is, additionally, a welcome change from most comparisons of the British and American economies in this period, which virtually rubber-stamped the deeply ingrained underlying assumption that America's economy *must* perforce have been superior. Michie's possibly surprising conclusion is the product of studying one of Britain's outstanding key financial institutions rather than its heavy industry, so often the subject of comparative examinations of this kind.[49] According to Michie:

> As a result of the New York Stock Market's restrictive policy on membership and quotation, its high and inflexible minimum commission rates and its methods of trading, the securities market in New York was fragmented into a number of distinct components, each dealing in the business the Exchange ignored. By persistently interfering in the relations between itself and these other markets, the New York Exchange reduced the efficient operation of the securities market, as a whole. . . . [T]he Stock Exchange's commitment to the daily settlement of trading, and its growing restriction of quotation to large, established corporations, did have profound influences upon the U.S. economy. The former was a destabilizing influence upon the financial system, tending to exaggerate crises, while the latter encouraged the creation of ever larger business units operating, first, in railways and, later, throughout manufacturing industry.[50]

Another related area in finance in which many would probably judge Britain's structure and performance to be historically superior to that of the United States is in the respective branch banking networks in each country. From the late nineteenth century onward, of course,

British discount banking has been overwhelmingly dominated by the Big Five (Big Eight prior to 1919; now the Big Four) high street banks, each with hundreds of branches throughout the country, and traditionally including some mortgage (especially commercial) finance and the accounts of local small- and medium-sized businesses as the backbone of their trade.[51] In the United States, however, banks were chartered exclusively by the states and until the 1960s were *not* permitted to operate in more than one state – a fact which is too little known, and even less appreciated, abroad. It is for this reason that American banks have the curious names they often do – the First National Bank of Topeka, Kansas; the Second Bank of Austin, Texas, and so on – while even a bank with a name like the Bank of America operated in one state, in this case California. The effects of this system upon finance in particular regions or states in America, especially those disproportionately affected by a regional depression, can readily be imagined: as all or virtually all of their depositors came from the immediate neighbourhood of the bank, and (until the New Deal reforms of the 1930s) individual banks had absolutely no way of securing further deposits in a state or region heavily affected by economic downturn, and no links to more successful banks in other cities or regions, bank closure and ruin were regularly the order of the day. During the Great Depression, heavily affected by a rural crisis in the South and Midwest, it is arguable that this factor alone magnified a normal economic downturn into a national and then international catastrophe of unprecedented magnitude. In contrast, Britain's branch banking system ensured that the worst-affected areas of Depression would continue to be linked financially with the more prosperous areas of the south-east, with an arguable result that Britain's experience of the Great Depression was much less severe than America's. This size differential in discount banking continues to the present day. In 1991 the largest commercial bank in the United States, Citibank NA of New York, held deposits of $155 billion. Citibank was outranked in size by *twenty-five* foreign banks, including Barclays (with deposits of $259 billion) and National Westminster (with deposits of $233 billion) and by *sixteen* different Japanese banks. The largest commercial bank in Texas, America's third largest state, NCNB Texas National Bank of Dallas, held deposits of only $27 billion, while the largest bank in Chicago, America's third largest city, held deposits of only $25 billion.[52]

A third area in which Britain's performance has been outstanding has been in the continuing centrality of the City as a major financial centre over the past thirty years. The City today is unquestionably one of the three great financial centres in the world, together with New York and Tokyo, and is likely to remain as such, despite the rise of instantaneous world-wide communications and the rivalry of Zurich, Paris, and

Frankfurt in Europe.[53] The City's traditional role re-emerged strongly in the late 1950s and early 1960s, with the rise of the Eurocurrency and Eurobond markets, in the wake of restrictions still imposed on American financial dealing and with the renaissance of Western Europe and the beginnings of large-scale investment and borrowings by Third World and Arab countries; Britain's residual links in the former Empire and the Middle East unquestionably stood it in good stead, as did the reputation of the City for total probity and of British bankers and public servants for traditional honesty and gentlemanly behaviour. The location of the marine and aircraft insurance industry at Lloyd's, and the time-zone centrality of London between America and the Far East were also powerful factors in this renaissance. So, too, in all likelihood was the relatively *laissez-faire* attitude of both Labour and Tory governments to the affairs of the City – in striking contrast to Labour's record of interference with industry.[54] Although some of these favourable trends were surely diminished by the Wall Street crash of 1987 and the subsequent mood of deep pessimism in City circles, in comparative terms the City remains one of Britain's few economic claims to being a great power, a claim which is universally respected.

In other respects, too, the economic decline of Britain, when the full range of business activities is considered, has been exaggerated, especially if one moves beyond the usual types of statistics by which economic performance is normally measured. In 1990, for example, Heathrow was the busiest airport in the world, with 43.0 million arriving and departing passengers, just ahead of Haneda airport in Tokyo (40.2 million), Frankfurt (28.9 million), Chicago O'Hare (25.6 million), and Orly in Paris (24.3 million). This is, surely, an excellent test of contemporary importance and centrality in the service sector. Even in the manufacturing sector where most of Britain's relative decline has occurred, Britain was still the ninth largest producer of motor vehicles in the world, while some businesses like ICI, Royal/ Dutch Shell, and Glaxo were still among the largest in the world.

The view of the development of the British economy outlined here has recently become popular among historians, although its implications for the 'cultural critique' have not properly been spelled out. In particular, this view is associated with the economic historian C. H. Lee, in his work *The British Economy Since 1700* (1986); P. J. Cain and A. G. Hopkins, in their study of 'Gentlemanly Capitalism and British Expansion Overseas', and my own research.[55] Lee has examined and contrasted the highly successful economy of the south-east of Britain, centred in London, compared with the fitful long-term growth of the north. According to Lee's careful research, Britain in effect contained two separate regional economies, an 'affluent economy . . . [with] an element of self-sustaining growth' in the south-east, based 'on the twin pillars of accumulated wealth from trade and finance and the land', and a low-income, relatively less significant industrial and manufacturing economy in the north.[56] Cain and Hopkins see 'gentlemanly capitalism', based, in their words, on 'land, finance, and commercial services', as the key to understanding the growth of the British Empire and its unofficial empire down to the Second World War, and minimize the role of British industry in this process. My own work has focused on the very rich and, as noted here, on the taxpaying middle classes.[57]

There is, in addition, another very important consideration, not normally adduced by those for whom Britain's long-term decline is assumed, which is of great relevance here, namely the initially high and continuously rising standard of living throughout modern history. It is well known that Britain was not, in terms of its living standards, the equivalent of a Third World country prior to industrialisation; its average living standards were, to use the well-known analogy of Phyllis Deane, around the same as that of Mexico at the time she was writing in 1965.[58] Nearly all European visitors to England, from the late Middle Ages to the nineteenth century and beyond, routinely commented on the amazingly uniform prosperity of England (if not of Scotland, Wales, or Ireland), and especially the lack of a desperately poor peasantry or artisan class visibly defined by their dress.[59] Perhaps the first class of foreign visitors to England regularly to dissent from this sanguine view of Britain's prosperity were middle-class American tourists of the nineteenth century, who were invariably appalled by the gross and degrading poverty of Britain's industrial towns and slums.[60] These travellers' tales probably conceal two underlying important facets of Britain's standard of living: first, down to after the Second World War, the average standard of living in Britain, even for its working class, was higher than anywhere else in Europe, higher than in countries like Germany which were making rapid economic progress. Second, it was lower than the standard of living in the United States (and perhaps one or two other countries like Australia), at least for America's urban white Protestants, although unprecedented population growth and an increase in income inequality in Britain as a result of industrialisation – whose maximum point was probably reached about 1870 – created an urban and rural proletariat with a significant portion continuously below the most minimal poverty line.[61] On any *European*-wide comparison, however, Britain down to the post-1945 period *always* had an average standard of living which continued to be higher than that of countries which were ostensibly industrialising more rapidly and to whose industrial growth British cassandras were continuously making invidious comparisons, Germany being the prime example. There is simply no sign that this was changing when the First and Second World Wars unexpectedly altered the course of European history: it is now a commonplace, for instance, that the inter-war period was a time when living standards rose for the whole British population, mass unemployment and the Depression notwithstanding; the dire primary poverty of Victorian England's slums all but vanished, while by the mid-1930s the middle and lower middle classes, and even a part of the working class, had entered the first stages of the 'affluent society', with widespread ownership of electrically powered consumer durables and classless expenditure patterns.[62].

The post-war era shows even more of a paradoxical picture, and one which is of great importance to the argument of this book, for per capita living standards in Britain have risen dramatically and uninterruptedly, at a time when the statistics of economic performance normally used by economists and public commentators have almost invariably shown Britain's economic performance to have been the worst of any comparable country. Furthermore, and more singularly still, quantitative indices of consumer living standards in Britain show them to be identical or virtually identical to those in other industrialised countries, including nations like Japan, Germany, and the United States to which Britain is adversely compared on a daily basis. These gains in per capita living standards, moreover, have come especially rapidly when Britain's ostensible economic performance, as measured by the normal indices of economic performance – rates of inflation, unemployment, economic growth, the balance of trade, etc. – has seemingly been most deplorable. Trends in the ownership of consumer durable goods (since 1973) and in housing tenure (since 1914) in Britain are spelled out in Tables 1.7 and 1.8.

The data here are indeed remarkable, and are in themselves surely quite sufficient to put the lie to, or at least greatly to qualify, any notion of a British economic decline in recent decades. There simply cannot be the slightest doubt that the past three decades have seen the most marked and singular rise in the standard of living for the ordinary Englishman and woman of any period in history, with levels of ownership of consumer durables, and even more significantly, home ownership, reaching levels virtually unimaginable a few decades before. Who, in 1950, would have believed that a few decades hence a majority of households would possess central heating, confined at the time to the mansions and exclusive apartments of only some of the very rich? A new household toy like the video, introduced only around 1980, was found within eight years in more than half the homes in Britain – and so on through the list of items.

Perhaps the most important comparative fact, however, which one might adduce about this data is that the figures for Britain are virtually identical for all industrial countries. In the United States, for instance, 65.6 per cent of all housing units were owner-occupied in 1980.[63]

Table 1.7 Trends in the ownership of consumer durables, Great Britain, 1973–88, by percentage of all households

	1973	1978	1981	1988
Vacuum cleaner	88	92	94	–
Refrigerator	78	91	93	–
Deep freezer	–	32	49	77
Washing machine	67	75	78	84
Tumble drier	–	19	23	42
Dishwasher		3	4	10
Telephone	45	–	75	85
Car	54	57	59	–
Central heating	39	45	59	–
Television:	95			
Colour		61	74	91
Black and white only		35	23	7
Video	–	–	–	53
Home computer	–	–	–	18

Sources: Central Statistical Office, *Social Trends 1983–1991*, p. 115; p. 101. Not all items are covered in every year.

Table 1.8 Housing by tenure, Great Britain, 1914–88, by percentage of all households

Date	% Owner-occupied	% Local authority	% Privately rented	Others
1914	10		90	
1938	25	10	65	
1951	29	18	45	8
1960	42	26	26	6
1970	50	30	15	5
1981	56	32	12	–
1988	66	23	12	–

Sources: 1914–81: David Butler and Gareth Butler, *British Political Facts, 1900–1985* (London, 1986), p. 334; 1988: Central Statistical Office, *Social Trends, 1991*, p. 146.

Differences between Britain and America in regard to housing tenure can probably be better explained by Britain's far-reaching rent controls and by relative age differences (Britain has significantly more elderly people, often living in local authority housing or nursing homes) and differential local customs (Scots and Northern Irish are more likely to live in council housing than are the English) than by differences in the standard of living *per se*. British levels of consumer durable ownership were remarkably similar to those in other industrialised countries and slightly better in some categories: only 82 per cent of French households owned a colour TV in 1989 and only 75 per cent of American households owned a washing machine in that year, for example. *All* industrialised countries have, for all practical purposes, virtually identical standards of living by these measurements, although contemporary Britain appears, if anything, to be on the more affluent end of the continuum.[64]

These extraordinary gains in the British standard of living have come about, it should be reiterated, at precisely the time when Britain's economic performance has been the subject of universal lamentation and hostile criticism. How can this be? How is it that the greatest gains for the standard of living of the average person in the history of Britain – for that is clearly what these statistics show – have occurred precisely when Britain's economy was the subject of perpetual derision? How is it that the standard of living of the average person is at least as high in Britain as in the United States or Germany? It is the sincere belief of the author that, in fact, the coincidence of the unprecedented rise in the British standard of living with the consistently disastrous figures of the normal indices of economic performance are so incongruous and anomalous that in themselves they constitute prima-facie evidence that the ordinary figures of economic performance simply do not measure what they are invariably taken to measure – the overall strength of the economy and the overall economic well-being of the population – and are, in fact, largely irrelevant to accurate analysis of a country's economic state of health. By any rational and objective criteria, I would submit, Britain's economy has never performed more strongly in its history than during the past twenty years, while its performance has enabled Britain to close the gap with those few countries which, it could be argued, formerly enjoyed a significantly higher standard of living. In the United States, for instance, owner-occupied housing constituted 45.6 per cent of all housing units in 1920 and 61.9 per cent in 1960, compared with Britain's *c.*15 per cent in 1920 and 42 per cent in 1960.[65] It might be more accurate, however, to describe this as the expansion downward of the consumer web of credit, and the expansion outwards of middle-class consumer expectations and patterns of behaviour to take in virtually the whole of the British working class and British regions beyond London and the south-east. All of this is powerful further evidence, in my view, of the superficiality of the 'cultural critique' and other views necessarily premised on the fact of Britain's economic decline.

Perhaps the most objectionable feature of the 'cultural critique' – and, indeed, of many other lines of criticism of Britain's economic performance during the past generation – is its obsession for manufacturing industry, its manufacturing fetishism. Tacitly, only manufacturing counts as a 'legitimate' business activity. This is especially curious as it is in direct contradiction of 'Petty's Law', the natural evolution of all economies, not in the long run toward manufacturing, but toward the services, commerce, and finance, which all cogent observers of modern economies are of course aware has been a general rule throughout modern history. It is also in direct contradiction of the common-sense evidence of regional differentiation in modern societies: prosperous cosmopolitan world centres like London, Paris, or New York comprise economies relatively less based in manufacturing industry than urban industrial centres which are renowned for their squalor and lack of amenities or diversity. It is difficult to believe that there is not some underlying sexual undertone to the widespread preference for manufacturing rather than the services, manufacturing industry being virile and related *inter alia* to military prowess, the services in contrast being seen as effete and non-productive, although they generate far more revenue. There is nothing privileged or preferable about manufacturing industry as compared to the services: a pound is always a pound, a dollar is always a dollar. Recently I asked the manager of a jet engine factory in England to show me a randomly chosen ten-pound note taken from the company's tills. I carefully compared this piece of currency to another ten-pound note taken from the revenue of a firm which provides bus tours of Stratford-upon-Avon and Blenheim Palace. Despite the most careful and searching examination, I was unable to discern the slightest difference between the two.

If the view of the evolution and nature of the British economy which has been put here is accurate, its implications for the 'cultural critique' are surely fundamental: the entire 'cultural critique' appears to be radically misconstrued, being based on a fundamentally inaccurate conception of the nature of the British economy over the past 150 years and offering reasons for its change and evolution which simply do not accord with the actual facts. The most fundamental proposition of the 'cultural critique', that Britain's was the first economy to industrialise but that it progressively declined as an industrial economy after 1870, is essentially flawed. Its second fundamental proposition, that British culture was and is anti-business and anti-industrial, is also incorrect, although demonstrating this will require separate discussions of the nature of British culture, of the educational system, normally a part of the socialisation process of the upper middle class and the elites, and of the structure of Britain's elites themselves. The rest of this book will discuss each of these matters in turn.

2

British culture and economic performance

A central contention of the 'cultural critique' analysis is that Britain's culture, especially since about 1870, is endemically anti-capitalist and in particular anti-industrial and anti-manufacturing. This is clearly an underlying and key presupposition of this viewpoint and no analysis of this critique can fail to address the matters raised by its proponents.

Among the historians we have encountered, the cultural dimension of the critique is most prominent in the writings of Martin Wiener. For Wiener:

> The children of businessmen were admitted to full membership in the upper class, at the price of discarding the destructive, production-oriented culture shaped during the century of relative isolation [i.e. post-1760 'isolation' from the gentry]. 'The main point about landowners – in England at least – is that they did not acquire their land in order to develop it, but in order to enjoy it', observed H. J. Habbakuk. The adoption of a culture of enjoyment by new landowners and aspiring landowners meant the dissipation of a set of values that had projected their fathers as a class to the economic heights, and the nation to world predominance. In its place, they took up a new ideal – that of the gentleman. . . . Through these mechanisms of social absorption, the zeal for work inventiveness, material production and money making gave way within the capitalist class to the more aristocratic interests of cultivated style, the pursuits of leisure, and political service. Similarly, the modern industrial town was abandoned, whenever the means existed, in favour of a rural, preferably historic home.[1]

At the heart of the complex, entrenched cultural syndrome, pervading 'educated opinion', which emerged triumphant in post-1870 Britain was the 'suspicion of material and technological development and [the] symbolic exclusion of industrialism'.[2] 'Old values and patterns of behaviour lived on within the new, whose character was thus profoundly modified. The end result of the nineteenth-century transformation of Britain was indeed a peaceful accommodation, but one that entrenched premodern elements within the new society and gave legitimacy to antimodern sentiments'.[3] In the late nineteenth century 'the myth of an England essentially rural and essentially unchanging' became all-pervasive, appealing to 'Conservatives and Imperialists, and to anti-Imperialists, Liberals and Radicals'.[4] 'The vision of a tranquilly rustic and traditional national way of life permeated English life.'[5] Economists, political commentators, and even businessmen almost invariably despised and attacked 'the snares of economic growth'.[6] This pervasive anti-business culture 'could not help but affect the world of action'.[7] In the twentieth century

> [British] politics and business . . . bore the imprint of a divided bourgeois consciousness. The nation that had been the mother of the industrial revolution was now uneasy with its offspring. The class that had reared industrialism seemed to wish to deny its paternity.[8]

Wiener examines and analyses modern British culture for over 200 pages in terms of how it worked – in his view – through politics, through intellectual life, through the educational system, and through the careers of businessmen and large corporations, to diminish the attractions of profit-seeking capitalism. In a very similar – indeed, almost identical – vein, another key writer responsible for the widespread acceptance of this viewpoint, Corelli Barnett, posits that

> The 'enlightened' Establishment had been a hundred years and more in the making, its ancestry beginning with (to put it in studbook form) romanticism out of emotion by idealism [!]. The early-nineteenth-century romantic movement had reacted against Georgian materialism and cold rationality; it turned away in disgust from the ugly visage of industrialising Britain and the coarseness of living humanity; and it found refuge in beautiful other worlds of the imagination. Where Wordsworth and Sir Walter Scott showed the way, Pugin, Morris and the Pre-Raphaelites followed with their stained-glass visions of the middle ages. . . .Round the turn of the twentieth century, men of letters, artists and architects had persuasively reinterpreted the earlier romantic conceptions of an ideal world, laying a new emphasis on the moral and physical beauty of an imagined rural life compared with the squalor and greed of urban Britain. . . .All these strands of romantic imagination move together to make the texture of the 'enlightened' Establishment's sensibility, explaining the aesthetic vision of New Jerusalem as a sun-lit garden-city society inhabited by a race at once comely and happy.[9]

When Anthony Sampson completed his original *Anatomy of Britain* in 1962, he concluded that

> All through this book I have been haunted by the Victorians, who invented so many of the institutions in which we now work – regiments, public schools, civic universities, the professional civil service, political parties, the Pru [Prudential Assurance]. . . . The dominating presence of the Victorians is enhanced by the traditional British habit of preferring to honour the old institutions, with their pageantry and rigmaroles, rather than the new more powerful ones. . . .The gap between pomp and power, between the 'dignified' and 'efficient' parts, is an immemorial British trait. . . .But after visiting the darker caves of government, I believe that this game has gone to ridiculous lengths.[10]

There is thus a consensus among the proponents of the 'cultural critique' that Britain's culture was profoundly affected during the nineteenth century so that it became an adversary of capitalist enterprise and innovation in the undisguised and dynamic form which was the hallmark of other, more rapidly growing economies.

These claims about Britain's culture are both far-reaching and complex; they also entail an understanding of the definition of culture, a term which is obviously ambiguous and multifaceted. 'Culture' can refer to a number of different things, superficially related but also widely varied in meaning and implication. One might speak of a national culture, the sum of prevalent and normal assumptions, habits, attitudes, and imagery in a particular country at a particular time which sets it apart from national cultures elsewhere, often in very subtle ways, and which might thus be well discerned by foreigners. It is clear that advocates of the 'cultural critique' have something like this in mind; they clearly suggest that Britain's prevalent post-1870 national culture is anti-industry, anti-modernisation, anti-profit, anti-urban and so on. This definition of culture is, however, conflated with others to which it may or may not be more than superficially related, if that. The clearest example of this is its conflation with what is often termed 'high culture', the prevalent schools, ideologies, genres, and trends of a country's leading intellectuals, especially its writers, university academics, artists, and highbrow editors. A 'national culture' might also be distinguished from a nation's 'mass culture' in the sense this latter term is usually meant today to denote the entertainments, unofficial activities, dress, speech, music, etc., of the majority of people in a society, especially those unaffected by 'high culture'. Although mass culture may be national-specific, it can often be exampled by cases with functional equivalents elsewhere – for example, baseball is the national summer sport in the United States and Japan, as is cricket in Britain,

Australia, and the West Indies. In contrast, many aspects of national culture in the first, most general sense we distinguished may have no ready functional equivalent but only represent national-specific modes of behaviour or patterns of thought. It is probably true, for instance, that the behaviour of a middle-class Englishman in the face of some unexpected adversity or crisis would be markedly different from that of a peasant from southern Italy met with the same crisis – or so the familiar stereotype would imply – with the Englishman stoic and rational, the Italian gesticulating and emotional. However offensive it is now regarded to talk in such terms, it seems obvious that such national cultural characteristics plainly exist. Similarly, men and women can probably be shown regularly to behave differently in different situations, the old and the young, and so on.

There are, however, difficulties in all this at several levels when these definitions are related to an argument about the economic decline (or rise) of Britain (or any other country). One, most obviously, is the lack of clarity and exactitude in relating the characteristics of a national culture – assuming they can be readily identified at all – to economic performance. Another is the relationship of examples taken from a country's high culture – or, indeed, popular culture – to a country's prevalent national culture, and the relationship of these to economic performance. Because the word 'culture' has several meanings in English, this difficulty is particularly insidious, since examples from a country's (highly unrepresentative and untypical) high culture may well be taken as characteristic of a national culture to which they are related only by the use of the term 'culture' in ambiguous ways. Another crucial difficulty lies in the hazards entailed in identifying a set of writers, intellectuals, or schools of thought in a country as being the mainstream of that society's high culture (or 'culture' defined in any other way). Normally, those who are known widely, either at that time or later, represent only a fraction of that society's artists and cultural figures.

It must seem apparent even to the most superficial student of the 'cultural critique' as it has commonly been presented in relation to Britain's economic 'decline' since 1870 that all of these difficulties and ambiguities – and probably others as well – are consistently present in the arguments of its advocates. There is, for example, a constant slide from high culture – the anti-business rhetoric and statements of intellectuals – to national culture, with these statements taken as typical of deeply held beliefs about the whole society. But, almost by definition, one would have thought, the writings of the intelligentsia are untypical of the views of the average person – most intellectuals are, almost by definition, at odds with the commonly held beliefs of the day. There is the selection of intellectuals to demonstrate the anti-business mood of the intelligentsia; how often are those with different views selected? Most importantly of all, there is the tacit assumption that the progenitors or organs of either high culture or national culture, even assuming they have been properly identified, are responsible for, and can accurately be held to be responsible for, an economy's failure to perform as well as its competitors: in other words, that there is a salient causal connection between the anti-industrial or anti-business climate of opinion found pervasively (it is argued) in high culture or national culture and the performance of its entrepreneurs.

Many of these points have been made in other critiques of (in particular) Wiener's thesis, although not with the emphases we wish to give here.[11] The theses which will be argued here are that Britain's high culture was, demonstrably, perhaps the least hostile to entrepreneurship and business life of any in Europe and perhaps in the world; its intellectuals were the least alienated of those of any leading society; and that Britain's culture was becoming more rational and positivistic rather than less from 1850 onwards, in a way which it is reasonable to link causally *with* support for pro-business values rather than as antipathetic to them.

One of the major problems inherent in any attempt to link cultural traditions with economics is the question of the selectivity of the evidence: more than in most historical questions, the evidence is extremely diverse and does not immediately select itself. It seems perfectly clear, as well, that the historian with a deeply held view on this question will be sorely tempted to select evidence to fit his views. In any society or nation which is reasonably diverse and multifaceted, and where a diverse intelligentsia has existed for some generations, virtually any intellectual tradition can be constructed by later historians in order to explain or account for that society's distinctive outcomes. The sage words of the American sociologist Peter F. Drucker, written in 1943, ably describe the pitfalls of ascribing national outcomes to a particular sequence of historical figures, deemed to be the most significant in that nation's history:

> If the national character explanation is untenable the national history explanations are meaningless. If the Germans instead of Nazism had developed a German form of Gandhi pacifism, we would now have many books showing the 'inevitability' of this development in the light of the Reformation, Luther, Kant, Beethoven or F. W. Forester; and there were a great many more devoted pacifists in the Germany of 1927 than there were devoted Nazis. If the English had developed a totalitarian philosophy, the pseudo-historian would have had a field-day with Henry VIII, that

great totalitarian Cromwell, Hobbes, Bentham, Carlyle, Spencer and Bosanquet.[12]

'National-history explanations' – clearly being used by Drucker in two of the senses we distinguished, to denote both national cultures and high cultures – are indeed so often a part of our common imagery of nations and national behaviour; how often does this popular imagery change! Compare, for example, the common and contrasting popular images of China and Japan: from 1931 to 1945 Japan was commonly (and correctly) seen as a military aggressor and fascist behemoth, China as a gentle land of peaceful peasants. Twenty years later, in the United States at least, the wheel had swung full circle, with Maoist China now almost invariably portrayed as a fanatical ideological aggressor, bent on Communising Asia at all costs, while Japan was known at the time chiefly for having renounced its army and for producing cheap, harmless, imitative junk. By the 1980s the wheel of popular perception in the west had swung again, with post-Maoist China until 1989 edging into alliance with the west and Japan increasingly feared as the world's economic superpower willing to do almost literally anything to augment its irresistible drive for export markets. Who can say how the two countries will be perceived a generation from now? During the whole of this period, hundreds of works, from learned treatises to pop journalism, were written to show the inevitability of the then-current set of perceived Chinese and Japanese national qualities, their roots deep in the national character – and culture – of either state. Many other similar instances can be adduced. In the early nineteenth century Germans were often depicted in English-speaking countries as impractical philosophers along the lines of Goethe and Kant or as peaceful, industrious peasants and villagers. This image changed, one need not say, in the years from Bismarck to Hitler. Few, however, could analyse the history of Germany since 1945 without once again paying tribute to their peaceful industry; nor would many nowadays claim that Germans were inherently warlike or authoritarian. Perhaps such examples show merely that 'national character', and the cultures presumably underlying these characteristics, can alter over time, but how deep or genuine is a conception of national culture likely to be if it can change fundamentally in less than a generation? We know, too, that there is often little difference between the popular image of a national culture and racist stereotyping: some might look for underlying cultural explanations for Japanese hard work and industrial perfectionism, but how many today would look for explanations of the 'shiftlessness' and criminality of blacks, the money-grubbing of the Jews, or the drinking habits of the Irish?

Any assessment of the attitude of a particular national culture toward capitalism, business life, or industrialism must surely be seen as a component of a much wider national culture which comprises a host of characteristic attitudes unrelated to these topics and whose relevance to them is, at first glance, far from clear. In the case of what characterises English national culture, there seems to be a wide consensus, revolving around such qualities as empiricicm, moderation, compromise, tolerance, and the relative absence, compared with other cultures, of extremism. There is also the deeply rooted conservatism of British life. These typically English qualities have been usefully summarised by Nikolaus Pevsner (like many another acute commentator on English life, a refugee), the great historian of art and architecture, in *The Englishness of English Art*:

> personal liberty, freedom of expression, wise compromises, that is the two-party system not shaken by communism or fascism, the democratic system of negotiating in parliament as well as on boards and committees, the distrust of sweeping statement (the kind of statement on which the present book relies) and of the demagogue. The eminently civilised faith in honesty and fair play, the patient queueing, the wisdom in letting go in Ireland, in India, a strictly upheld inefficiency in the little business-things of everyday, such as the work-man's job in the house, windows that will never close and heating that will never heat, a certain comfortable wastefulness and the demonstrative conservatism of the wig in court, the gown in school and university, the obsolete looking shopwindow in St. James's Street, the Steward of the Chiltern Hundreds, the Keeper of the Queen's Swans, the Portcullis Pour-suivant, the City Companies, and L.s.d., and yards and acres and Fahrenheit. All these things seem as eternal as the rock of Gibraltar.[13]

Pevsner goes on to explain that 'in fact they are not', and that Alexander Hertzen, the Russian emigré philosopher, stated in the 1850s that 'nowhere is there a crowd so dense, so terrifying as in London, yet it never in any circumstances knows how to queue'.[14] In the years since 1955 when Pevsner delivered the Reith Lectures from which this extract was drawn, a good deal has changed, too: most English houses today have double-glazing and central heating; most (but not all) 'obsolete looking shopwindows' in St James's Street and elsewhere have been modernised; the 'gown in school and university', if it survives anywhere at all, is a studied affectation; L.s.d. has given way to the strict rationality of the decimal; yards, acres, and Fahrenheit are no doubt also in the process of going west. Yet there is surely an underlying element of continuing truth in much of this description, battered as even such matters as 'wise compromises' and 'the eminently civilised faith in honesty and fair play' have undoubtedly been over the past quarter-century.

Given that there are continuing and discernible underlying patterns in British culture, the fundamental question must be addressed: is British culture anti-capitalistic and anti-business? It seems difficult properly to answer this question unless it is situated in a comparative national framework. Here we come to a crucial point, for on any fair-minded international comparative basis it seems unarguable that British culture is far less anti-capitalistic and far more sympathetic to business life and entrepreneurship than virtually any other national culture in the world, and certainly more sympathetic to capitalism than any other European culture. To take high culture first – the writings of intellectuals and attitudes of the intelligentsia – it is probably no exaggeration to say that the thrust of intellectuals throughout the western world over the past 150 years has been consistently and pervasively anti-capitalistic; indeed, western high culture in its ideological substance has *consisted of* attacks upon capitalism, and on the liberalism with which it is strongly associated, from a right-wing perspective, pre-industrial and anti-modernist (and, in this century, anti-liberal authoritarian); from a left-wing perspective, socialist and collectivist; or from a more generalised anti-urban, anti-technological standpoint, sometimes associated with the right, sometimes with the left, now in full flow as environmentalism. On any comparative basis British culture has been markedly less strident in its condemnation of capitalism than any other European culture and, indeed, presents one of the rare cultural traditions where capitalism and business life have been advocated and defended by leading intellectuals. There is virtually nothing whatever in British culture, at any stage of its modern evolution, to set beside the cosmic anti-bourgeois sarcasm and distilled hatred and loathing emanating from Germany's Brechts and other Marxist writers on the left, or its right-wing proto-fascist proponents of 'cultural despair' and radical nationalist authoritarianism, traditions which are also well represented in all other European cultures.

The German cultural tradition here is the crucial comparative case, for it is Germany which so often is posited as Britain's European nemesis and its prime economic exemplar and rival. Yet it is absolutely apparent to anyone with even the most cursory knowledge of German culture that anti-capitalism, together with its apparent comrades-in-arms, anti-modernism and anti-liberalism, present an ever-recurring triad of values more persistent and more resounding than any *leitmotif* in a Wagner opera. Fritz Stern, the brilliant historian of the interface between German Jewish capitalists like Gerson von Bleichroder and traditional German aristocratic society, has concisely summarised the perpetual affinity of this perverse triad:

Money, so the saying went, was something one had but did not talk about. Under the new system, exemplified by Bleichroder [Bismarck's financial advisor, a German Jew who was eventually ennobled], the Junker stood in danger of not having money, and so they were condemned to talk about it, at least in private, while publicly maintaining the stance against Mammon. The more capitalism altered the physiognomy of Germany, the more the Junker were forced to do battle in the material arena, to mobilise their political power in order to defend their declining economic interests. All of this hardened their prejudices against the grasping money-man who had but one value, that of ruthless profiteering. If only there had been a Marxism for nobles. As it was, they had to make do with their own harsh mixture of the idealisation of rural life and the denunciation of urban, rootless capitalism, for which Jews seemed to have a most uncommon penchant.[15]

This hostility to capitalism was fully shared by the majority of Germany's notable intellectuals and well-known writers during the past 200 years, for whom (to right-wingers) liberalism, rationalism, modernity, and capitalism represented a pot-pourri of destructive and foreign intellectual influences, to be removed by the surgeon's blade of radical nationalism and true German values, or for whom (to left-wingers) capitalism and liberalism represented degenerative and atavistic forces, destructive of the German working classes, to be removed by the scalpel of revolution. For Paul de Lagarde, one of the prophets of what Stern has termed a radical nationalistic 'German religion',

> Liberalism was also blamed for promoting materialism and Philistinism, for destroying metaphysics, converting scientists and educated men into mere fact finders, for encouraging dilettantism. The Liberals eschewed the total view, the whole picture and hence had no thorough-going *Weltanschauung* and no understanding of the religious life. . . .His denunciation of Manchesterism, of the unfettered capitalistic society was entirely in keeping with the dominant mood of German conservative critics. It is an important fact that at the very moment when German capitalism entered its exuberant maturity, German intellectuals and industrialists fumed strongly against laissez-faire and condemned it as a foreign importation.[16]

The other extreme of the German spectrum was, needless to say, no more charitable in its attitude toward capitalism than was the extreme right. By definition Karl Marx, Friedrich Engels, Rosa Luxembourg, and all other German Marxists viewed capitalism as the root of all modern evil which would vanish in comprehensive fashion with the coming of socialism, brought about by a revolution which might well begin in Germany itself. Although some German social democrats such as Edward Bernstein – like social democrats everywhere – no doubt were willing to compromise to some extent with the status quo, Germany long continued to contain more than its share of acidic left-wing intellectuals who could speak of capitalism and capitalists only as the enemy and only as forces to be destroyed and purged on the day of revolutionary reckoning – thus Kurt Tucholsky depicted Weimar captains of industry as pigs, George Grosz invariably drew the Weimar German bourgeoisie as pimps and the clients of prostitutes, and Berthold Brecht, into the post-Stalinist period, used whited faces and bizarre lighting in his plays to heighten hostility to the bourgeoisie – a hostility insufficiently deep, however, to prevent Brecht from holding a Swiss bank account where his West German-copyrighted royalties were paid.[17] Nor were examples of extreme intellectual hostility to capitalism confined to the fringes. If one were to make a list of, say, the ten or twenty most influential German writers of the past 200 years, a list which would certainly include Kant, Hegel, Goethe, Nietzsche, Rilke, Thomas Mann, and others, not one was particularly enamoured of capitalism and capitalists. Most thought capitalism either irrelevant or evil, and even the liberals on such a list were unfriendly to capitalism. Thomas Mann, for instance, often depicted as a kind of old-fashioned liberal conservative representative of the old established German bourgeoisie, a 'good German' who emigrated to America after 1933, despite his Aryan origins, purely out of hostility to Nazi totalitarianism, was himself the author in 1901, at the age of 26, of *Buddenbrooks*. This novel has given its very title to the syndrome of intergenerational dynastic decline in a capitalist family. Its theme has been described as 'a novel of death, resignation and extinction [in which] the heir of the great nineteenth-century mercantile family dies simply because he has not the will to survive':[18] hardly the greatest encomium to capitalism since Adam Smith. Although *Buddenbrooks* is sometimes compared to Galsworthy's *The Forsyte Saga* (whose famous first novel, *A Man of Property*, appeared in 1906) there are crucial differences: Mann's essential pessimism about, if not hostility to, the old German bourgeoisie remained unaltered throughout his career, while in the later components of *The Forsyte Saga* Soames Forsyte and his London upper-middle-class family are clearly portrayed in a far more sympathetic light.[19] Indeed, the soap-opera-style empathy generated by Galsworthy toward the Forsytes is the very opposite of Mann's caustic hostility; one is as typically English as the other is typically German. The most careful and specific examination of German literary attitudes towards businessmen and capitalism, by Harold James, has highlighted the almost universally negative light in which businessmen have been depicted over the past 200 years.[20]

Significantly, too, the post-Nazi period has seen no real modification of the anti-business tradition in German literary culture, with two provisos: the right-wing German critique of modernity and liberalism, totally discredited by the enormities of the Nazi regime, has disappeared, while businessmen are somewhat less visible in the writings of leading post-war authors like Böll and Grass than the 'acquisitive society' as such.[21] Certainly there is no evidence in recent German high culture of any bias in favour of businessmen or capitalism, and the German 'economic miracle' has proceeded without the creation of literary or cultural role models, to the extent that Neil McKendrick claimed that 'in the Germany of the economic miracle Brecht and Grass and Böll have savagely criticised those in charge of industry'.[22] The situation over the past forty years, in other words, appears a continuation of Germany's time-honoured tradition, with the qualification that the Nazi experience and the existence of a Stalinist East Germany have eliminated, in the Federal Republic, the more extreme manifestations of the cosmic loathing and hostility toward capitalism and liberalism hitherto so marked a feature of German culture. Yet Germany's left-wing terrorists of the Baider-Meinhoff type, right-wing neo-Nazis, and its ecological extremists have been no less strong than anywhere else in post-1960 Europe.

There are, too, a number of other notable features of German capitalism which are relevant to any comparison with Britain. German capitalism, like other continental capitalism, was hallmarked by a smaller pre-industrial capitalist class and much less private capital than was the case in Britain, as Gerschenkron made the basis of his wide-ranging analysis of economic development thirty years ago.[23] In comparison with Britain – which, as we have seen, was always a commercial/financial based economy – Germany probably had a relatively more significant industrial and manufacturing sector than did Britain. By 1910–13, for instance, 44.6 per cent of German net domestic product was in the industry, handicrafts and mines sector, compared with 32.0 per cent in transport and services and 23.4 per cent in agriculture.[24] A recent careful study of the 502 wealthiest German entrepreneurs alive in 1912–14, drawn from the statistics of the German wealth tax, showed that 50.0 per cent were industrialists and manufacturers and 47.0 per cent active in banking, commerce, and the service sector.[25] Among wealth-holders the manufacturing sector, especially heavy industry, was thus arguably larger than in Britain although the statistics we have are not comparable.[26] In Britain, too, the landed aristocracy was much wealthier than in Germany, and traditionally more liberal and broad-minded: The Whig aristocracy masterminded the Great Reform Bill and led virtually all British governments, including Liberal governments, down to the Edwardian era. Germany's Junkers, in contrast, were by repute poor, narrow-minded, provincial and reactionary. This combination of factors – the enhanced role of the German state, an economy whose comparative advantage lay increasingly after 1870 with heavy industry, especially in military production, steel, chemicals and electricity, and a reactionary, impoverished nobility – combined with Germany's traditional author-itarianism to give it the peculiarly perverse character its national history assumed from 1848 until 1945, of which the Nazi epoch represented an ultimate extreme, a parody at midnight.

The other side of this coin was the well-known weakness of German liberalism and the domination of its middle classes by the Prussian aristocracy. Professor Wiener does discuss this in his book; it would be odd for a book whose thesis is that Britain's culture was anti-business and anti-industrial to fail to comment on the obvious and manifest anomaly that in Britain's great European rival, a country whose industrial efficiency and economic growth are supposedly everything that Britain's is not, the ruling elite of the country and its ethos unarguably seemed more hostile to businessmen and capitalism than was the case in Britain. Although Wiener does not address this point directly, his comments on a related matter, the social and political distance between Germany's new industrialists and its old aristocracy, is quite cogent, and deserves to be noted:

> Aristocratic hegemony persisted also – indeed, more obviously – in Britain's emerging rival, Germany. Because the political histories of the two nations contrasted so dramatically, for a long time Britain was wrongly seen as taking a path of development opposite to that of Germany – a path of complete bourgeois triumph as against Germany's holding onto 'feudalism'. Britain was supposed to be the archetypal 'nation of shopkeepers' – a Napoleonic gibe that was false when first uttered, and still false, if less obviously so, when repeated by German writers before and during the first World War. In truth, Britain and Germany both underwent powerful industrial revolutions in the midst of strong and resilient aristocratic societies.

> That this encounter of industry and aristocracy led to different economic (not to mention political) outcomes in the two countries can be explained by many factors, chief among them the chro-nology of economic change, the degree of aristrocratic openness, and, perhaps most crucial, the character of each aristocracy. Because the industrial revolution in Germany took place later and more suddenly than it did in Britain, the German industrial

bourgeoisie had less time to become accepted by and absorbed into the older elite. Second, the Prussian aristocracy, in particular, was less ready than the English aristocracy to accept wealthy businessmen into its ranks, regardless of how much they hastened to remake themselves on the Junker model. For both these reasons, the new industrialists and entrepreneurs of Imperial Germany were more likely than their longer-established English counterparts to retain their preoccupation with production.

Beyond this, however, the two aristocracies were different enough to influence their respective middle classes in quite distinct ways. The Prussian aristocracy was still an aggressive, authoritarian military caste: English lords and gentry had, with prosperity, long since shed that character. Moreover the Junkers, for all their caste pride, were not wealthy on the English scale, and had to continue to struggle ruthlessly to protect and develop their economic and political position. In spite of their romantic pretensions, the Junkers became, as Fritz Stern observed, ever more 'agrarian industrialists'. It was perhaps this combination of militarism and economic pressure that made Bismarck's government appreciate the geopolitical value of economic development, and that underlay the historic arrangement of 1878-9, in which industry traded political support for the economic support of tariff protection (and, ultimately, *Weltpolitik*). Particularly after 1879, the industrial bourgeoisie in Germany was moving toward an aristocratic model less hospitable than the English to 'free enterprise' or political liberalism, but more suitable to maintaining a fierce drive toward economic growth (closely associated with national power). In Germany, thus, capitalism and liberalism were devalued far more than industrialism, whereas in England it was industrialism and not capitalism or liberalism whose development was inhibited. In this way, the conjunction of modernisation with an entrenched aristocracy led in Germany to obstructed political development, and in Britain to inhibited economic development.

(Wiener, op.cit., pp. 8-9)

There are several important difficulties with this explanation. First, and most clearly, is its striking tacit denial that Germany's anti-business culture affected its rapid economic growth after 1870. If the culture of a nation crucially affects its economic performance, how can it be that Germany, with its deep hostility to capitalism, liberalism, and modernity, saw such rapid economic development? And if the nexus here was not crucial – if (as seems to be the case) Germany made extraordinary economic gains despite its anti-business culture – how can its culture be linked to economic development as a crucial causal factor in the British case, as is the very thesis of Wiener's book? Wiener's attempt to get round this seemingly fundamental objection is that German culture, or at least its elites, favoured industrialism rather than other forms of capitalism linked more squarely with liberalism. (Although he does not elaborate on this, he may have 'cosmopolitan' commerce and finance in mind.) As we have seen, this is an accurate description of German capitalism, but it assumes that historical actors like 'Bismarck's government', the 'industrial bourgeoisie [with] an aristocratic model. . . . More suitable to maintaining a fierce drive toward economic growth' deliberately and knowingly drove this peculiar mode of development. There may be some truth to this view, but it is also the case that Germany, no less than Britain, enjoyed a specific set of comparative economic advantages and disadvantages of which its entrepreneurs took advantage. These were determined by a wide variety of specific historical, geographical, sociological, and resource conditions which were, almost certainly, far more significant than governmental policy goals. It is also the case that the evident prevalent cultural mood of anti-capitalism and anti-liberalism in Germany throughout most of its history could not be manipulated or induced by the Junkers or 'Bismarck's government'. Left-wing cultural anti-capitalists were as bitterly opposed to them as to capitalism, while far right proto-fascists and Nazi theorists would increasingly have regarded these traditional German conservatives as far too moderate.

Virtually everything which has been said here of Germany can be repeated, in somewhat modified form, of the other European countries. On the Continent, where the Anglo-American tradition of liberalism and pluralism was weak or non-existent, the political left was chiefly represented from 1870 to 1960 or later by socialist anti-clericalists, doctrinaire theoretical champions of revolution, and the right, throughout the nineteenth century and down to 1945, by royalist, clericalist, or authoritarian anti-modernists. Few intellectuals were comfortable with capitalism, and few saw in it the dynamic force for creating near-universal affluence which its champions in the English-speaking world proclaimed. If intellectuals in Italy, France, or pre-1917 Russia lacked the ideological extremes of their German counterparts (which is arguable), they fully partook in their general outlook.

Britain is usually compared adversely to Germany by advocates of the 'cultural critique', but it is just as common to draw an invidious comparison with the United States. It is with the vigorous, permanently innovative, user-friendly, clever, dynamic and most of all successful capitalism of America and its business culture that advocates of the 'cultural critique' evidently have as their continuous central point of reference and comparison. Unquestionably, both the legal and informal structures of the United States have been, almost by definition and at many levels, bound up with capitalist expansion and the promotion of free enterprise. Without doubt that commitment to capitalism has been both deeper and more genuine than anywhere else in the world, with the possible exception of a number of places on the rim of east Asia during the past generation, like Singapore and Hong Kong. It cannot seriously be contested that the standard of living for the average person in America was, until the 1960s, higher than anywhere else in the world (Canada and Australia possibly excepted) or that dynamic capitalism was seen as the vehicle which produced this generally happy state. There is no question that businessmen, especially 'self-made' men who rose in the great 'rags-to-riches' manner, were widely admired, or that feudal distinctions of rank based on birth were both unknown and deprecated, except in the case of black slaves. The widespread notion of American 'exceptionalism', of a country 'born free' without Europe's atavistic, pre-modern feudal class structure and aristocracy, and without a significant socialistic or revolutionary tradition, has at the very least a large element of truth.

Having said all this, however, it is also necessary to add many qualifications to this benign depiction. Differences between America and Europe in wealth, income, and living standards actually predated the rise of the United States to world industrial pre-eminence and were already evident in colonial times; American businessmen were already wealthier than their richest British counterparts by the 1840s or even earlier.[27] The happy outcome of the American economy thus antedated any official American commitment to capitalism (indeed, it antedated the concept of capitalism) and was evident while the future United States was part of Britain's old mercantilist system of Empire. America's fortunate ratio of arable land to population, its unclaimed resources, already high literacy rates, and geographical locale probably had more to do with this outcome than its culture, although the popular image of the shrewd acquisitive Yankee came early.

America's prosperity was, of course, never universal. Until the 1960s it almost totally excluded blacks, who were legally debarred from full participation in most of the services provided to white men throughout the South and virtually excluded from all salient opportunities for upward mobility in the rest of the country. Even in the prosperous 1920s and later still, millions of farmers, miners, immigrants, slum dwellers and many other groups failed to share in the bounty of American prosperity. As recently as 1929–30 only 17.1 per cent of Americans aged 15–17 were enrolled in any secondary school. In 1988 only 53.8 per cent of all Americans aged 65 or more had completed secondary school; nearly half, in other words, of Americans born prior to 1923 had 'dropped out' of school. To be sure, the percentage completing school among this age-cohort is probably far higher than in any other country, but it indicates that social mobility in America was anything but genuinely universal until very recently, if it can be so described today. (By 1988, among those aged between 25 and 34 – born between 1954 and 1963 – this percentage had climbed to over 86 per cent.) As we have seen, too, although America clearly pioneered the 'affluent society' (if the many exceptions to its universality be overlooked), during the past generation other countries have caught up, even those like Britain hallmarked by allegedly terrible economic performances, and now have virtually identical statistics of consumer ownership patterns.

From the viewpoint of this discussion, however, the most important point which ought to be made about America's 'exceptionalism' is that American high culture was not 'exceptional': its intellectuals and leading writers have demonstrated much the same hostility toward capitalism, industrialism, the consumer society, and urbanism as have Europe's, bearing in mind that American culture partook of the Anglo-American empirical tradition, always adverse to ideological doctrines or abstract political theories, while its political culture normally confined both socialism and anti-modernist authoritarianism to the far fringes. While American intellectuals and writers from Jefferson to Thoreau, Emerson, Whitman, Jack Kerouac and Alan Ginsberg have certainly sung the virtues and merits of extreme individualism and personal freedom, few of them gave explicit endorsement to capitalism. Just as in Europe, from the 1880s onward two broad schools of writers and intellectuals emerged who were bitterly hostile to capitalism and the market economy, one representing a left-wing 'progressive' or socialistic attack on capitalism, the other a right-wing anti-democratic anti-'mass society' critique. Both were also tied up with a deep-seated anti-urbanism and with a surprising degree of animosity toward technology. All of these critiques have been familiar and ever-recurrent themes in American literary culture. Left-wing writers like Theodore Dreiser, Sherwood Anderson, John Steinbeck, John Dos Passos and many black and immigrant writers were as scathing (though perhaps better-mannered) about the consequences and human waste produced by American capitalism and consumerism as were Brecht or Sartre about their own bourgeoisie. A significant anti-modernist, anti-capitalist extreme right also emerged in America in this century, the expatriates T. S. Eliot and Ezra Pound being the best-known (Pound, of course, was jailed as an active wartime supporter of fascism). According to the literary critic Gerald Graff,

> We can ... delineate a twentieth-century literary Right [in America]. It would include the New Humanism, Eliot's classical royalism, and the Southern Agrarian wing of the New Criticism.

But these writers are 'reactionary', not 'conservative'. They are almost as extreme in their opposition to the status quo as are their counterparts on the Left. In so far as they defend 'established society', it is an established society that no longer exists. In this respect they could not be more remote from the so-called New Right of today's *National Review* and Moral Majority, who are unqualified apologists for corporations. How different from such apologetics was the attitude of the self-styled reactionary Allen Tate, for instance, who in 1939 noted 'the iniquity of finance capitalism' and proclaimed that 'our social-economic system, with its decadent religion, depraved morals, and disorganised economics, is thoroughly rotten'. To be sure, the neoconservatism of such journals as *Commentary* and *The New Criterion* is markedly more benign toward capitalism than was Tate (or the editor of the original *Criterion*). Yet in their cultural judgments, if not their political ones, these neoconservatives tend to be more anti-Left than pro-American or procapitalist.[28]

Classical American writers from Thoreau to Mark Twain, Robert Frost, and William Faulkner have also glorified the rural life, condemning urban America, machinery, and technology as inherently corrupting; this tradition lives on in pro-environmental works like *Silent Spring*, *The Greening of America*, and indeed, in a sense in anti-business jeremiads like *Unsafe at Any Speed*, which are stocks-in-trade of the contemporary American scene. American high culture also has been hallmarked by the phenomenon of the American cultural expatriate. Legion indeed are the American writers and artists who viewed their homeland as so much the spiritual and cultural desert that they preferred to go abroad, whether this be to Paris with Ernest Hemingway and Gertrude Stein, to London with Henry James and T. S. Eliot, to visit the future in the Soviet Union, or the Far East to reach Nirvana. It seems safe to say that in no other significant nation has so large a portion of its productive intelligentsia abandoned its homeland. Nor was harsh and sarcastic criticism of the American bourgeoisie confined to leftists, ultra-conservatives, and exiles. Perhaps the most scathing and successful negative depiction of the American bourgeoisie appears in such works as *Main Street*, *Babbitt* and *Elmer Gantry* by Sinclair Lewis, a classical middlebrow Midwestern writer who never left home.

If American high culture has had little good to say of American capitalism and its works, it has had arguably even less support among its leading academics and university teachers. Far from being a hotbed of the fomentation of a pro-capitalist ideology, America's universities have for several generations been widely known for their highly critical attitude toward American capitalism and most other aspects of

American society. American conservatives have long perceived the leading universities in the United States in this light. In 1951 the youthful William F. Buckley Jr, later editor of the *National Review* and one of the most renowned media champions of American conservatism, published *God and Man at Yale*, in which he 'strove to document the monumental anti-Christian and collectivist bias' at America's second oldest university, a pillar of the Ivy League hitherto known for its 'privileged clientele, exclusivity and conservatism'.[29] Throughout the 1950s and 1960s works appeared by conservative writers with titles like *Collectivism on the Campus* (by E. Merrill Root, 1955) and *Conquest of the American Mind* (by Felix Wittner, 1956). Such careful survey research as has been undertaken has documented as beyond question the left–liberal ideological beliefs of most American academics, especially at the most 'elite' of universities and particularly in the arts and social sciences (as opposed to the pure and applied sciences) with the possible exception of economics and related disciplines. One important survey of the backgrounds and attitudes of 60,028 college and university academics at the end of the 1960s found that of 7,023 academics in the humanities and social sciences at the 'elite colleges and universities' in America, nearly 69 per cent defined themselves as 'left' or 'liberal' in their political outlook.[30] This survey showed that 51.8 per cent of all academics had voted for Hubert Humphrey in 1968 – the Democratic party's very liberal candidate – compared with 34.7 per cent for Richard Nixon, the Republican candidate and winner, 1. 3 per cent for George Wallace, and 1.9 per cent for left-wing minor party candidates like Eldridge Cleaver, while 10.4 per cent did not vote.[31] In the 1968 Presidential election, Nixon received 43.4 per cent of all votes cast, Humphrey 42.7 per cent, Wallace 13.5 per cent, minor candidates 0.3 per cent. According to the same survey of academics, only 19.2 per cent of all faculty members had voted for Barry Goldwater, the arch–conservative Republican candidate, in 1964, compared with 67.0 per cent for President Lyndon Johnson, the Democratic candidate.[32] In the actual election, Johnson had received 61.1 per cent of the total national vote, Goldwater 38.5 per cent. Although many self-defined 'liberal' American academics probably desired nothing more than an extension of New Deal Government programmes to institute measures like a national health system, as well as a more vigorous attack on racial prejudice, rather than a revolutionary attack on the capitalist system, anyone familiar with the humanities and social sciences faculties of America's leading universities at the time (or, probably, today) will know that it was easier to find an avowed Satanist than an avowed conservative in many college departments. Of course most academics with a strong view on a particular subject will bend over backwards to present alternative opinions, but some will not and no one can fairly say that America's elite universities worked to enhance the reputation of unreformed capitalism. Student newspapers, student councils, and student activities on many American campuses (as elsewhere in the western world) were, for decades, overwhelmingly dominated by the left, invariably with an anti-capitalist, anti-militarist, and anti-western agenda and outlook. Since the late 1960s it seems reasonable to believe that the growing centrality of the neo-conservative intellectual position, as well as the discrediting of Marxism, have made supporters of capitalism more visible, while economics and business departments have always been notably more conservative than other arts faculties. Yet complaints about the left-wing bias of the syllabus of America's universities have, if anything, grown since the 1950s, most recently in Allan Bloom's *Closing of the American Mind* and in widespread accusations that only the 'correct' (i.e. leftist) line on issues like reverse racial discrimination and feminism need be tolerated on some campuses. In any case, it seems abundantly clear from all this that arguably the most significant and influential formulator of the attitudes of the next generation of Americans, the 'elite' colleges and universities of the United States, have simply not acted to further the reputation of American capitalism and, if they have, this has been despite rather than because of the attitudes of the majority of their academics. If the 1980s witnessed the rise of the 'yuppie' generation of students, committed to Business School followed by easy money on Wall Street or in corporate America, wallowing in their material values, in the context of the 'Reagan revolution', this was entirely unexpected – utterly unlikely, in fact, given the mood of America's campuses only fifteen/twenty years before – and a wholly unintended consequence of the attitude of most university teachers.

The attitudes of both America's leading writers and leading university academics have thus been demonstrably hostile to capitalism, and have in no sense acted to propagandise for the free enterprise system or its values. Their typical attitudes seem in fact to be closer, in their attitudes towards capitalism, to those of Germany's feverish and malignant twin traditions of right-wing anti-modernism and left-wing revolution than to anything one might expect in the homeland of triumphant capitalism. If this be so, it is again powerful prima-facie evidence that the power of high culture and the intelligentsia to influence economic performance is extraordinarily limited – indeed, virtually non-existent – entirely apart from any more fundamental dispute one might have with the prevalent interpretation of the nature of a national economy, or its actual performance.

There is finally the case of Japan, and a consideration of the Japanese case is highly instructive. Any linkage of Japanese culture with Japan's stellar economic performance since the 1950s must come to terms with the self-evident fact that Japan's historical development was entirely separate from the evolution of European culture, and clues to any postulated causality must look for entirely different modes of thought, religion, and ideology, at least prior to the 1860s. In dealing with Japanese success, too, and in reviewing the recent comment and literature which accounts for it, one is struck by a failure persuasively to explain it in a full and comprehensive way. This in my view is because the best-known characteristics of Japan's 'national character' and its cultural underpinnings would certainly appear to any objective observer to consist largely of values most likely to work *against* rapid and triumphant economic success – the pervasive survival of pre-modern quasi-feudal and neo-feudal qualities and beliefs, an apparently obsessive conservatism, an abiding concern for hierarchy and traditional ceremony, and, in particular, self-effacement and a deep antipathy to public eccentricity, visibility, or self-publicity which makes the Englishman's alleged preference for these characteristics appear very half-hearted.[33] Indeed, in reviewing these well-known national characteristics one will be clearly struck by their close resemblance, in Oriental guise, to the values regularly ascribed to the English as highly typical of their nation and culture, quite often by proponents of the 'cultural critique' who view them as the very cause of Britain's economic decline! When one recalls that Japan is also an island, once possessed a great empire acquired by force, is renowned for its technology, remains a monarchy, etc., the resemblance becomes even more striking.

The inability of even acute observers cogently to explain Japanese success leads commentators to proffer explanations such as the following:

> Why has Japan succeeded? Because of the Japanese. For the Japanese make up an intensely industrious nation, filled with a tenacious desire to get on, to progress, enthusiastically devoted to everything new, and capable of tireless exertion in order to succeed; they will work with a disciplined, obstinate steadiness and they will live with a frugality that is scarcely ever seen in the West today.[34]

Each of these points would appear to be either manifestly tautological or direct contradictions of other widely held images of contemporary Japanese society.

Japan's rise to economic leadership if not supremacy is a *tour de force* which is extremely difficult to link plausibly to any cultural explanation, in my view. Some points about this rise can, however, usefully be made. The first is that it is really quite recent. Although a number of writers have drawn attention to Japan's very strong manufacturing growth before 1939, and its industrial growth rate was indeed extremely impressive in the inter-war period (starting, of course, from an extremely low base), even in 1955–60 Japan was not a first-ranking economic power and its 'economic miracle' occurred later than Germany's or Italy's.[35] Japan's spectacular performance is almost wholly a product of the period since only the mid-1960s and would seem to rest upon two major pillars. The first has been an uncanny perception that consumers in the affluent west, especially the United States, wanted universally high quality consumer goods, especially those with an outstanding record of freedom from servicing, and in particular goods incorporating the latest technology. Japan has thus waxed rich from being the first to perceive the economic importance of 'yuppies' (and their like-minded elders) and their values, especially a mistrust of and an eye for shoddiness and its purveyors. Japan has been fortunate, too, in that its entrepreneurial *tour de force* has enabled at least one such new consumer good or development to be successfully marketed and exported every few years from the late 1960s to the late 1980s: among them the 'walkman', the CD, and reliable mass-market cars incorporating a host of superior consumer features like air-conditioning. Significantly, the late 1980s and early 1990s have seen an apparent hiatus in this seemingly endless stream of new products. Second, Japan has acted as an integrated national system, much as Britain did in the late eighteenth century and then in the 1880–1940 period, with a linkage of state, industry, and bureaucracy made possible by the lack of an effective political opposition and a quiescent labour force.[36] This Japanese 'system' has effectively exploited world pressures for free trade, while erecting enormous barriers in practice to hinder foreign manufactured imports from entering Japan.

It should seem apparent to any clear-minded observer that, successful as both of these strategies obviously have been, they are fraught with potential danger for the future. The method chosen by Japan for economic success, the export of a succession of high quality consumer goods on a grand scale, has been a *tour de force* dependent wholly upon a fortunate series of outstanding triumphs; miss a beat and the pattern is shattered, at least temporarily. The existence of a previously successful, linked 'system' of control is no guarantee of future success and works against independent initiatives. Should this occur – as arguably seems to be the case since the 1980s – Japan becomes more dependent than before on an economy of a very different type, perhaps based (like Britain after 1870) on the export of capital and the remission of overseas profits. A phenomenal export surplus, too, automatically makes for currency appreciation and a comparative rise in labour costs, making Japan even more reliant on either a continuation of its *tour de force* or compensation in other directions.

As the decline in its Stock Market shows, Japan in my view is already showing many of the warning signs of an economy due to decline, at least by the conventional measurements of decline, and I shall not be surprised if the performance of the Japanese economy is not markedly and perceptibly worse twenty years from now than it is today. Central to this decline will be the working of 'Petty's Law', the inevitable movement of an economy from the primary to the secondary to the tertiary sector unless checked by still more *tours de force* in the form of successors to the transistor radio and portable colour television, innovations of which even the Japanese do not seem capable. There is every sign, instead, that Japan will increasingly resemble the Britain of Hobson's day, with revenue drawn from the remittance of overseas investments. Indeed, Japanese economic activity now revolves increasingly around the purchase of shopping centres, office blocks and department stores throughout the world.[37] Japan's richest men increasingly hold their fortunes in urban property rather than in industry or finance, perhaps to an even greater extent than is the case in Britain. Japan's two richest men at present, Yoshiaki Tsutsumi and Taikichiro Mori, worth $30 billion and $23 billion in 1987, are primarily Tokyo property developers, as are many other Japanese billionaires. These trends need not be disastrous: as we have seen in the British case this type of economy is both perfectly normal and takes on a successful life of its own. Japan also enjoys many underlying advantages, especially a well-educated, homogeneous labour force, consistently high levels of savings, and no overseas military commitments. Presumably, too, Japan will not in future have to fight in two world wars within thirty years, as Britain did after 1914. But Japan also suffers from equally clear-cut disadvantages apart from those we have mentioned, such as a complete lack of natural resources or agricultural self-sufficiency, unsatisfied consumer demand which could become a tidal wave of discontent, a population ageing at a rapid pace, and growing evidence of chronic financial and political scandal and corruption at a very deep-seated level within Japan's 'Establishment'. In particular, the Japanese consumer has failed to share in the Japanese economic bonanza, especially in the key area of housing. A tiny two-bedroom flat in central Tokyo costs over $700,000, a price vastly in excess even of its Mayfair equivalent. As is well known, Japanese home buyers now often secure mortgages extending over two lifetimes and frequently commute for over two hours in either direction. Too, there is little love lost for Japan in Asia, Europe, North America, or almost anywhere else in the world, but rather enormous muted resentment directed either at memories of Japan's brutal imperialism from 1931 to 1945 or jealousy toward its recent economic success, or both. In my view few outsiders will shed many tears for future Japanese misfortunes. Japan's very ambiguous cultural presuppositions, especially a value-system seemingly opposed in many respects to economic success and to capitalism, will no doubt be drawn upon to account for this decline, just as they are now used to explain its success.

There is another facet of Japanese culture and its cultural heritage which is highly relevant, in my view, to this description of Japan's recent success as a *tour de force*. It is common to link a nation's economic success with its cultural hegemony, so that countries which are markedly successful and internationally of the first importance in the economic sphere almost automatically put their stamp upon the world's culture and often serve as 'homelands of the mind' for the international intelligentsia. France in the eighteenth century, Britain in the nineteenth, Germany under the Kaiser, and the United States since the First World War (especially since 1945) are obvious examples of this nexus. Japan in contrast presents an example perhaps without parallel in modern history of a nation whose economy has been extraordinarily successful – arguably the strongest and most dynamic in the world over the past thirty years – but whose cultural influence has been for all practical purposes non-existent. Remarkably few Japanese writers, intellectuals, or artists have proven central to the contemporary world's culture and, indeed, remarkably few are known outside of Japan. Of course, there are exceptions like Akira Kurosawa the film-maker, and of course Japanese artistic motifs and even philosophies, like Zen Buddhism, have had their influence. Yet the same might be said of virtually any country or national culture in the world. The impact of Japanese culture on the rest of the world, and especially on the west, has probably been less significant than, say, the impact of Mexico or Australia, semi-peripheral countries lacking a modicum of Japan's economic strength or influence. Only one or two Japanese writers, most notably Kawabata Yasunari and Mishima Yukio, have made the slightest impact on the outside world, and only four Japanese scientists have won Nobel Prizes since 1950 (compared with, for instance, no fewer than thirty-three British scientists).

One central test of the real influence of a nation's culture is the international use of its language. To be sure there may well be a significant time-lag in the manifestation of influence: via the Church, Latin remained perhaps the most significant international language for well over a millennium after the fall of Rome; in our time French was, and to a certain extent remains, a central language of diplomacy more out of habit and courtesy than from any widespread illusions about the might of twentieth-century France. Yet a comparison of English and Japanese here is extremely revealing. English is today beyond any doubt whatever the world's *lingua franca*, the successor to Latin, whose influence is today probably without equal in modern history among any living languages. When the leader of a coup in central Africa speaks to the world's media and press, he speaks English, just as do the Prime Ministers of Israel and Egypt, the President of the Philippines, the Foreign Minister of Indonesia, the head of the United Nations. One interesting but little-noticed result of *glasnost* and decommunisation in the former Soviet Union and eastern Europe has been a steady rise in the use of English in its media and a major increase in the teaching of English in its schools (in the former satellites, in place of Russian). Should Britain decline to the status of minor power – indeed, should it sink beneath the waves – the English language is one legacy which it has truly given to the whole world, perhaps for ever. The use of English as the world's international language has, if anything, grown (perhaps markedly) over the past thirty years, despite the alleged economic decline of Britain in relative terms and the apparent decline of the absolute power of the United States during this period. If anything, knowledge of English as a sign of individual *savoir-faire* and cosmopolitanism has increased markedly in the recent past. Zimbabwe, the African nation formerly known as Southern Rhodesia, saw a fifteen-year struggle between the British, white colonists, and its black majority. When independence finally came in 1979, Zimbabwe's first President, Robert Mugabwe, was a self-proclaimed Marxist who established a one-party regime. Yet by 1991, according to one black Zimbabwean magazine, knowledge of English had become a central indicator of sophistication among the black majority:

> Also, our parents are responsible for, and stimulate the attitudes and behaviour we have adopted or has been imposed on us youths. For example, to be accepted into elite society, one has to speak perfect English, preferably with a touch of special accent, so that at social gatherings, mothers can proudly boast, 'Mwana wangui haagoni chiShona.' (My child cannot speak Shona.) Already at a tender age, this child . . . develops an air of superiority over her other black relatives and friends. Often that child will tend to associate with white children and completely absorb their culture.[38]

In complete contrast, familiarity with the language of Japanese beyond Japan, let alone any wider influence or usage in international affairs of any kind, remains very nearly as limited as was the case in 1960, before the economic ascendancy of Japan. It is safe to say that the ratio of Japanese schoolchildren learning English to schoolchildren in Britain or the United States learning Japanese is of the order of a thousand to one, and is likely to continue in these proportions for an indefinite period. Japanese scholars and scientists wishing to make an international impact of virtually any kind must perforce write and communicate in

English, just like most scholars in Denmark, Peru, Portugal and other minor countries. To be sure, Japanese is said to be a very difficult language for foreigners to learn, but so is English. To be sure, Japanese is spoken in only one country while English is spoken in many, but so are Spanish, Arabic, French, and several other languages, and Mandarin Chinese has more speakers than English and Japanese combined. The international influence of English over the past generation has not diminished, but probably has grown, because the central determinants of what is knowledge, what is news, and how these are disseminated, remain in geographical terms exactly where they were a generation ago, on the east and west coasts of the United States with secondary annexes in London, Oxbridge, and Paris. Tokyo has no more achieved even junior ranking among these centres of influence than has New Delhi or Buenos Aires. Significantly, however, the cultural influence of Britain remains unquestionably very great: greater, probably, than any country except the United States.

Each of these countries and their cultural features have been discussed as a contrast to Britain. When one turns from any of these countries to Britain itself, perhaps the clearest impression which must be made on any fair-minded observer is that British culture represents an exception to many of these trends. More certainly than in any of the countries we have examined here, Britain lacked a truly radical anti-capitalist left or an anti-modern extreme right of any significance. Of course Britain had its Fabian socialists and its reactionary 'royalists' à la T. S. Eliot as well as its Kiplingesque imperialists, anti-urban anti-industrial champions of art and natural living like William Morris, and those half in love with, half hating modern science and technology, like H. G. Wells. The point is, in comparison with any other advanced society, even the United States, Britain's milk-and-water Nietzsches, Brechts, Dostoyevskys, Sartres, and Pounds lacked either the sheer venom or the sheer extremism of their opposite numbers almost anywhere else. The terms which have been used over and over again to describe the typical ambience and institutions of British society are terms like 'moderation', 'common sense', 'compromise', 'persuasion by reason, not fiery rhetoric', along with the celebrated facets of British 'character', the hiding of emotions, the stiff upper lip, *sang froid*, kindness to animals, the shyness, the satisfied introversion, the preference, when striking up a conversation with a stranger or a chance acquaintance, for discussing the weather or sport, and not (as on the Continent) whether God exists. There is a general impression that these characteristics are of relatively recent origin and that the English, prior to the nineteenth century, were an unusually violent, quarrelsome, cruel, and riotous people whose national characteristics changed fundamentally around the middle of the nineteenth century.[39]

For advocates of the 'cultural critique' this change in characteristic behaviour has been a fundamental hallmark of the 'gentrification' of industrial leadership and entrepreneurship in British society allegedly so injurious to England's economic performance.[40] No doubt there is a strong element of accuracy in historical accounts of this change in British character, although the underlying spirit of compromise surely has much to do with the empiricist tradition in British philosophy, a product of the late seventeenth century if not earlier.[41]

More importantly, while many have seen in these features of Britain's national character the seeds of England's allegedly pusillanimous entrepreneurial performance, it is just as easy to view them as markedly less hostile to capitalism and Britain's economic performance than those characteristically found on the Continent and elsewhere. As remarked, one can search Britain's modern cultural history in vain to find the equivalent – any equivalent – of the extremist critics of capitalism, liberalism, and modernity found almost everywhere else. In Britain, these values had triumphed in the seventeenth and eighteenth centuries and were supported ubiquitously across the British political and intellectual spectrum. An interesting and significant minor aspect of these critical differences may be found in the relative lack in Britain of anti-semitism which viewed Jews as capitalist exploiters and money-sucking usurers, so powerful a component of both right- and left-wing intellectual assaults on capitalism throughout Europe, as the German extracts above illustrate. In Britain, however, the role of Jews as money-lenders and capitalists was often, indeed regularly, performed by native-born Dissenters and Presbyterians, and by Anglicans, especially in the City of London; indeed, modern British capitalism had its origins in the long period from 1290 to 1656 when Jews were officially barred from living in England, while Britain rose to economic supremacy between 1700 and 1850 when the Jewish population of Britain was insignificant. British Dissent's 'Cousinhood' dynasties of wealthy Quakers, Unitarians, and Congregationalists often exhibited those group characteristics attributed to Jews elsewhere – great wealth, clannishness, intermarriage, perverse religious heterodoxy, general alienation from the mainstream of belief – while Britain's Anglicans exhibited no hostility to money or trade whatever and most wealthy men in modern Britain were almost certainly Anglicans.[42] While Jews comprised about 10 per cent of all British business millionaires and half-millionaires born in the nineteenth century, and many other foreign-born groups were disproportionately wealthy, Jews and foreigners certainly experienced much less hostility in Britain than on the Continent.[43] The modernist values and attitudes allegedly borne by Jews on the Continent were in Britain assented to universally, not least of all by the Anglican majority.

Intellectuals in Britain demonstrated markedly different characteristics from their colleagues elsewhere. A strikingly high share of major writers in modern England emerged from the upper middle classes, especially the wealthier professional classes. They were largely university educated, and enjoyed some degree of affluence and success in their careers.[44] It is a myth that British writers and intellectuals live in garrets and die in poverty. This may have been a common pattern in Paris or Vienna, but in Britain most very notable writers have earned a good deal of money from their efforts and died in comfortable circumstances, not deigning to accept the fruits of their labour. Shakespeare, who apparently became the richest man in his home town chiefly by writing plays, is the progenitor of this pattern. Dickens, who left £80,000 when he died (over £3 million in today's money), rising above his humble origins by his pen, was a notable Victorian example. Many important British writers, too, were officially honoured in their lifetimes and most were widely known by literate people; a great British writer who remained genuinely unknown in his own lifetime, like Gerard Manley Hopkins, is certainly a rarity. The three best-known intellectual coteries in Britain during the past century have probably been the early Fabian Society, the Bloomsbury group, and their close colleagues, the interrelated Cambridge intellectual 'aristocracy' comprising the Darwins, Trevelyans, Wedgwoods, Vaughan Williamses, and Russells. Each of these groups was drawn substantially from the Victorian upper middle class verging on wealth, while members of these coteries not strictly from a similar background, like Sidney Webb among the Fabians, quickly married into it or adopted its mores. Other well-known cultural circles and groups, from the 'Souls' to the left-wing poets and authors of the 1930s, have come from broadly similar backgrounds and, perhaps more significantly, never succeeded in genuinely breaking with their pasts in lifestyle or aspiration. Arguably from the early nineteenth century to the 1960s there has never been a successful intellectual group in Britain entirely outside of and apart from this class seed-bed of the British intelligentsia, and arguably during this long period, too, there has never been a significant group among the British intelligentsia which truly wished to overthrow the status quo, either from a left- or a right-wing direction. Most intellectuals in modern British history have, in fact, spoken a common language with common tacit assumptions and sub-texts, all normally at least recognisable by the British upper middle classes despite their preference for reading Dorothy Sayers rather than T. S. Eliot. All operated, broadly, within a common problematic. Until the 1960s, and with a few feverish exceptions, most British intellectuals were, to a remarkable degree, non-political and certainly did not regard politics as the mode of addressing first-order questions. As is well known, there was hardly a British intellectual tradition of Marxism until the 1960s and certainly the Marxist intelligentsia in Britain, when it existed at all, was less original and prepossessing than in virtually any other western country. As is well known too, Britain until the 1960s notably lacked the unemployed and unemployable university graduate, a type notoriously over-represented among radical movements in Europe and the Third World. Britain's university graduates were relatively smaller in number than elsewhere, and as a rule rapidly found employment in industry, the professions, the civil service, or overseas in the Empire.[45] The social dimensions of the British intelligentsia reinforced Britain's lack of ideological extremes and its empiricist tradition, and was itself reinforced by it. These were surely powerful forces in sustaining the status quo, which essentially accepted capitalism and certainly had no deeply held wish to replace it.

The lack of an indigenous Marxist or truly 'adversarial' intelligentsia in Britain is, in fact, a commonplace of most recent Marxist analyses of modern Britain, especially from writers like Perry Anderson.[46] Anderson and others have argued that the lack of a radical intelligentsia in Britain is among the major causes of the salient linkage between the English bourgeoisie and the aristocracy. This postulated connection is not wholly accurate in my view, as will be explored later in this work, but all observers of the British intellectual tradition have consistently been struck by the lack of radical thought or thinkers in the European sense. Again, it seems perverse to posit a connection between British culture and Britain's alleged anti-industrial spirit without noting British culture's even more striking lack of significant radicals.

It is also mistaken in my view to see any significant part of the British political tradition as essentially hostile to capitalism, even the Labour tradition – although Labour, especially when out of office, often enunciated a rhetoric and programme of socialism. Professor Wiener's case is in significant part built around the contention that the British Conservative party was never a party committed to capitalism and industrialism (although widely assumed to be by the left), much less to *laissez-faire*, but was always, throughout its whole history until 1979, a paternalistic, essentially rural, largely aristocracy- and gentry-run political organisation with a pre-modern ideology revolving around 'one nation', *noblesse oblige*, church and monarchy, and traditional patriotism.[47] Certainly this is a widely held view of the Conservative party and one which the Conservative party itself has often been keen to enunciate as proof that it deserved working-class support. It is also probably quite true that most self-made northern manufacturers were much more likely, in the nineteenth century, to have been Liberals than Tories, Cobden and Bright being the ideal types here (although Bright ended his life as a Liberal Unionist ally of the Conservative party). It is also significant that the Conservative party always contained more than its share of important spokesmen, such as many associated with the Anglican church and the traditional aristocracy, who preferred a modified capitalism, or even a moderate socialism, to *laissez-faire*. From time to time, for example during the Second World War and during the post-war Labour period, the Conservative party took pains to give much publicity to the social reforming spirit in the party, chiefly, it must be stated, to promulgate the impression that it was no longer a reactionary party of hard-faced capitalists whose solution to uppity trade-unionists was a whiff of the dole queue. (The implication being that this had once been the case, but Conservatives had now repented and saw the error of their ways.)

However popular this view of the history of the Conservative party has been, and may still be, it is one which in my view is essentially misleading. Although the Conservative party has possibly never been a party of *laissez-faire* in the same sense as the radical wing of the mid-Victorian Liberal party, and has always been willing to enact measures of social reform and social welfare, through most of its modern history it has constituted the party of the Establishment functioning as a coherent, successful national system – the party, as it were, of Great Britain Ltd. The Conservative party has always viewed both commercial and manufacturing capitalism as elements *par excellence* of the Establishment's coherent system, along with other non-business elements such as the Anglican Church, the professions, universities, and Empire interests. Within this overall matrix, it is probably true to say that it has favoured (perhaps strongly favoured) London-based financial and commercial capitalism at the expense of manufacturing industry in the north. While this has been widely seen as a terribly wrong choice for the successful performance of the British economy, it reflected what as we have seen was simply the 'natural' working-out of Britain's post-1870 comparative advantage and, if anything, demonstrated a shrewd appreciation of the real strengths of Britain's economy, far shrewder and more realistic, in fact, than the understanding of most recent political and economic commentators. Within that overall matrix, too, it is simply false to assert that the Conservative party was ever in any sense anti-business or anti-capitalist. The idealisation by many Conservatives of Disraelian social reform as anything more than a tendency within the Conservative party's many strands is certainly an exaggeration.[48] Lord Randolph Churchill's radical programme of 'Tory democracy' certainly represented the mainstream of the modern Conservative party far less accurately than the successful unification of the traditional aristocracy and the business and professional middle classes, especially in the south of England, chiefly engineered by his victorious adversary Lord Salisbury. The legacy of this merger was a party which was always pro-business, in the context of the Conservative party's overriding purpose and its other interests. As Mathew Fforde has aptly noted:

> A hostility to industrial and commercial growth cannot be detected in the late-Victorian and Edwardian Conservative party's general attitude toward the economy. After all, had not abundant wealth and global power resulted from the existing system? The nationalist party would be unlikely to repudiate the economic bases of national greatness.[49]

Even when Conservatives were keenest to show that a 'one nation' philosophy, inclusive of a deep commitment to social reform, comprised the most significant part of the Tory agenda (and, moreover, always had), their leading spokesmen also none the less took great pains to emphasise the value they also placed on business life and capitalism, and the benefits for the working class which had always accrued from capitalism. An example here is Quintin Hogg's *The Case for Conservatism*, a Penguin paperback expounding the basic ideas and viewpoint of the Conservative party which was published in 1947. *The Case for Conservatism* appeared at a time which probably coincided with the absolute nadir of Toryism in modern times, less than two years after a disastrous and totally unexpected defeat by the Labour party. Labour then seemed destined to stay in office for twenty years and the Conservatives' defeat was occasioned in large part by memories of mass unemployment and heartless industrial capitalism in the previous decade; Communism was then literally sweeping through Europe and Asia. Moreover, 1947 was also the year before impoverished, bomb-bestrewn Britain surrendered India and faced virtual national bankruptcy. One can hardly imagine a time less propitious for works of proselytising zealotry for capitalism. Indeed, while Quintin Hogg's tract does indeed emphasise 'the religious basis of society', 'the organic theory of society', 'authority' and 'country' as pillars of Tory philosophy, nevertheless a major portion of the work is taken up with explications of 'enterprise', 'property', 'incentive', 'trading for profit', and 'competition' as equal pillars.[50] As to, for example, private property,

> Private property is a natural right. . . . [T]he Conservative consistently supports private enterprise against state monopoly, and he does so not because of a bigoted or pedantic hatred either of monopoly or State enterprise (although he does dislike them both) . . . [but] because, as a general principle, he regards private enterprise as a positive good, and more likely to serve the public interest than monopoly of any kind, or in particular than state monopoly. . . . [T]he Conservative believes that the existence of

powerful and independent trading interests, though never without danger, is a public advantage as tending to the diffusion of power and therefore to the perpetuation of freedom in society.[51]

While Quintin Hogg is often quoted as a philosopher and advocate of a 'one nation' traditionalist philosophy of Conservatism that differs widely from an enterprise-based free market ideology, as Lord Hailsham of St Marylebone he remained a senior pillar of the Thatcher revolution many decades later. By the mid-1980s he was indeed virtually the only remaining Thatcher cabinet minister whose background lay in the old-fashioned elite of Eton and Oxford. Hogg, presumably, saw no inconsistency between enunciating a conservatism based on Burkean-Disraelian traditionalist principles, and one which centrally advocates a *laissez-faire* enterprise culture.

It is also important to note that while individual Tory intellectuals unquestionably harboured romantic visions of a traditionalist premodern, neo-feudally hierarchical conservative ideology animating the Conservative party, in the normal and influential realms of politics, with its lobbies, influence-peddling, and realistic economic calculations, business groups have always been far more powerful than romantic dreamers. The Federation of Business Industries (now the Confederation of British Industry, or CBI) founded in 1916, has long been recognised as the most powerful lobbying group on the employers side in economic matters. By 1939 membership already consisted of 2,900 individual firms and 180 trade associations. It lobbied the Chancellor of the Exchequer on a regular basis, apparently with considerable success.[52] By the 1930s, too, a host of other industry lobbying groups had grown up (some founded earlier), among them the National Union of Manufacturers, the Association of Chambers of Commerce, the Chamber of Shipping, the British Iron and Steel Federation, the British Employers Confederation, the National Chamber of Trade, and many others. All non-Labour MPs, and many Labour MPs as well, had perforce to take the views of such organisations into account, especially where they spoke for important local trades. Britain has always had, too, a well-organised series of lobbies dedicated to protecting and advancing *laissez-faire* capitalism, such as the Liberty and Property Defence League, founded in 1882, the British Constitution Association, founded in 1905, and the Anti-Socialist Union, founded in 1908.[53] Until recently, scholars devoted far less attention to right-wing organisations of this kind than to, say, the Fabian Society or the Independent Labour Party, doubtless reflecting the pro-leftist agendas of so many social historians, but they were, none the less, extremely influential in their day. Even at the very zenith of British collectivism in the 1940s, new pro-enterprise bodies like Aims of Industry, founded in 1942, and the British Institute of Management, formed in 1947, came into existence.

If such bodies remain surprisingly little known, there is perhaps less need to emphasise the intellectual tradition of support for the free market, *laissez-faire* and upward mobility through dynamic capitalism found in a full-blown form possibly only in Britain and the United States. Adam Smith, David Ricardo, Samuel Smiles, Herbert Spencer, W. H. Mallock, and Alfred Marshall are all British names, a formidable tradition notably absent from any continental economic culture. In recent times, F. A. von Hayek's *The Road to Serfdom* appeared in wartime Britain and largely addressed the growth of British state controls. Karl Popper's *The Open Society and Its Enemies*, also by a refugee of distinguished intellectual gifts, provided, jointly with the later novels of his English contemporary George Orwell, the most seminal discrediting of totalitarianism of the right and left, especially among Stalin's fellow-travelling British intellectuals, so significant a force from about 1930 to 1956. More recently, a new group of proponents of *laissez-faire*, like Ralph Harris and Sir Keith Joseph, created much of the intellectual climate of opinion which led to Thatcherism, as have new organisations like the Centre for Policy Studies. The point here is not that this tradition has always been in the ascendancy – there were many decades, especially around the Second World War, when its ideology was so marginal as to seem thoroughly quixotic – but that, weak as it might have been in the first sixty years or so of this century, it was always stronger than its equivalents anywhere else, with the solitary exception of the United States. Even in America, too, during the same period, collectivism certainly occupied the intellectual high ground in virtually all facets of informed debate on public policy.

For decades, too, perhaps the major intellectual and political effort among, especially, younger and less orthodox Conservative thinkers and politicians aimed at reforming the ills of *laissez-faire* capitalism went not to instituting some variety of social democratic collectivism, but to enacting Tariff Reform, the erection of a tariff wall around the whole Empire with the joint aims of reviving British industry, consolidating the Empire into one immensely vast and powerful economic unit able to equal the size and strength of America, Russia, and Germany, and 'making the foreigner pay' for social reform at home. Tariff Reform captured the imagination of several generations of enthusiasts in the Conservative party, from Joseph Chamberlain, Bonar Law, and Lord Milner to men like L. S. Amery. Its actual enactment, after the three decades of struggle, to meet the challenge of the Depression in 1932, probably did help in reviving British industry; those who labelled it a way to enrich inefficient British manufacturers without any effort on their part forget that both the United States and Germany (and most other countries) had effectively used high tariff walls to become economic superpowers, while, of course, Britain had virtually no tariffs at all from 1846 to 1932. While advocates of the 'cultural critique' often view the Conservative party as long dominated by effete unworldly aristocrats and landed gentry utterly unsuitable to the rough-and-tumble of modern international economic competition, those actual aristocrats in the Conservative party who might credibly be described in these terms viewed their party in a very different light indeed, as essentially a businessman's party whose leaders and rank-and-file alike regarded the old aristocracy as grotesque fossils. By the mid-1920s a bona-fide aristocratic Conservative of long lineage like Lord Hugh Cecil thought that in Baldwin's Cabinet real power lay with the 'middle class monsters' and 'pure party politicians'; by the late 1940s his brother Lord Robert Cecil thought that the Conservative front bench in even the House of Lords was, except for Lords Salisbury and Munster, 'occupied by capitalists'.[54] As a proportion of the occupations among Conservative MPs, landowners declined from 23 per cent of Tory MPs in 1914 to 19 per cent in 1939, while businessmen rose from 24 to 51 per cent.[55] In the post-war period the Conservative party's MPs and leaders have chiefly consisted of businessmen and lawyers. A landowner of impeccable lineage like Francis Pym or Lord Carrington (whose ancestors were in any case bankers) has become an oddity in a Conservative Cabinet, especially since the 1960s, with the majority of the party middle class or even lower middle class in origin.

It is with the knowledge that throughout its modern history the Conservative party has remained centrally a pro-business party that apparently quite deviant examples of anti-business rhetoric and ideology should probably be viewed. Most dedicated advocates of 'Tory democracy' or 'Tory radicalism' who emphasised the radical or quasi-socialistic element in Conservatism were marginal figures, especially during normal times. Often, too, the rhetoric of leading Conservatives who employed what Professor Wiener has termed the 'rural myth' should in my view be read in a quite different sense from that which advocates of the 'cultural critique' have suggested. When Conservatives and others appeared to voice a widespread 'criticism of city life by those whose way of life was essentially urban' (as Wiener has put it),[56] in my view, they regularly meant something quite different and their remarks should certainly not be taken literally. Stanley Baldwin is clearly a case in point. Wiener devotes several pages to Baldwin's love of the countryside and rural England, enunciated in frequent speeches and essays, in passages recalling such things as 'the tinkle of the hammer on the anvil in the country smithy, the corncrake on the dewy morning, the sound of the scythe against the whetstone, and the sight of a plough team coming over the brow of a hill'[57] – images which by the mid-1920s when they were written already recalled a *rural* way of life which was rapidly vanishing through mechanised farming. Some of the best-known photographs and newsreels of Baldwin deliberately show him in his favourite guise, a typical Worcestershire farmer and squire mucking about with his pigs. He was, indeed, John Bull incarnate, bearing more than a passing resemblance to the familiar cartoon depiction. But what inference should we draw from Baldwin's self-image and rhetoric? That he was opposed to the creation of the giant chemical firm, Imperial Chemical Industries, formed under his Premiership? That he had something against the growth of 'semi-detached London' which, during his term at Number Ten, transformed hundreds of square miles of outer London farmland into the Metropolis's newest suburbs? That he regarded the glitzy world of the West End, from the newly created BBC to Noel Coward's Mayfair to Lord Louis Mountbatten's thirty-room penthouse apartment, as inherently depraved? Perhaps, but is it not far more plausible that Baldwin was quite deliberately signalling, to a Britain undergoing enormous and unsettling political, social, and economic change, that the Conservative party, at least, understood and remembered England's great and glorious traditions and appreciated its time-honoured values and heritage? At exactly the same time as Stanley Baldwin was mucking about with pigs in Worcestershire, his opposite number in America, Calvin Coolidge, was receiving enormous publicity from functionally equivalent newsreels and photographs depicting him out West in cowboy costume and in Indian gear and head-dress. Did 'Silent Cal' really believe that Americans should exchange their tin Lizzies for Conestoga wagons or that tepees and log cabins were to be preferred to apartment houses and California bungalows? Is it not rather more likely that Coolidge was signalling precisely the same thing, using American idioms and icons, as was Stanley Baldwin: that the Republican party at any rate deeply valued the central symbols of America's heritage, founded in values which were then being called into fundamental question by unprecedented cultural, social, and economic change? And surely Stanley Baldwin no more wished to return to the rural England of Squire Western and Jethro Tull than Calvin Coolidge – whose most famous remark was that 'the business of America is business' – thought that the time of Davy Crockett and Daniel Boone should reappear. Certainly there is nothing whatever in any actual policy pursued by either man to suggest that they confused symbol and reality in any facet of economics or social life. There is, indeed, nothing whatever in any aspect of the history of the Conservative party to suggest that it ever confused symbol with reality in any economic policy.

In a similar manner, although the Edwardian Liberal party has often been seen as a radical party which initiated the Welfare State and set the stage for Labour, in no sense was it anti-business or anti-capitalist. Lloyd George's radicalism was chiefly directed against landowners whose profits came without effort and with few gains for the nation or the ordinary person, unlike the profits of businessmen. As a recent historian of 'collectivism' in this period has noted, specifically addressing the points raised in *English Culture and the Decline of the Industrial Spirit*

> Wiener's thesis may also be contested with regard to the Liberals. The assertion that the appealing values of landed society came to dominate the British elite sits unevenly with Liberal anti-landlordism. The Liberal Party's land policies were intended to increase economic growth, not least in the countryside, by setting the people free from retardive and regressive land laws.[58]

Reviewing the policies of both parties in this period, Fforde also found that

> Both Conservatives and Liberals promised that their policies would encourage industrial, commercial, financial and agricultural prosperity and progress. There is no evidence that in the period 1886–1914 mainstream Conservatism or Liberalism sustained an anti-industrial or anti-growth political culture. It is certainly tempting to observe a common love of the countryside amongst the Victorian politically active and to invoke it as evidence for anti-industrialism. But to admire rivers, trees or mountains did not mean to reject cities, factories or banking-houses. Ecologism is a rather recent force.[59]

Post-Edwardian Liberalism became strongly associated, from the 1920s onwards, either, in its progressive ranks, with an early acceptance of Keynesian reformist capitalism (via Keynes himself) or, among its business right wing, with an increasing tendency to merge openly with the Tories, most notably in 1931. Had the Liberals remained the largest left-of-centre party in Britain after the First World War, it might well have evolved into something very like the post-New Deal Democratic party in the United States, committed to both a dynamic, progressive capitalism and considerable measures of social reform. Only during the past thirty-five years has the residual Liberal party embraced the package deal of ideas and programmes commonly associated today with the 'green left', but still in the context of a party which is explicitly anti-socialist and anti-Labour.

The case of the Labour party is, of course, more complicated. From 1918 onward the Labour party was officially committed to a policy of mass nationalisation 'to secure for the producers by hand or by brain the full fruits of their industry . . . on the basis of the common ownership of the means of production, distribution and exchange'.[60]

Especially in the troubled period from 1918 to 1926 and whenever it was out of office in the 1930s, some Labour politicians and many Labour intellectuals produced a steady stream of anti-capitalist and anti-business pamphlets, books, and diatribe which must have put the fear of God into many a businessman and wealthy *rentier*. The Left Book Club and other bodies of this kind published dozens of works with titles like *Britain Without Capitalists*. Labour's annual conferences were almost invariably occasions for ritual and extreme denunciations of capitalism and of entrepreneurs, while giving a platform to those who loudly foreshadowed the Commonwealth to come where socialism and co-operation replaced the jungle of the market-place. Conservative newspapers regularly gave maximum publicity to extreme attacks on the established order by Labour figures, the wilder and more over-the-top the better. A Labour intellectual like Sir Stafford Cripps, later a pillar of the Churchill and Attlee government, in the 1930s advocated the immediate enactment by the next Labour government of an Emergency Powers Act, restricting the movements of capital, placing restrictions on press reports of the government, and immediately abolishing the House of Lords.[61] Many more sober Labour figures advocated similar measures. Whenever Labour has been in Opposition since 1945, its left wing has gained the upper hand or come close, proffering a wide-ranging socialist platform and denouncing the half-hearted moderation of the previous Labour government. Each generation has seen the functional equivalent of its predecessor, from the Bevanites of the 1950s to the Bennites and the 'loony left' of the 1980s. It is at least arguable that the Labour party's long-standing apparent commitment to extreme socialism in the event it came to power with a working majority has had an adverse effect, conceivably a most adverse effect, upon the actions of British businessmen: why invest, why build up a successful concern, if Labour might at any time grab the lot?

Nevertheless, the record of Labour in power has been, as everyone knows, altogether different in kind. The first two Labour governments lacked a majority in the House of Commons and were unable to enact measures of socialism even if they had so wished. Ramsay MacDonald's first Labour government in 1924 was determined to prove its respectability; MacDonald and Philip Snowden, his Chancellor of the Exchequer, were both made Freemen of the City of London for their services to financial normality. The second Labour government of 1929–31 fell over MacDonald's commitment to rigid treasury orthodoxy. Labour's reputation as a radical party in practice is based chiefly, if not wholly, on the Attlee government's performance in 1945–51. The post-war Labour government is rightly regarded as one of the great reforming governments of the century, nationalising the coal mines, railways, and the Bank of England, giving independence to India, enacting the National Health Service and other social security measures. Beyond this, however, it did not go, and it was in no real sense anti-business nor, except in the limited areas where it extended state control, anti-capitalist in any sense. This is now readily admitted by all left-wing historians of the Attlee government. According to the Marxist academic David Coates,

> Far from weakening private capitalism, Labour Party nationalisation after 1945 actually *strengthened* it as a system, and reinforced the economic and social position of its ruling groups. It did this by relieving them of the responsibility for derelict industries, by removing from them the economic consequences of low investment and inefficient management, and by providing them instead with an infrastructure of publicly owned basic industries whose pricing policies could be designed so as to subsidise the private sector on which economic growth and export earnings so critically depended.[62]

Even the wider list of industries to be nationalised after 1950, had Labour returned with a working majority, was highly empirical in nature – or so the Labour party took pains to claim. In his speech to the 1950 Labour party conference at Blackpool, Herbert Morrison explained that

> We have not made an abstract list of industries for socialisation. We have considered them in relation to various parts of the programme in a natural way. For example, the proposals with regard to making industrial assurance into a public concern are made primarily on the basis of rounding off the social services and completing that great edifice. Water is in the programme [of industries to be nationalised] primarily in relation to agriculture and life in the rural areas, which have the greatest interest in the development of water supply. Similarly, cement is there in relation to the cost of building operations.[63]

In two other areas the post-war Labour government does appear far more radical than any other government before or since – although here too, a closer look might provide a different view. Labour used an extensive array of government mechanisms to apply a variety of unprecedented peacetime controls on the economy. Many of these were far-reaching indeed, entailing a degree of economic regulation previously unknown. For instance, no factory building or repair work in excess of £1,000 could be undertaken without a licence, and all such requests were rigorously vetted.[64] The Capital Issues Committee effectively controlled the flow of most new capital investment, new issues being directed almost exclusively at export-earning or import-saving industries at the expense of distribution, entertainment, and the service sector.[65] The fact that, prior to the Attlee government, the war had seen the institution of a far-reaching system of controls over the economy without precedent, itself led to the readier acceptance of these controls in peacetime than would, in all likelihood, have otherwise been the case. Denis Healey's observation that *laissez-faire* again became a viable political option in Britain only after those who had participated in the war at a decision-making level had passed from the scene appears especially acute. Even more saliently, rates of personal taxation reached levels without any precedent in history. A bachelor earning £10,000 had retained £6,222 after income tax and surtax in 1937, but only £3,501 in 1948, despite the fact that inflation had nearly halved the value of the pound.[66] The maximum rate of death duties on a millionaire estate passing for probate reached 75 per cent in 1946–9, whereas it had been taxed at only 50 per cent in the period 1930–9 and only 65 per cent during the war. It was in this period that the wealthy, especially those who had inherited landed wealth, appeared to be a doomed species, scheduled for extinction. The war and post-war era probably witnessed the end of 'Society' in its traditional sense, with its 'network of country houses' and widespread servant-keeping. Yet both of these extremes in Labour policy plainly grew out of the regulations and laws in force during the war, and chiefly remained in place because of the parlous state of the British economy and the need for extreme measures in the period of post-war reconstruction. Labour's extraordinary rates of personal taxation of course represented an ideological commitment to achieving forcible equality, but it seems difficult to believe that had Labour come to power with a working majority in a Europe always at peace in this period, it would have raised taxation rates to anything like these levels, rates which would almost certainly have proven to be electoral suicide and the occasion for widespread and deliberate avoidance. It should also be noted that the need for massive rearmament so soon after a devastating world war, and greatly increased government social security responsibilities everywhere, saw unprecedented taxation almost everywhere as well. In the United States, for instance, top marginal rates of income tax exceeded 70 per cent during the Korean War.

On all other fronts, however, the post-war Labour government supported British industry and left British capitalism alone. Some franker conservatives, indeed, wondered that Labour, with its enormous electoral mandate in the context of an exhausted Britain and a radicalised Europe, with conservative forces almost everywhere totally discredited or marginalised, did not do far more. In 1945, for example, the *Economist* magazine noted that Labour's list of industries to be nationalised 'is most moderately short':

An avowedly Socialist Government, with a clear Parliamentary majority, might well have been expected to go several stages further. There is nothing in the list about the land . . . ocean-going shipping . . . merchant shipping . . . [or] petroleum, which, in its domestic aspects, might be thought the most obvious target of all.[67]

In particular, the post-war Labour government left the City and finance virtually alone, being far more concerned with labour-intensive extractive industries and other parts of the national infrastructure. Despite all the government restrictions and confiscatory rates of taxation, too, money, indeed fortunes, could readily be earned. Perhaps as many self-made men, especially in property and service industries, began in the post-war era (often with their demob. payout) as at any time in British history. Angus Maude's well-known summary of the situation – 'Since the war ended it has been easier to make higher profits without being really efficient than probably at any period in my lifetime' – came from a perceptive right-wing Tory, not a socialist.[68]

In most other respects, too, the post-war Labour government was remarkably conservative and simply followed in the pathways of established British policy. Indeed, looking at the well-known group photograph of the 1945 government – perhaps the last occasion at which some gentlemen wore wing collars – one has the uncanny impression that one is looking at a late Victorian government, transported in time. Sir Stafford Cripps, for example, *seems to be* William E. Gladstone in mid-twentieth-century disguise. It was, too, the last British government to operate wholly before television, before the ubiquitous employment of public opinion polls, and before the age of the pervasively mendacious public relations machine; the last, perhaps, to use words – at least part of the time – in other than manifestly Orwellian ways. In its foreign policy the Labour government was instrumental in founding NATO, containing Communism, building a British atom bomb, and entering the Korean War as a matter of course. It retained conscription in peacetime and still-vast Commonwealth responsibilities. Its domestic social policies had virtually nothing to say about such matters as feminism, sexual reform, abortion, environmentalism, privacy, restrictions on government secrecy, and other social issues later so important a component of the left-liberal agenda; indeed, its attitudes on these issues appear to be nearly identical to those of previous Tory governments. Anthony Howard remarked that 'the overwhelming Labour victory of 1945 brought about the greatest restoration of social values since 1660'.

Even more than the Attlee governments, the Wilson (1964–70, 1974–6) and Callaghan (1976–9) Labour administrations can in virtually no sense whatever be seen as anti-business or anti-capitalist. Wilson's government was committed upon its narrow election victory to pursuing Keynesian economic growth as a panacea to Britain's perceived economic woes and backwardness. Its policies were continuously derided by the left, both within the Labour party and outside of it. When its growth policies were sidetracked around 1966 due to a continuous balance of payments crisis, its chief aim became producing a trade surplus. Renationalisation of steel (1967) was its sole concession to doctrinaire socialism. Wilson's own imitation Churchillian rhetoric, emphasising 'modernisation', technology and growth as a substitute for traditional socialism, was especially scorned by the left, while his personal entourage of wealthy self-made businessmen, former army officers, and public relations specialists has generally been regarded with a mixture of contempt and prurient interest.[69] James Callaghan's government was notable chiefly for its total failure to achieve anything at all, although it was probably the first British government to use monetarism as a deliberate policy, before 'Thatcherism'.[70] Since 1979, Labour has responded to Opposition and to the 'Thatcher revolution' with, first, a sharp move to the left and then an equally extreme move to the right, virtually ditching any residual obeisance to achieving 'socialism' after about 1987, in the context of the collapse of Communism and socialism in Europe. Labour's move to the extreme left from 1979 to about 1984, accompanied by unprecedented internal tension and the secession of many leading party moderates to the Social Democrats, of course produced its worst electoral results in many decades. It thus seems extremely difficult to see anything in Labour's record apart from some aspects of its great 1945–51 government which can properly be termed anti-business or anti-capitalist, and these must be seen as a small part of a larger picture of a party committed to social democracy and then to Keynesian reformist capitalism. Committed socialists like Ralph Miliband long recognised the sharp limitations invariably placed on the achievement of socialism in Britain through parliamentary means.[71]

Proponents of the 'cultural critique' are thus quite wrong in linking Britain's allegedly poor economic performance in this century with an anti-capitalist mainstream polity. Indeed, with British politics, as with so much else in British society, the most striking impression made on any historian is surely its moderation, the continuous eschewing of extremes and extremists, unlike the long experience of the continental countries. Perhaps the clearest example of this occurred at the 1931 General Election, held at a time when unemployment had climbed to nearly three million, or 21.5 per cent of the insured workforce. At this election the National Government received 14.5 million votes out of 21.7 million cast, or 67 per cent, the Labour opposition 6.6 million votes, or 33 per cent. Sir Oswald Mosley's New Party, the direct predecessor to the British Union of Fascists and already heavily imitative of Mussolini's Fascists, received exactly 36,377 votes, or 0.2 per cent of all votes cast. At the other extreme of the spectrum, the British Communist party did rather better, receiving no less than 74,824 votes, or 0.3 per cent of all votes cast – these figures despite unprecedented unemployment and all the despair which accompanied it. In fact, in its entire history the British Communist party has succeeded in electing just four MPs (one in 1924, one in 1935, two in 1945), while no right-wing extremist party, or any other Marxist party of the left, has ever elected a single MP at any time. The contrast here with the continental countries is impossible to exaggerate: at the 1930 German election the Nazis and Communist parties between them received 31.4 per cent of the total vote (13.9 million votes out of 35 million), at the 1932 German election 52.0 per cent, then 56.2 per cent at the final Weimar election in 1933. The French Communist party polled 15.3 per cent of the vote in 1936, and then, consistently, between 26 and 29 per cent of the total vote throughout the remaining years of the Fourth Republic. The pattern found in British politics, of the consistent marginalisation of extremist parties and leaders to the far fringes of political life, seems to be a prominent hallmark of the English-speaking democracies, in sharp contrast to the continental countries throughout much of their history, and Britain should probably be seen here as part of a pattern of electoral behaviour analogous to that in the United States and the white Commonwealth, rather than that in the rest of Europe until well into the post-war period.

Turning elsewhere, the 'cultural critique' is also misleading in its assessment of the effects of British culture on profits and profitability, another key plank in the agenda of this interpretation. As Professor Wiener has claimed, 'However many businessmen's sons entered [the public schools], few future businessmen emerged from these schools, and those who did were "civilised"; that is, detached from the single-minded pursuit of production and profit.'[72] If this were the case, the profits of Britain's major firms, increasingly dominated by public-school-educated 'gentlemen' should have declined over time. Such was, in fact, not the case. The overall *raison d'être* of all economic activity by all British firms remained – and, virtually by definition, most remain – the 'single-minded pursuit of profit'. Historical studies of the profitability of British firms in this century have shown, first, that the overall rate of profits varied directly with general economic conditions, peaking during the inter-war period in the 1919 boom and during the late 1920s and late 1930s, declining by roughly 40 per cent in the 1920–2 and 1929–33 depressions, but then recovering satisfactorily.[73] Possibly in contrast to America and Germany, profitability continued throughout the British economy during the very worst part of the Great Depression. Net true income assessed under Schedule D of the income tax (the tax on company profits) for all firms in all industries totalled £934.3 million in 1927, £665.6 million in 1932, and £948.8 million in 1936.[74] No single industry in Britain actually reported a negative income in 1932 except for shipping (£870,000), even textiles, where income for all companies declined from £30.0 million in 1927 to £11.3 million in 1932, still a positive figure.[75] The dividend issued by Imperial Chemical Industries, Britain's largest company, was 8 per cent in 1928 and 1929, 6 per cent in 1930, 4.5 per cent in 1931, and 8 per cent during 1934-6.[76] Continuing profitability was achieved in part, of course, by rationalising and shedding excess labour, but it is such relentless efforts in heartless profit-seeking which, presumably, the 'cultural critique' argues formed no part of the behavioural code of the gentleman-capitalist. In the post-war years, rates of company profits were remarkably high – indeed, extraordinarily high – until the late 1960s, when a severe 'profits squeeze' became evident. According to Andrew Glyn and Bob Sutcliffe, two Marxist economists, the share of profits in British company net output stood at the remarkable level of 25.2 per cent in 1950-4, but declined steadily to 20.2 per cent in 1965 and only 12.1 per cent in 1970.[77] They attribute this decline to 'wage pressure, economic stagnation and international competition', to which might be added the beginning of the oil and commodity crises.[78] Whatever the causes of this decline in profits, chronologically it is very difficult to attribute it to any effect produced by public-school-educated 'gentlemen' of the traditional kind, for the decline seems clearly to coincide with the passing of such men from the scene. D. C. Coleman, for instance, pinpoints 1962 as the year when the traditional British bifurcation of 'gentlemen' and 'players' perhaps became obsolete.[79] The mid–late 1960s would indeed mark the last date at which there would be active senior businessmen who clearly remembered England prior to the First World War, and the first date at which younger men raised in the wake of the 1944 Education Act and the new realities of the post-war world reached middle management positions in numbers. In any case, profits rose again in most sections of the British economy under Mrs Thatcher, although not evenly throughout all sections of the economy.[80] By the later 1980s rates of return in British industries 'caught up with those in other industrial countries'.[81] Again, it seems quixotic to attribute any of this to deep-seated cultural changes in the British psyche, although no doubt the 'enterprise culture' underlying the 'Thatcher revolution' legitimated a strong entrepreneurial response by British companies and businessmen. In the later 1970s, however, when a minority Labour government was in office, overall profits also rose strongly, before dropping sharply in the 1980-1 recession.[82]

Both British culture and British politics have thus clearly worked to limit and to marginalise the intellectual and ideological extremes which threatened to undermine the cultural foundations of capitalism in other societies. As we have seen, too, it is simply unreasonable to link British culture and the typical upper-class products of its elite culture with any alleged decline in profitability. There may, as well, be other more subtle and less familiar cultural factors operative in modern Britain which may have assisted, in a positive way, to create a climate more favourable to capitalism and its attendant values than elsewhere, and which certainly contradict on other grounds the 'cultural critique'. One of the most interesting of these subtler areas is, in my view, the changing use of syntax and diction in established and educated English prose and discourse. In the course of the nineteenth century, I would contend, educated English prose and discourse manifestly evolved in the direction of much greater clarity, cogency, and conciseness, to give it the elegance and precision which one now associates with the best English prose, and which is normally the wonder of visitors from other parts of the world (especially America) who encounter it for the first time. The evolution of this typical pattern of syntax may, perhaps metaphorically, be seen to have evolved in an 'anti-gentry' direction, away from slovenliness and imprecision to those precise, well-defined, and well-delineated modes we may associate with rationality and modernity. This change appears to have occurred rather suddenly in the late Victorian and Edwardian period, such that good and clear prose of 1925 differed palpably from its equivalent seventy years before. Take for example, Thomas Carlyle. Carlyle might be seen by some as an extreme and eccentric advocate of a viewpoint whose prose style mirrors his other eccentricities. Yet there is not that great a difference between Carlyle's prose and that of other leading authors of his day, while he was, as an advocate of a viewpoint, obviously trying to convince his readers of its merits. Consider, for example, Carlyle on the rich and poor in Scotland, from *Past and Present* (1843):

> So many hundred thousands sit in workhouses: and other hundred thousands have not yet got even workhouses; and in thrifty Scotland itself, in Glasgow or Edinburgh City, in their dark lanes, hidden from all but the eye of God, and of rare Benevolence the minister of God, there are scenes of woe and destitution and desolation, such as, one may hope, the Sun never saw before in the most barbarous regions where men dwelt. Competent witnesses, the brave and humane Dr. Alison, who speaks what he knows, whose noble Healing Art in his charitable hands becomes once more a truly sacred one, report these things for us: These things are not of this year, or of last year, have no reference to our

present state of commercial stagnation, but only to the common state. Not in sharp fever-fits, but in chronic gangrene of this kind is Scotland suffering. A Poor-law, any and every Poor-law, it may be observed, is but a temporary measure; an anodyne, not a remedy: Rich and Poor, when once the naked facts of their condition have come into collision, cannot long subsist together on a mere Poor-law. True enough: – and yet, human beings cannot be left to die! Scotland too, till something better come, must have a Poor-law, if Scotland is not to be a byword among the nations. O, what a waste is there; of noble and thrice-noble national virtues; peasant Stoicisms, Heroisms; valiant manful habits, soul of a Nation's worth, – which all the metal of Potosi cannot purchase back; to which the metal of Potosi, and all you can buy with *it*, is dross and dust!

Charles Dickens, too, wrote in a style not that dissimilar to Carlyle's – garrulous, allusive, unskimmable, seldom getting quite to the point – which was a characteristic feature of everything he produced. Evidently this style did Dickens no harm: he was the most popular author of his day and virtually from his earliest works was freely compared to Shakespeare. This passage, from *Our Mutual Friend* (1864), is pure Dickens and a true artefact of its times:

The great looking-glass above the sideboard reflects the table and the company. Reflects the new Veneering crest, in gold and eke in silver, frosted and also thawed, a camel of all work. The Herald's College found out a Crusading ancestor for Veneering who bore a camel on his shield (or might have done it if he had thought of it), and a caravan of camels take charge of the fruits and flowers and candles, and kneel down to be loaded with the salt. Reflects Veneering; forty, wavy-haired, dark, tending to corpulence, sly, mysterious, filmy – a kind of sufficiently well-looking veiled-prophet, not prophesying. Reflects Mrs. Veneering; fair, aquiline-nosed and fingered, not so much light hair as she might have, gorgeous in raiment and jewels, enthusiastic, propitiatory, conscious that a corner of her husband's veil is over herself. Reflects Podsnap; prosperously feeding, two little light-coloured wiry wings, one on either side of his else bald head, looking as like his hair-brushes as his hair, dissolving view of red beads on his forehead, large allowance of crumpled shirt-collar up behind. Reflects Mrs. Podsnap; fine woman for Professor Owen, quantity of bone, neck and nostrils like a rocking-horse, hard features, majestic head-dress in which Podsnap has hung golden offerings. Reflects Twemlow; grey, dry, polite, susceptible to east wind, First-Gentleman-in-Europe collar and cravat, cheeks drawn in as if he had made a great effort to retire into himself some years ago, and had got so far and had never got any farther. Reflects mature young lady; raven locks, and complexion that lights up well when well-powdered – as it is – carrying on considerably in the captivation of mature, young gentleman; with too much nose in his face, too much ginger in his whiskers, too much torso in his waistcoat, too much sparkle in his studs, his eyes, his buttons, his talk, and his teeth. Reflects charming old Lady Tippins on Veneering's right; with an immense obtuse drab oblong face, like a face in a tablespoon, and a dyed Long Walk up the top of her head, as a convenient public approach to the bunch of false hair behind, pleased to patronize Mrs. Veneering opposite, who is pleased to be patronized. Reflects a certain 'Mortimer', another of Veneering's oldest friends; who never was in the house before, and appears not to want to come again, who sits disconsolate on Mrs. Veneering's left. . .

Now consider some equally typical passages from good mid-twentieth-century prose, one by a writer unknown except within a particular special interest group, the other by a man who is often regarded as the greatest English prose writer of the century, and perhaps the most famous:

On the morning of October 8th, 1952 in weather that was seasonable but which could not be called foggy, an early suburban train, from Watford to Euston, was making its usual stop at Harrow and Wealdstone; and at the up main line platform many passengers were joining the train. It was fully protected in rear, with the distant, outer home, and inner home signals all correctly at danger. Then, inexplicably and at full speed there bore down upon that standing train the up Perth sleeping car express running 1½ hours late, and headed by the Stanier 'Pacific' No. 46242 *City of Glasgow*. There was scarcely time to comprehend the full horror of what had happened before the 7.55 a.m. express from Euston to Liverpool and Manchester, double-headed with a 'Jubilee' class 4–6–0 *Windward Islands* piloting the brand new 'Pacific' No. 46202 *Princess Anne*, came tearing in from the south end at about 60 m.p.h. and ploughed into the wreckage of the first collision.

The result was indescribably terrible. In many ways the two collisions were a ghastly echo of Quintinshill, except that in the first one the fast-moving express struck the rear of a standing train instead of a massive locomotive, and the casualties were mainly in the 'local'. But the down express, double-headed as at Quintinshill, struck a far more formidable obstacle than the scattered wreckage of the troop train, and under the footbridge at Harrow there piled up the most terrible wreck seen on a British railway.[83]

In our time it is broadly true that political writing is bad writing. Where it is not true, it will generally be found that the writer is some kind of rebel, expressing his private opinions and not a 'party line'. Orthodoxy, of whatever colour, seems to demand a lifeless, imitative style. The political dialects to be found in pamphlets, leading articles, manifestos, White Papers and the speeches of under-secretaries do, of course, vary from party to party, but they are all alike in that one almost never finds in them a fresh, vivid, home-made turn of speech. When one watches some tired hack on the platform mechanically repeating the familiar phrases – *bestial atrocities, iron heel, bloodstained tyranny, free peoples of the world, stand shoulder to shoulder* – one often has a curious feeling that one is not watching a live human being but some kind of dummy: a feeling which suddenly becomes stronger at moments when the light catches the speaker's spectacles and turns them into blank discs which seem to have no eyes behind them. And this is not altogether fanciful. A speaker who uses that kind of phraseology has gone some distance towards turning himself into a machine. The appropriate noises are coming out of his larynx, but his brain is not involved as it would be if he were choosing his words for himself. If the speech he is making is one that he is accustomed to make over and over again, he may be almost unconscious of what he is saying, as one is when one utters the responses in church. And this reduced state of consciousness, if not indispensable, is at any rate favourable to political conformity.

The first extract here is from O. S. Nock's *Historic Railway Disasters* (London, 1970), and is a description of the horrible train wreck at Harrow in 1952 in which 112 people were killed. Nock, a railway signal engineer, wrote over eighty books on railway history but his writings will probably be unknown to those without an interest in this topic. The second extract is from George Orwell's famous essay 'Politics and the English Language', originally published in *Horizon* in April 1946. Perhaps the most glaring feature of a comparison of these two passages is that Nock's description is, by any test, at least as well written as Orwell's, although Nock was an engineer who turned to writing as an enthusiastic amateur in a specialised field, while George Orwell is universally regarded as one of the best writers of our time, the author of two among the ten or so most important English-language novels of the century, and a man who would certainly have been awarded the Nobel Prize in Literature had he not died at the age of 47. Both are typical examples of conspicuously good writing by Englishmen in recent times, although neither is materially better than any of thousands of extracts from articles, essays, editorials, or even speeches which would show much the same features: the extraordinary clarity of expression, the cogency, the gift of always getting straight to the point without dissimulation, perhaps above all the control demonstrated over language, with the deliberate and extraordinarily effective use of meiosis, litotes, and hyperbole, as at the end of the passage here by Nock.

It is also self-evident that both recent passages differ most fundamentally from the extracts by Carlyle and Dickens quoted just before them. The difference between the earlier and more recent extracts consists, evidently, in the fact that the latter extracts are, to a very large degree, more cogent, lucid, and precise, although no doubt many will prefer the charms – very different charms – of the earlier classics. Both sets of quotations are in my view typical of their time and place – which is not of course to say that there were not writers, contemporary with Carlyle and Dickens, like Macaulay or perhaps Newman, whose works are cogent, concise, and lucid, and not to say that there are not tens of thousands of English writers during the past generation who write appallingly; indeed, paradoxically, the excellent and famous passage by Orwell quoted here makes this very point and regards bad writing (wrongly in my view) as virtually ubiquitous.

It seems abundantly clear, however, that the *general direction* of good prose writing in England over the past 150 years has been in the direction of consistently increasing clarity, cogency, and simplicity, compared with the norm in previous times. It also seems apparent that this change crystallised only recently, probably just before or just after the First World War, and that even good late nineteenth-century prose was far more verbose than that of our time. This evolution in the direction of simplicity in prose had its roots in several distinct and important causes. The art of advocacy in the English courts with the necessity to persuade and convince through evidence and inference from evidence is perhaps one important cause. Another is the successful House of Commons style as it evolved in the nineteenth century, with its tacit aim of persuading an unseen but ever-present reasonable man (personified by the Speaker) through reasonable argument rather than succeed by bombast, bullying, or demagoguery. The clever-clever Oxbridge High Table manner, so prominent a feature of university life in this century, was nevertheless unremarked on prior to the secularisation of Oxford and Cambridge in the late nineteenth century, although what A. L. Rowse has termed the 'unbearable brilliance' of the Oxford Union may have a longer pedigree. Perhaps the most important factor in this evolution, however, was the rise of the public schools with their heavy emphasis on the classics, and the growth of grammar schools for the bulk of the middle classes in which a similar curriculum was emphasised. This evolution was materially assisted by the appearance of widely-known and best-selling guidebooks to good style, of which H. W. Fowler and F. G. Fowler's *The King's English*, first published in 1906, is perhaps the best known. This work was compiled by two brothers, the sons of a Tunbridge Wells clergyman. The surviving brother, Henry Watson Fowler, who was educated at Rugby and Balliol and then served as an Assistant Master at Sedbergh School, noted in the preface to the third (1930) edition of *The King's English* that 'It has sometimes seemed to us, and to me since my brother's death, that some of the conspicuous solecisms once familiar no longer met our eyes daily in the newspapers. Could it be that we contributed to their rarity?'[84] *The King's English* consists in large part of examples of 'conspicuous solecisms' drawn chiefly from the press, novels, and politicians of the 1900–6 period; by the 1930s, examples of blatantly poor writing from these sources were much more difficult to come by. *The King's English* opens with the celebrated advice which serves as a capsule guide to cogent writing and is the scourge of the obfuscator: 'Prefer the familiar word to the far-fetched; Prefer the concrete word to the abstract; Prefer the single word to the circumlocution; Prefer the short word to the long; Prefer the Saxon word to the Romance.'[85]

This increasingly pervasive emphasis in good English writing on rationality, concision, and clarity sits uneasily, it seems to me, with a society whose elites are, it is urged, increasingly anti-rational, gentrified, unrealistic, and, most of all, unable or unwilling to face the actual realities of industrial society in the twentieth century. A hegemonic elite truly bent on fostering the 'cult of the gentleman', the 'rural myth' and 'a counter-revolution of values' would, it would surely seem, be reluctant to further a ubiquitous form of discourse increasingly rational and clear-eyed. For many years, too, many sociologists starting with Max Weber have seen just these values as a salient causal factor in engendering capitalism, Weber linking both with the rise of Protestantism. Indeed, Weber's celebrated thesis was as much an attempt to demonstrate a nexus between rational, modern values and habits of behaviour and 'the spirit of capitalism' as to link it specifically with the growth of a particular religion, a claim which is clearly much more problematical.[86] If this be so, it is surely curious, to put it no more strongly, that these values should be increasingly emphasised in good writing at a time marked, it is urged, by 'the gentrification of the industrialist'.

Another similar and very distinctive feature in British habits of thought is the attempt to be comprehensively accurate and even-handed in assessing the world. British commentary on events is notably marked by its great fairness and pains to achieve great accuracy – or so it seems to this writer, who has had a wide experience with the cultural habits of several English-speaking countries and with several others. In this century at any rate English culture has placed a distinctive and readily perceptible premium on accuracy. A good example of what I have in mind here is the *Guinness Book of Records*, the all-time best selling reference book first produced in 1954 by twin brothers in London, Norris and Ross McWhirter, and now produced annually in thirty-five different languages.[87] Unlike similar books of 'amazing events' and happenings the aim of the *Guinness Book of Records* is to publish only totally verifiable information. This frequently entails rejecting rather than accepting inaccurate tall tales and Sunday supplement-type reports. Thus, the oldest known person in history, according to the *Guinness Book*, was a Japanese fisherman who died at the age of 120 in 1985 (he was listed by name and age in the 1870 Japanese Census), not some alleged inhabitant of the Caucasian mountains or the Amazon jungle aged 170 or so – all such claims being either exaggerations or unverifiable. The longest snake ever known was about 32 feet long, not 75 or 100 feet as in legendary travellers' tales – and so on, through each category of superlative. The nearest American equivalent of the *Guinness Book of Records* was probably the 'Ripley's Believe It or Not!', newspaper cartoons which were published from 1919 until the 1970s. In contrast to the stark accuracy of the *Guinness Book*, they sailed very close to the wind in what they alleged, and frequently depicted human 'freaks', reputed religious miracles and supernatural events, and the like. Today, dozens of radio stations in the United States have late-night talk programmes devoted largely to the occult and the supernatural, while virtually every bookshop in the United States has a major section devoted to astrology, tarot reading, UFOs, the 'Bermuda Triangle' and subjects of this kind – fascinating stuff to many, no doubt, but grossly inconsistent, one might assume, with the rational values which allegedly serve as the seedbed of capitalism.[88] Many other standard reference works in a wide variety of fields published in Britain have also put an all-embracing premium on accuracy, from the *Encyclopaedia Britannica* to the *Oxford English Dictionary* to *Keesing's Contemporary Archives* and the *Statesman's Year-Book*, their reputation deriving entirely from their accuracy and objectivity. Similarly, British institutions of information dissemination of every kind, from *The Times* – long the world's newspaper of record – to the BBC have acquired a very similar reputation around the world. It is also a most characteristic feature of academic or quasi-academic presentation of any kind in Britain to eschew exaggeration, to present the small-scale searching piece of analysis or research rather than the grand idea or theory, especially when these cannot be verified by clearly appropriate evidence. Grand Theory is, for better or worse, much more a feature of both continental and American scholarship and philosophising than a feature of English intellectual life.

It seems curious to this writer that these features of British culture and British discourse in modern times, so characteristic and unmistakable, should seldom be proffered by English commentators on British culture as significant. Many English writers on their culture, in fact, point to diametrically opposite features as more common. To George Orwell, the 'mixture of vagueness and sheer incompetence is the most marked feature of modern English prose, and especially of any kind of political writings.'[89] It is safe to say that Orwell never made a more inaccurate or misleading observation. Many other commentators on modern Britain have perceived a decline in the typical cogency of expression among good writers. Yet there really is no compelling evidence for this view, while Britain stands out in the English-speaking world for the clarity of expression among its writers, politicians, and journalists. A comparison, say, with typical American or Australian levels of expression is quite laughable. Among American politicians and public figures, for instance, one who can speak and express himself elegantly and intelligently, like Adlai Stevenson and John F. Kennedy, is so unusual that he is remembered for these qualities many decades later. Popular writing in the United States is universally regarded as abysmal while simple literacy is a quality as rarely imparted at many American schools as the ability to levitate.

The British cultural emphasis on rationality, clarity, and accuracy also has obvious affinities with the long-standing British tradition of excellence in science. The British contribution to science of course began centuries earlier than the more decent penchant for clarity of expression. Perhaps indeed clearness and accuracy in writing is a broadening out of the scientific habit of mind to the generality of the educated population. Possibly this occurred via the imparting of at least some science to most middle-class males in the public schools and grammar schools (as was increasingly the rule), and often in the universities. Possibly this was brought about by an increasing interest in and fascination with the speculative aspects of science on the part of the general public, for instance by scientific lectures and demonstrations so popular in the mid-Victorian era. However this process occurred it shows that the 'cultural critique's' understanding of middle-class British education is indeed misleading, for a central tenet (arguably the central one) of the 'cultural critique's' thesis is that classical education as imparted in the public schools and universities has been intrinsically hostile to science, as has been post-industrial British middle-class culture generally. But this assertion ignores the extraordinary British contribution to science over the past 300 years, with giants like Harvey, Newton, Faraday, Darwin, Huxley, Lister, Kelvin,

Rayleigh, Fleming, Crick, Hawkings and so many others making profound and fundamental contributions in a wide variety of fields. Most of Britain's scientific giants came, broadly speaking, from the same backgrounds of the middle-class and above as other important cultural achievers, although science probably always produced more self-made men than other areas, like Michael Faraday. Darwin, for example, was educated at Shrewsbury and Cambridge, and came, of course, from a family already eminent and established. There has always been a surprisingly strong aristocratic and gentry nexus with science in Britain, with figures like the Hon. Henry Cavendish (1731-1810, the discoverer of oxygen), Sir George Cayley (1773-1857, inventor of the glider), John William Strutt, third Baron Rayleigh (1842-1919, discoverer of the rare gases), and Bertrand Russell, among others, drawn from a remarkably small demographic base. In his recent book *Britain's Prime and Britain's Decline: The British Economy 1870-1914*, the eminent economic historian Sidney Pollard has examined in great detail, and completely exploded, the myth that German scientific training and education was markedly superior in either quality, funding, or status, to Britain's efforts in these areas in the period 1870-1914.[90] If anything, on closer inspection the British educational expenditure on science and closely related fields appears the more impressive, while an objective examination of German science in this period reveals many disturbing faults.[91] Pollard's clear-headed revisionist analysis is especially impressive in coming from a distinguished historian of truly remarkable erudition who was born in Austria and recently taught in German universities, while lecturing for many decades at British universities.

In this century, British basic science has always been remarkably strong. Taking the awarding of the three Nobel Prizes in science as a rough indication of merit, from 1901 to 1990 British scientists have won 22 Prizes in Chemistry, 24 in Medicine, and 20 in Physics (total 66). German scientists' totals have been 27 in Chemistry, 13 in Medicine, and 17 in Physics (total 57). Only the United States, with its 36 awards in Chemistry, 45 in Medicine, and 57 in Physics (total 138) has been significantly ahead, while other countries have trailed far behind. French scientists, for example, have been awarded 22 Nobel Prizes in science, while only five Japanese scientists (one in 1949) have been Nobel laureates. Cambridge University, in particular, has emerged as one of the pre-eminent centres of scientific research in the world, with many scientific chairs and research institutions. Since 1917, only eight Soviet scientists have won a Prize, despite the great emphasis placed on science in the Soviet Union throughout most of its history. Several of these were educated under the Czarist regime or abroad (1978 physics laureate Peter Kapitza, for instance, at Cambridge). Britain's record in science is one which, on a population basis, arguably outstrips that of any other country including the United States. This extraordinary record certainly continued until at least the Second World War: of the five most important inventions or discoveries to emerge from or be developed during the Second World War (the jet engine, radar, penicillin, the computer, atomic energy), four were essentially British discoveries while the fifth, atomic power, was developed with a considerable British input. The notion that British culture is adverse to science is thus surely quite absurd, as misleading as the positive image of the formidable German, or still more, Russian scientist.

Some will argue that while it might be true that British scientists have made an extraordinary number of basic discoveries, these were often, and now regularly, employed in profitable technological innovations only in foreign companies. The saga of the jet engine, where by the late 1950s the early lead Britain had built up had been partially lost to the United States, is an obvious example; so is the growth of the computer industry, chiefly outside of Britain. Three replies should be made to this argument, which admittedly has a major element of truth in it, especially in the period from the early 1950s to the 1980s. First, the argument we are specifically examining here is that British culture is adverse to science. This argument is surely without merit. Second, in so far as there has been a failure in the development and manufacturing in Britain of British scientific and technological discoveries, all that we have said about the *nature* of the British economy since 1870 should be kept in mind: Britain's comparative advantage strongly favoured other forms of business life, no less lucrative or entrepreneurial. Third, the argument above may have its merits but it also has its faults, for (at the time of writing) Britain does have – to use the cases we have just mentioned – a significant aerospace industry, including a very major jet engine sector, and an internationally significant computer industry. It is simply not the case that Britain has 'deindustrialised', even by the terms in which this argument is usually made, which ignores the satisfactory condition of its service sector and, indeed, the existence of this sector. As with the evidence on economic strength, many comparative determinants of scientific ability are still far more favourable to Britain than is often realised. For instance, in 1989 Britain was fourth in the world in the number of influential patents held, according to one American study, behind the United States, Japan and Germany but ahead of France, Italy, Switzerland and all other countries. Among the articles published in the world's 40,000 journals of science and mathematics, the plurality (30–40 per cent) were written by Americans, but those by British authors amounted to about eight per cent of all such articles. By nationality British authors were in joint second-fourth place, tied with Japan and the Soviet Union. These figures have been stable for the past twenty years.

Along with the extraordinary British contribution to science at the level of high culture was a popular culture which always was surprisingly friendly to science and felt an affinity to science and science-related modes of thought, an affinity clearly related to the rational elements in British culture and to increasing emphases on clarity and accuracy. For the past century or so, the imaginative life of middle-class boys and youths in Britain has comprised an important measure of science and science-related matters, among them science fiction stories from H. G. Wells to *Dr Who*, Meccano sets and toy trains, mathematical puzzles, secret codes, and brain teasers of the type favoured by the pre-adolescent, constant speculation on space travel and on life on other planets, the collection of rocks and animal specimens, train spotting, nature field trips, and a host of other similar activities and preoccupations which will be very familiar to most British readers. The popularity of these activities is perennial and may very well loom larger than all sporting activities, at least for boys aged 7–14; probably they have always been more popular than scouting. These pathways of hobby and imaginative life among British boys became set, in all likelihood, in the late nineteenth century, when secularised leisure-time activities became thoroughly acceptable. H. G. Wells's *The Time Machine* appeared in 1895, his *War of the Worlds* in 1898, both following on the American Edgar Allan Poe (1809–44) and the Frenchman Jules Verne (1828–1905), who wrote most of his famous novels in the period 1863–90. Boys in other societies probably have had very similar imaginative interests in this century, and, normally, much of this interest of course becomes desultory or non-existent upon adolescence or young adulthood. Nevertheless, it is again simply misleading to assert that British culture marginalises or excludes the sciences and the scientific consciousness: on the contrary, it brings it into the deepest places of the imagination of much of the population.

The other side of the coin of the spread of a scientific, positivistic culture at both the high and mass levels has been the near-total secularisation of British society and the reduction, virtually to the vanishing point, of the force of organised religion. Britain differed, of course, from the Catholic countries of the Continent in adopting an Established religion of compromise, which had from its start made its peace with science and the newer forms of learning. Saints' icons, prayers to the Virgin, miraculous cures and places of pilgrimage which loomed so large in continental Catholicism had no place, or only the most minimal one, in post-Reformation Britain. As a result, the congruence of continental liberalism with anti-Catholicism and the deep animosity of the established Catholic Church to all forms of modernity, regarding it as heresy, also had little or no role in post-1750 Britain. Indeed, an intolerant anti-Catholicism, which condemned the Roman Church as a sinister, primitive, corrupt medieval bastion of superstition, was prevalent in Britain at both the elite and mass level, mixed in with patriotic hostility to France and ethnic hostility to the Irish. Nevertheless, the Anglican Church did, until the Age of Reform, hold a formal monopoly on religious prestige, status, and power in England, and enjoyed some of the privileges associated with an established continental church. Until surprisingly late, too, the clerical profession was virtually the only profession which a man of learning could pursue, a fact which is not sufficiently appreciated now. Neither university teaching nor the civil service could provide more than a tiny portion of the places available in the Anglican Church while journalism and the free professions were fraught with uncertainty. Until the 1870s, more than 60 per cent of the graduates of Oxford and Cambridge became Anglican clergymen, the old universities being chiefly, in effect, religious seminaries. The loss by the Anglican Church of its former role as the national church was profoundly traumatic to men of ideas like John Henry Newman and William E. Gladstone. The Church had also continued to benefit from a remarkable residual role in secular affairs. For instance, until 1858 the Church was solely responsible for the probating of wills in England and Wales, an extraordinarily lucrative perquisite which generated an army of officials and lawyers in the Ecclesiastical Courts (as the courts of probate were known), dealing with matters which would thereafter be regarded as totally secular in nature. It was because of the continuing central role of the Anglican Church, too, that the appointment of any of the two archbishops and twenty-four bishops in England and Wales was always the subject of such interest and controversy: both because men continued to regard religion as central, and because appointment to the most senior positions of the Church, so limited in number, marked the zenith of one of the few learned professions. If, today, England's universities had only twenty-six chairs in all of the subjects they taught, from nuclear physics to the history of art, and these went, by unsolicited appointment, to a scholar in any disipline, each new appointment would also be discussed and debated as vigorously. Beyond the Church of England, too, were the Nonconformist sects, each with its own history, sociology, and legions of congregants. Religious debate and discourse were not merely significant in Britain through the late nineteenth century, but arguably paramount, religious publications of all sorts probably outnumbering all other kinds of publication combined, in both circulation and range.

From 1870 onward, and especially in this century, it goes without saying that this situation has utterly changed. Religion today is chiefly a ghettoised embarrassment, its leaders and spokesmen seen in the media's public eye only when one says something especially radical or especially stupid. The appointment of a new Archbishop of Canterbury is the occasion of major media interest, but often, recently, as the opportunity for a frank discussion of his inadequacies. Media present-ation of religion and religious questions is largely confined to the 'graveyard' slot on early morning television and radio when no one is likely to listen, while church attendance since 1918 has gone from weakness to weakness, broken only by slight rises in the early 1950s and perhaps at the present time. The situation of the Nonconformist sects is even more parlous, with dissenting life having virtually disappeared in many places. Only the Catholic Church and immigrant religions appear to be healthy, and then perhaps chiefly as a mode of ethnic and national identity.

While secularisation has of course occurred throughout the world in this century, particularly in Western Europe, in Britain it may well have gone further than almost anywhere else; certainly active participation in the Anglican Church and the other Protestant churches has declined fairly dramatically.[92] Religious belief and the whole field of religiosity are notoriously difficult matters to be accurate about; the point here is that, once again, the available statistics all seem to be grossly at variance with the central thesis of the 'cultural critique' that modern Britain has moved *away from* rationality and science to a glorification of pre-modern and anti-modern values in its cultural life. On the contrary, these statistics seem highly consistent with the growing acceptance of secular and positivistic values throughout virtually the whole of society – assuming that any links at all can be drawn between them and the British economy, which is highly arguable in any case.

It is, for instance, proverbially argued that Protestant dissenters 'sparked' the industrial revolution, and the decline of Nonconformity might be linked with the decline of pro-capitalist values and of entrepreneurship. Although plausible, this argument is probably quite misleading. First, and contrary to popular belief, there is absolutely no reason to suppose that the percentage of successful businessmen who were Dissenters in the period 1800–1939 was higher than a random figure. The notion that very disproportionate numbers of successful businessmen were Dissenters is a misconception based on counting only well-known industrialists and manufacturers and ignoring equally or more successful merchants, bankers, and entrepreneurs in other occupations who were largely Anglican.[93] The fallacy of the 'Weber Thesis' as it has been applied to the British experience is, in truth, very close to the central misconception underlying the 'cultural critique', that Britain was an *industrial* economy derailed by the anti-entrepreneurial code of the 'gentleman'. In fact, very nearly the opposite seems to have been true. Second, Nonconformity included far more than businessmen whose religion might have motivated them to become successful entrepreneurs. Nonconformity – especially Methodism, but also Quakerism, Unitarianism, and most other sects – certainly fomented a radical and anti-capitalist ideology among many of its adherents. The close connection between Methodism and the Labour party is legendary, as is the participation of Quakers, Unitarians, and adherents of many other sects in radical movements of all kinds, from the campaign for nuclear disarmament to colonial independence movements. The decline of Nonconformity might thus just as readily have acted to dilute and diminish attacks on capitalism as to decrease the number and quality of Britain's entrepreneurs.

The importance of science and positivistic values in modern British culture, and even the decline in overt religiosity have also been consistent with a deeply humanistic element in the British character and culture, another facet of the effectiveness with which extremes and extremism have been marginalised in British politics and ideology. From Chaucer and Shakespeare onwards, there has been a deep humanism about most English cultural artefacts which is a distinctive feature of England's national culture. Whether this be in the music of Vaughan Williams and Walton, the architecture of Wren or Capability Brown, the poetry of Keats or Wilfred Owen, Wordsworth or Edward Thomas, this deep and genuine humanism is perhaps the most evident single characteristic of what is distinctively English in the cultural sphere. As usual, the deep humanity of English culture is perceived most clearly and enunciated most movingly by foreigners. Karel Capek (1890–1938), the Czech writer who coined the word 'robot', remarked about the 'gentleness of the English' that,

> Sometimes you have a sense of uneasiness at feeling so solitary in the midst of these kind and courteous people; but if you were a little boy, you would know that you can trust them more than yourself, and you would be free and respected here more than anywhere else in the world; the policeman would puff out his cheeks, to make you laugh, an old gentleman would play ball with you, and a white-haired lady would lay aside her 400 page novel to gaze at you winsomely and with her gray and still youthful eyes.[94]

Since Britain emerged in the eighteenth century as the world's leading economic power, and has always remained a leading economic power, there has evidently been no underlying inconsistency between its deeply humane culture and its capitalist economy, while an inability to perceive this is one of the failings of the 'cultural critique'.

A number of factors have led many observers of Britain's economic and social history over the past century to draw some very misleading inferences about British culture and its relationship to British capitalism. At the centre of the confusions which surround this relationship is the profound misunderstanding concerning the very nature of the British economy, with its false tacit assumption that the relative decline of British industry is congruent with a decline in Britain's overall economic performance. As we have seen, this ignores the growing importance of Britain's financial and commercial sector. Equally important is the linkage of this decline to Britain's allegedly anti-business culture. But British culture is neither anti-business nor anti-scientific. On the negative side it plainly contains fewer anti-capitalist cultural traditions, signposts, and cues than virtually any other society; on the positive side, its cultural base is founded not in anti-rational, anti-modern 'gentry' values but, on the contrary, on a value-system and thought patterns which emphasise positivism and rationality to a remarkable degree, a culture based on reason and ratiocination which is fully congruent with its economic comparative advantage as an economic and financial power, but which was also remarkably humane.

These observations are certainly not in themselves the whole story. There is Britain's educational system to consider as it affected the upper middle-classes. Then there is the evolution of Britain's elite structure and the bearing this had on Britain's economy.

3

Education, the 'gentleman', and British entrepreneurship

The typical education received by the sons of Britain's industrialists from the early Victorian period onward – specifically, education at a fee-paying public school and (less often) at one of the two older universities – is at the heart of all variants of the 'cultural critique' of British economic decline posited by historians, for here is the actual mechanism of the process of socialisation by which the progeny of hard-nosed, profit-maximising, often self-made industrialists were allegedly transformed into effete and soft-hearted 'gentlemen', unfit by outlook, training, or behaviour for the rough-and-tumble world of the factories. Professor Wiener has put the case against the public schools clearly and succinctly:

> For all their vaunted independence, the public schools, through new institutions like Headmasters' Conference, converged on a common model. Despite the absence of state direction, they came to constitute a system, one that separated the next generation of the upper class from the bases of Britain's world position – technology and business.

> The most obvious example of the public schools' detachment from the modern world was the virtual absence of science of any sort from their curricula. In the teaching of science the public schools lagged far behind the schools of lesser social standing. . . . [I]t was a normal part of the curriculum . . . in many grammar schools. Yet it did not penetrate the schools of the upper class for some years thereafter, and then only over determined obstruction.

> The public schools gradually relaxed their entrance barriers. Boys from commercial and industrial families, however, were admitted only if they disavowed their backgrounds and their class. However many businessmen's sons entered, few future businessmen emerged from these schools, and those who did were 'civilized';

that is, detached from the single minded pursuit of production and profit.[1]

Although chiefly writing of the baneful effects of the public schools on the quality of British political and military leadership after 1900, and acknowledging (p. 36) that 'for most boys school was a memorably happy experience', Corelli Barnett fully shares in this indictment:

The late nineteenth century was a time of intense scientific progress and intellectual speculation – a time of colossal industrial developments and social change. All of this bore crucially on the future of Britain and the British Empire. Awareness of little or none of it penetrated into the public schools. The growing threat of other great nations to British predominance, for example, did not lead to a comparative examination for the benefit of pupils of the strategic and industrial foundations of British power and the power of her rivals. It merely led – in some schools – to an uncritical patriotism, in which other great powers were looked upon rather as rival schools, to be humbled by 'pluck' and team spirit.

[T]he generation of boys who were to reach leading places in British life in the 1920s and 1930s were the products of the public school at this period of greatest regimentation, stuffiest self-satisfaction and conformity, and most torpid intellectual life – midway between the Arnoldian era of experiment and growth, and the reforms of the mid-twentieth century.[2]

The harmful effects of the public schools persisted long past the inter-war era, according to Anthony Sampson, and were at the heart of the malaise that permeated post-Suez Britain, despite some efforts at modernization and reform:

In the Victorian ethos it was by uprooting boys from their parents, and forging them into a tough society, that imperial leaders were created. Many Victorian schools were built round imperial service, or the army. . . . In Britain itself, the segregated world of public schools crops up in all kinds of institutions: a boy can pass from Eton to the Guards to Oxford to the Middle Temple to Parliament, and . . . need never deal closely with other kinds of people.[3]

It has become normal in discussing the history of the public schools to periodise their evolution in modern times according to a well-known pattern. Until the early nineteenth century, the public schools were remarkably anarchistic, with an extraordinary degree of freedom from the regimentation of student life which so characterised them for most of the Victorian period. The very symbol of this anarchistic period was the Long Chamber at Eton, a 'barn-like room, where fifty-two scholars slept . . . it was unheated until 1784 when two fireplaces were put in; the windows were broken. It was filthy, stinking of corrupting rats corpses, ordure and urine.'[4] The boys – extraordinary as this must sound – were completely unsupervised, and 'scenes of the coarsest and most flagrant orgiastic indulgence took place, of a sort that participants (or victims) could later barely bring themselves to describe.'[5] Apart from homosexual abuse, torture, beatings, burnings, and drunken mayhem were daily occurrences. *The Lord of the Flies* was alive and well in Georgian England. One 'alumnus' of the Long Chamber applied to an insurance company in 1826 and mentioned that 'he had slept in the Long Chamber for eight years'. On hearing this, the chairman of the company – instead of requiring a medical examination – passed the applicant without further ado: 'We needn't ask him any more questions.'[6] Rioting and student rebellion were common – the 1960s had nothing on Georgian England. The best-known student rebellion was organised by Byron, the poet, at Harrow in 1805.

The celebrated reforms of the early Victorian age must be seen against this background of incredible anarchy and corruption. The chronology and leadership here is easy to establish, so often have they been reiterated. The great reforming headmasters of the mid-nineteenth century, led by Thomas Arnold of Rugby – whose reforms have been described by G. C. Coulton as 'probably the greatest educational movement of nineteenth-century Europe' – as well as his contemporaries, predecessors, and imitators from Samuel Butler at Shrewsbury, C. J. Vaughan and Henry Montagu Butler at Harrow, Edward Thring at Uppingham, F. W. Walker at St Paul's, and many others – transformed the old system into the regimented, christianised, recreationised, imperialised public schools of legend and actual fact, founded (it is usually stated) in an impressive if arguably pedantic classical scholarship, muscular Christianity, and the ethos of competitive games – the backbone of the system whose aim was the production of Christian gentlemen, serving the Empire and bringing honour and glory to the schools.[7] The recreated and reconstituted system of the public schools reached its majestic apogee between, roughly, 1880 and 1914: by this time, it is frequently suggested, virtually all sons of upper-class and upper-middle-class families attended such schools, and their influence on the British Establishment of the day – and since – was utterly fundamental and certainly multifaceted.

Of the manifold influences of the public schools at their zenith only one concerns us here: the celebrated 'haemorrhage of talent' (the phrase is David Ward's)[8] through which the sons and other relatives of successful Victorian entrepreneurs were transformed into effete 'gentlemen', normally leaving business life entirely or, if remaining, manifesting clear business incompetence, unlike their forebears. This is perhaps the crux of the argument presented by advocates of the 'cultural critique', the essence of the mechanism wherein Britain's anti-industrial and anti-business attitudes are engendered and spread.

The alleged role of the public schools in engendering the decline of British entrepreneurship is a complex matter which can be divided into questions which are empirically testable by historians and those which are not; both of these categories must themselves be broken down into a series of more fundamental questions. About the process of engendering entrepreneurial decline, four important questions which can be empirically tested may be asked: first, was public school education common enough, in the late nineteenth century, possibly to instil a 'spirit of anti-industrialism' into the middle classes as a whole? Second, was it common enough crucially to affect the sons of industrialists and manufacturers (as opposed to other types of businessmen)? Third, was there in fact a 'haemorrhage of talent' whereby the sons of successful businessmen left business life for other fields? And, fourth, can anything be said with certainty of the entrepreneurial abilities of those educated at public schools who remained in business life? There are, in addition, a host of other relevant questions which are less amenable to comprehensive empirical testing but which are equally crucial to sustaining the position enunciated by the 'cultural critique': for instance, did the public schools actually offer a sustained agenda or curriculum which was anti-capitalist and anti-business? Did its typical curricula always, indeed, ignore science, and what is the relevance of this to entrepreneurial performance? Were there important relevant changes in typical curricula and can their chronology be linked with entrepreneurial performance a generation or two later?

To ascertain the accuracy or otherwise of the 'cultural critique's' view of the public schools, the author, as part of a larger research project concerned with the Victorian middle classes, has made an extremely detailed study of random samples of entrants at eight major public schools, and the fathers of these entrants, with the aim of determining the occupation, career pattern, and probate valuation of each person in this study, and of the father of each such person. The eight schools in this study were Eton, Harrow, Winchester, Rugby, Cheltenham, St Paul's, Dulwich, and Mill Hill, and the samples consisted of between 60 and 100 boys, randomly selected from school registers and alumni books, entering each school in 1840, 1870 and 1895/1900, roughly generational intervals, a total of 1,802 entrants in all.[9] The schools selected for study consisted in part of obvious and necessary choices – any such study must include Eton, Harrow, Winchester, and Rugby, normally regarded as the most prestigious of the so-called Clarendon schools, with Rugby the domicile of Dr Arnold and his revolutionary approach to public school life and ethos – and in part by the limitations of the sources.[10] To obtain the necessary samples, as well as some minimal information on each entrant, it was necessary for a school to have, first of all, an alumni register, which not every public school has compiled (there is, for instance, no post-1910 Eton alumni register), and, second, that the register be arranged chronologically by entrance dates, and contain some minimal biographical information on each entrant including, very preferably, the name and occupation of the entrant's father and information about the entrant's career, with his date of death. It is also preferable that the school's register be compiled well into the twentieth century, at a date when something substantial might be said of the careers of the 1895/1900 entrants. While many public school registers did possess all of these desirable characteristics, many others did not: the alumni registers of Charterhouse and Westminster, two obvious possibilities for a study like this one, for example, are arranged in strictly alphabetical order, making it virtually impossible to abstract entries from the three particular classes from the thousands of alumni names. In the end, Cheltenham, St Paul's, Dulwich, and Mill Hill were selected as both providing a useful range of types of schools and possessing very usable alumni registers. Regrettably, no school in the north of England likely to attract significant numbers of businessmen's sons possessed a usable alumni directory. Possible schools of this type were, in any case, very few in number. Bootham, the Quaker school in York, might possibly have been chosen, but its alumni directory is arranged in alphabetical order rather than chronologically by class. The inclusion of Mill Hill, the Congregationalist school founded in 1808, does compensate in part for the omission of a northern school of this type. While Mill Hill is located in London, it took Nonconformist boarders from all over the country. In any case, a careful study of the sons of businessmen at Eton, Harrow, Winchester, and the other highly prestigious schools included in this study is central to the case made by the 'cultural critique', and should go far to proving or disproving its case.

Before turning to the evidence from this study, something more must be said of each school whose entrants have been included. As noted, Eton, Harrow, Winchester, and (increasingly from Thomas Arnold's reign as Headmaster which lasted from 1828 till 1842) Rugby were generally regarded as the premier boarding schools in England in the nineteenth century, although Westminster was probably on a par with Eton in the eighteenth century – thereafter it ran downhill – and a number of newer boarding schools, most notably Marlborough, Wellington, Clifton, and possibly Cheltenham, challenged the pre-eminence of these four by the late nineteenth century. Among these four schools, too, there were very significant differences in the typical social class, wealth, and occupational backgrounds of entrants' families. Eton was, then as now, clearly the most prestigious school, the school where bona fide aristocrats and millionaires – though mostly well-established aristocrats and millionaires – were likely to send their sons. Especially in the political sphere, it produced, of course, more leaders than any other, with an average of five Etonians in twentieth-century British Cabinets whose median size was twenty.[11] Among its products since 1830 have been ten Prime Ministers. Generally, Harrow, its great rival, ranked second to Eton in these characteristics, although it appeared to be more open to new money than did Eton, and had a reputation for being a 'Whig' school as opposed to Eton's leanings toward Toryism. Among the fathers of 1895 Harrow entrants in our study, for instance, were Baron Leopold de Rothschild, the merchant banker who left £1.5 million, and Sir James Joicey, first Baron Joicey, the great colliery magnate who also left £1.5 million. Both were much more typical of the parents of Harrovians than of Etonians, as was Alfred Baldwin, former Methodist, ironmaster and Chairman of the Great Western Railway, whose son Stanley – not included in this sample – attended Harrow in the 1880s. Together, Eton and Harrow produced a grossly disproportionate share of the political and public elite. In 1831, 20 per cent of members of the House of Commons had attended Eton and 11 per cent Harrow. In 1865 these percentages were, respectively, 16 and 8. In 1906, 8 per cent of Liberal MPs and 42 per cent of Unionist MPs had attended Eton.[12] Among the 294 Cabinet Ministers holding office between 1868 and 1955 (including Labour Ministers), 75 were educated at Eton and 27 at Harrow.[13] Winchester and Rugby were somewhat similar in drawing chiefly from poorer, but still well-established, sections of the gentry and (especially) the professional classes – vicars, lawyers, army officers, colonial administrators and civil servants – but lacked a nexus with the political elite on the scale of Eton and Harrow.

The four other schools in this study were, however, substantially different in nature. Cheltenham, established in 1841, was originally a 'proprietary school': shareholders – there were originally 650 – could each nominate one pupil. Initially it drew chiefly from retired colonial administrators resident in the area, it became known as a feeder-school for future army officers and had strong links with the Anglo-Irish elite. As the century wore on, however, it probably became more similar, broadly speaking, to the other boarding schools in its social clientele.[14] St Paul's, in complete contrast, was a London day school of great antiquity whose eminent alumni included John Milton, Samuel Pepys, and the great Duke of Marlborough. Until 1877 the school's location was adjacent to St Paul's Cathedral; as the nineteenth century progressed and fashion deserted the city, it drew from a much lower social class than the other schools in this study, with a good many fathers in low-status clerical occupations and none, or very few, from the wealthier classes. In 1877 the school moved to Hammersmith, initiating a remarkable renaissance under F. W. Walker, High Master 1877–1905, becoming one of the leading schools in England in academic terms and drawing its recruits from London's upper middle classes. G. K. Chesterton, E. C. Benson, Leonard Woolf, Compton Mackenzie, G. D. H. Cole, and Edward Thomas, the poet, are only some of the very distinguished authors produced by St Paul's in this period or just after.[15]

Dulwich College, located in the middle-class suburb in south London, was founded by the will of Edward Alleyn, the Elizabethan actor-manager who may have employed Shakespeare at one time. It languished under the curious and absurd provisions of his will – the headmaster, for instance, always had to be a man surnamed Alleyn! – until the school was reconstituted in 1857 as two separate schools, the more famous classical school Dulwich College, and Alleyn's school, a day school with a modern education; it is the classical school which is considered here. (Because of its reconstitution in 1857, there is no 1840 cohort for Dulwich College in the data considered here.) It grew rapidly, typically drawing on the south London middle class in a similar way to St Paul's, but with rather more businessman fathers. It produced C. S. Forester, G. E. Moore and that curious trio of Old Alleynians who found fame and renown across the Atlantic, P. G. Wodehouse, Raymond Chandler and Ray Noble, the band leader who wrote *The Very Thought of You* and many other hits of the 1930s.[16]

The final school we examine here is Mill Hill, also a London school, but one distinguished, as noted, by the fact that it was a public school for Dissenters, chiefly Congregationalists. As a boarding school it attracted Dissenters from around the country. As a dissenting school, too, it also had, probably, the widest range of wealth and income among the parents of its entrants of any school studied here, with the sons of dissenting millionaires classmates of the sons of dissenting small tradesmen and ministers. Among the fathers of entrants in this study were Roger Cunliffe, whose son became Governor of the Bank of England, and Henry Overton Wills, the Imperial Tobacco millionaire; Sir George Wills, his son, who is one of the 1870 entrants, also Chairman of Imperial Tobacco, left £10 million. Among his classmates were the sons of a draper from Lee, Kent, of a mercer in Newport, Monmouth, and of a ship's ironmonger living in Upper Holloway.

The vast differences in the social clientele of these schools can be seen in Tables 3.1, 3.2 and 3.3, which respectively detail the number of

Table 3.1 Titled fathers of public school entrants, 1840–1895/1900

Date	Peer	Baronet	Knight	Total	N	%
			ETON			
1840	8	7	3	18	100	18.0
1870	10	4	1	15	101	14.9
1895/1900	12	7	3	22	102	21.6
			HARROW			
1840	4	2	2	8	60	13.3
1870	3	4	2	9	100	9.0
1895/1900	3	6	2	11	100	11.0
			RUGBY			
1840	1	2	1	4	61	6.6
1870	2	2	1	5	81	6.2
1895/1900	0	2	4	6	80	7.5
			WINCHESTER			
1840	0	2	3	5	60	8.3
1870	–	–	5	7	100	7.0
1895/1900	3	4	3	10	102	9.8
			CHELTENHAM			
1840	0	1	0	1	60	1.7
1870	0	3	2	5	80	6.3
1895/1900	0	0	3	3	82	3.7
			ST PAUL'S			
1840	0	0	1	1	61	1.6
1870	0	0	0	0	73	0.0
1895/1900	0	1	3	4	100	4.4
			DULWICH			
1840	–	–	–	–	–	–
1870	0	0	0	0	60	0.0
1895/1900	0	0	1	1	59	1.7
			MILL HILL			
1840	0	0	0	0	60	0.0
1870	0	1	2	2	60	3.3
1895/1900	0	0	0	0	60	0.0

fathers of entrants at each school who either inherited or were granted a title, the number who left an estate (in constant terms) of £100,000 or more – an enormous fortune, placing its holder among the wealthiest one-tenth of one per cent of all deceased adults – and, as well, the median probate valuation of all fathers of entrants.

Probably the strongest impression made by these tables is the extraordinary position of Eton as the school *par excellence* of aristocrats and the wealthy. These figures, indeed, probably understate the

Table 3.2 Fathers of public school entrants who left £100,000 or more in constant terms,* 1840–95

Date	Number, £100,000	N	%
	ETON		
1840	42	100	42.0
1870	49	101	48.5
1895	33	102	32.4
	HARROW		
1840	19	60	31.7
1870	35	100	35.0
1895	19	100	19.0
	RUGBY		
1840	8	61	13.1
1870	15	81	18.5
1895	11	80	13.8
	WINCHESTER		
1840	11	60	18.3
1870	11	100	11.0
1895	16	102	15.7
	CHELTENHAM		
1840	2	60	3.3
1870	13	80	16.3
1895	6	82	7.3
	ST PAUL'S		
1840	0	61	0.0
1870	0	73	0.0
1895	1	100	1.0
	DULWICH		
1870	2	60	3.3
1895	1	59	1.7
	MILL HILL		
1840	4	60	6.7
1870	7	60	11.7
1895	5	60	8.3

*Based upon the Rousseaux Index, in which an average of 1865 and 1885=100. Includes the capitalised value of land.
Sources: B. R. Mitchell and Phyllis Deane, *Abstract of British Historical Statistics* (Cambridge 1971), pp. 471–3; David Butler and Gareth Butler, *British Political Facts, 1900–1985* (London, 1986), pp. 380–2; *Return of Owners of Land, 1873–76*.

situation, for they record these social characteristics only for the fathers of entrants: but many Etonians were closely related to titled persons or the very wealthy in other ways. Perhaps the second most interesting impression is the opposite, the complete lack of aristocratic or wealthy fathers at schools like St Paul's or Dulwich College.

Table 3.3 Median probate valuations of fathers of public school entrants, 1840–95

	Current values (£)			Constant values (£)		
	1840	1870	1895	1840	1870	1895
Eton	80,000	88,463	64,184	71,483	103,100	46,377
Harrow	25,000	47,653	41,978	20,833	58,113	23,337
Winchester	37,500	21,317	15,513	32,355	25,669	16,646
Rugby	10,000	30,929	25,291	8,930	31,888	15,802
Cheltenham	7,000	10,000	7,858	6,605	9,755	4,695
St Paul's	1,516	2,000	3,778	1,651	1,903	2,633
Dulwich	–	3,238	5,192	–	4,139	4,104
Mill Hill	5,451	8,234	24,949	5,162	11,071	22,976

Although education at a public school is often taken as *ipso facto* synonymous with a wealthy or established social background, the great majority of public schools, even among the most famous of public schools, were attended almost entirely by the sons of the middle classes, few of whom were from wealthy or gentry backgrounds.[17]

The claims made by proponents of the 'cultural critique' thesis can in part be tested by a searching comparison of the fathers of the entrants in this study and the entrants themselves, with the aim of examining just how public school education, with its alleged anti-business, anti-profit, and pre-industrial syllabus and biases, affected the careers of those who experienced this type of education. If the public schools imparted such a bias, either through the overt values taught in the classroom or through more subtle factors of socialisation and peer-group attitude formation, this would necessarily be reflected in the career patterns among these samples of public school entrants in later life, with distinct and significant swings away from business in the case of businessmen's sons (and all others), and a decline in business acumen among the minority who none the less took up a business career, their ability at profit-making (and their interest in business profitability) severely dented by their educational experiences. In particular, there should be a pronounced swing away from industry and manufacturing, as totally ungentlemanly trades, by the sons of northern manufacturers and industrialists. One of the great virtues of a precise and comprehensive set of samples of entrants and their fathers of this type is that it allows us to test the 'cultural critique' argument in an exacting way.

Before considering what these samples show, two prior points should be made. First, although the 'cultural critique' thesis must crucially be dependent upon empirical evidence of this kind, it would seem that only a few previous studies of the intergenerational effects of public school education have ever previously been made, the most important a study of all 7,105 Wykehamists and their fathers born between 1820 and 1922 carried out by T. J. H. Bishop and Rupert Wilkinson.[18] The results here are hardly encouraging to the 'cultural critique' thesis, for these researchers found that although 11.1 per cent of the fathers of Wykehamists in their study were businessmen, 16.4 per cent of the Winchester entrants themselves became businessmen in their own careers! Nevertheless, one must treat these findings with some caution: they are based exclusively upon the Winchester alumni registers which may well systematically overstate the gentry and leisured percentages of both fathers and sons and are, in any case, self-descriptions. Moreover, 1,082 Wykehamists were excluded from the study – 13.2 per cent of the grand total of 8,187 entrants born 1820–1922 – because their occupations were unknown, while no fewer than 28.5 per cent of the Wykehamist fathers were of unknown occupation.[19] Nevertheless, Bishop and Wilkinson do note very clearly that 'there is no *statistical* evidence that Winchester helped turn the sons of businessmen to more gentlemanly careers than "Trade" ', and that 'from the 1870s on, the number of Wykehamists entering business continued to inch upward'.[20] It thus seems clear not only that the 'culture critique' thesis has been only inadequately tested by empirical research, but that such research as exists lends it no support.

Before coming to the main evidence in this study, another point must be made, relating to the first of the general queries raised above: even if public school education indeed was just as deleterious in its effects upon the entrepreneurial interests or abilities of its products as its harshest critics argue, was education at any fee-paying public school widespread or common enough to affect a significant portion of the sons of the middle classes? Almost certainly, the answer throughout the nineteenth century was clearly 'no'. In the early 1860s, only 2,741 boys attended any of the nine 'Clarendon' schools (Eton, Harrow, Rugby, Merchant Taylors', Winchester, St Paul's, Westminster, Shrewsbury, Charterhouse), of which only five were boarding rather than day schools.[21] There are, apparently, no comprehensive figures for attendance at all British public schools – whose definition was often a matter of dispute – but in the mid-1860s, the thirty-four public schools which, on one definition, existed at the time enrolled about 7,500 boarders; many of these schools probably catered for the local middle classes and occasionally for the lower middle classes. By 1902, on Professor Honey's estimates, it seems that there were sixty-four recognisable public schools with an enrolment of about 20,000.[22] The annual number of male births in Britain averaged around 375,000 in the early 1850s and 510,000 in the mid-1880s, although from this number must be subtracted all childhood deaths, the severely handicapped, etc.[23] Perhaps 300,000 boys of those born in the early 1850s survived into their teens and were healthy, and 450,000 of those born in the mid-1880s. If around 20 per cent of these belonged to middle-class households (probably an understatement), the suggested total number of middle-class boys born in any one year would therefore have been around 60,000 in the early 1850s and 90,000 in the mid-1880s. These figures, however, must themselves be multiplied by three or four (at least) to compare with the enrolment totals, for a school enrols three or four annual classes of boys at any one time – thus, the 'universe' of boys from which the public schools could potentially draw would probably have numbered 200,000 in the mid-late 1860s and 300,000 at the end of the nineteenth century. But *fewer than 4 per cent* of this possible figure attended any public school – much less Eton or Harrow – in the 1860s, and *fewer than 7 per cent* at the end of the nineteenth century.

It is obvious from these figures that unless the public schools attracted the sons of the country's leading businessmen in grossly disproportionate numbers it would have been *ipso facto* impossible for the public schools to have had the profoundly deleterious effects often attributed to them: demonstrably, too few middle-class boys attended a public school for this to have occurred. (The same, *a fortiori*, was true of Oxford and Cambridge, which enrolled only a few thousand students at any one time.) Moreover, public school attendance was not randomly distributed throughout the middle classes. It seems highly likely that, proportionately, many fewer sons of northern manufacturers and industrialists attended a public school at this time: for one thing, disproportionately more northern manufacturers were dissenters, while nearly all public schools were of Anglican foundation; most public schools were physically located in London, the Home Counties, and the south-west, remote from the northern cities. If this be the case, small as the percentage of public school entrants among all middle-class sons evidently was, it was likely to have been lower still among the sons of northern industrialists. Such research as there has been on this subject has clearly shown the great rareness of public school education among northern industrialists before the twentieth century. Dr Hartmut Berghoff's painstaking study of 754 leading businessmen in Manchester, Birmingham, and Bristol, active between 1870 and 1914 found that 3.6 per cent attended Eton, Harrow, or Westminster, 4.9 per cent any of the other six Clarendon schools, and a further 9.5 per cent any other public school.[24] Even these percentages probably exaggerate public school attendance by a significant amount, for Dr Berghoff could trace no educational information on a further 574 leading businessmen from the total of 1,328 in his study; it seems certain that very few of these attended a public school, for obituaries and accounts of the careers of these businessmen would certainly have mentioned any elite schooling, had it occurred, in most cases.[25] Dr Berghoff concludes that 'the overall impact of these schools on the entire business class must have been very limited indeed'.[26] Among the businessmen included in the five-volume *Dictionary of Business Biography* edited by D. J. Jeremy, only 12.7 per cent of those born 1840–69 attended a leading public school and another 7.9 per cent a lesser public school.[27] Other studies of industrialists born in the mid-late nineteenth century, and thus allegedly responsible for Britain's industrial decline, show much the same thing, the startling rareness of public school education among manufacturers and industrialists.[28] This pattern was found to be much the same in a study of Mayors and Lord Mayors of six leading British cities who held office between 1832/5 and 1914 – the Mayors and Lord Mayors of London, Manchester, Liverpool, Leeds, Birmingham, and Newcastle-upon-Tyne – carried out by the author of this book. Although some Mayors were professional men engaged in other spheres apart from business life, or occasionally members of the gentry, most were local businessmen, generally among the most prominent local businessmen who, by definition, constituted a major part of the local civic elite. Some, like Joseph Chamberlain and William Kenrick in Birmingham, and Sir William Forwood in Liverpool, became nationally synonymous with the 'thrusting', northern new business elite. Once again, it is the extreme rareness of public school education, even at the end of this period, which is so striking: of 378 men serving as Mayors or Lord Mayors of these six cities in this period, just 17 (4.5 per cent) attended either a Clarendon school or another leading boarding school (such as Clifton or Radley), and only 26 others (6.9 per cent) attended any public school, including local old-foundation grammar schools like Leeds Grammar School which only joined the Headmasters' Conference of officially designated public schools long afterwards. Only about one-half of this small group of public-school-educated Mayors, moreover, were local businessmen; the others were solicitors, or the occasional aristocrat like the two successive Earls of Derby who served as Lord Mayors of Liverpool in 1895 and 1911. It thus seems extraordinarily unlikely from all of this evidence that the very limited percentage of the northern elite who were educated at a public school down to the First World War could possibly have been responsible for Britain's industrial decline, even if the public schools induced all of the anti-business and anti-industrial qualities often assigned to them.

We come here, too, to a central paradox in the 'cultural critique' argument, for although there can seemingly be no doubt whatever that even Edwardian industrialists attended a public school only infrequently and in a small minority of cases, it was also the case that many more bankers and those engaged in established financial and commercial activities were typically educated at a public school: *yet it was industry which declined* and finance and commerce which continued to prosper. Every study of leading bankers, especially in London, since the mid-Victorian period, has emphasised their exclusivity, especially the consistency of their privileged educational backgrounds. For example, the study conducted by Philip Stanworth and Anthony Giddens of 460 leading company chairmen holding office between 1900 and 1972, found that over 80 per cent of the merchant banking and clearing banking chairmen, even those born in the earliest cohort in their study, 1820–39, were educated at a public school.[29]

We are now in a better position to consider in a precise way, and with new evidence, what were the intergenerational effects of the public schools on the careers of our samples of entrants. The evidence is set out in Table 3.4, which records, for each of the public school samples, the occupations of the fathers of each boy in the sample, and the later occupation of each entrant himself. It is very important to note that the evidence here was derived not only from the alumni registers of the schools where these were available, but from the comprehensive use of birth, marriage, and death certificates, of local directories, genealogies, probate records, and other biographical sources, as well as alumni registers of the universities where these were helpful, and many other records. Not only is the information here more wide-ranging and precise than in any previous study, it is probably as comprehensive as any research on this subject can be, and – as will be clear from the limited number of unknowns – in all likelihood cannot be much improved upon without grossly diminishing returns.

The varying occupations of both fathers and sons have crucially been grouped into three basic categories, landowners, professionals, and businessmen. Those active for the whole of their careers abroad are not included in any category or with the known totals; those described on their death certificates or other sources as 'gentlemen', of 'independent means', 'no occupation' and the like are not included with any of the three categories but are included in the known totals and percentages.[30] A principal aim in all of this research was precisely to diminish the number of unknowns and unclassifiable 'gentlemen', usually so common a feature of studies of this kind, and to ascertain the occupation of each man in a searching way. Very few public school graduates were unemployed throughout their lives, passing their days as idle gentlemen of leisure in the manner often suggested. Nor does an address at a named country house often indicate bona fide landowning or gentry status: the extent of actual landownership can be ascertained from a variety of sources, while detailed research in local directories

Table 3.4 Occupational categories of entrants at major public schools and their fathers, 1840–1895/1900

ETON

	Land	Professionals	Business
		Fathers	
1840	36 = 37.5%	45 = 46.9%	15 = 15.6%
	known 96; unknown 4		
1870	35 = 34.7%	38 = 37.6%	27 = 26.7%
	'esq.' 1 = 1.0%; known 101		
1895/1900	28 = 28.0%	44 = 44.0%	22 = 22.0%
	'gent.' 6 = 6.0%; known 100; unknown 2		
		Sons	
1840	28 = 30.4%	57 = 6.20%	5 = 5.4%
	abroad 5; unknown 2; none 2 = 2%; known UK 92		
1870	18 = 19.8%	52 = 57.1%	20 = 22.0%
	abroad 3; 'ind. means' 1; unknown 7; known UK 91		
1895/1900	17 = 18.1%	57 = 60.6%	16 = 17.0%
	abroad 4; 'ind. means' 4; unknown 3; known UK 94		

HARROW

	Land	Professionals	Business
		Fathers	
1840	18 = 34.0%	21 = 39.6%	11 = 20.8%
	'gent.' 3 = 5.7%; known 53; unknown 7		
1870	18 = 18.6%	36 = 37.1%	36 = 37.1%
	'gent.' 8 = 8.2%; known 97; unknown/abroad 3		
1895/1900	12 = 13.0%	35 = 38.0%	41 = 44.6%
	'gent.' etc. 4 = 4.4%; abroad 5; known 92; unknown 3		
		Sons	
1840	9 = 17.3%	34 = 67.3%	7 = 13.5%
	Abroad 5; known UK 52; unknown 3		
1870	14 = 15.2%	42 = 45.6%	25 = 25.0%
	'gent.' etc. 13 = 14.1%; abroad 6; known UK 92; unknown 2		
1895/1900	7 = 8.6%	48 = 59.3%	24 = 29.6%
	abroad 17; known UK 81; unknown 2		

RUGBY

	Land	Professionals	Business
		Fathers	
1840	18 = 34.0%	21 = 39.6%	11 = 20.8%
	'gent.' 3 = 5.7%; known 53; unknown 7		
1870	18 = 18.6%	36 = 37.1%	36 = 37.1%
	'gent.' 8 = 8.2%; known 97; unknown/abroad 3		
1895/1900	12 = 13.0%	35 = 38.0%	41 = 44.6%
	'gent.' etc. 4 = 4.4%; abroad 5; unknown 3; known 92		

	Sons		
1840	9 = 17.3%	34 = 67.3%	7 = 13.5
	abroad 5; known UK 52; unknown 3		
1870	14 = 15.2%	42 = 45.6%	23 = 25.0%
	'gent.' etc. 13 = 14.1%; abroad 5; unknown 2; known UK 92		
1895/1900	7 = 8.6%	48 = 59.3%	24 = 29.6%
	abroad 17; known UK 81; unknown 2		

WINCHESTER

	Land	Professionals	Business
	Fathers		
1840	13 = 23.7%	33 = 58.9%	8 = 14.3%
	'gent.' 2 = 3.6%; unknown 4; known 56		
1870	5 = 5.3%	60 = 63.8%	28 = 29.8%
	'gent.' 1 = 1.1%; known 94; unknown 6		
1895/1900	8 = 7%	62 = 60.8%	32 = 31.4%
	known 102		
	Sons		
1840	7 = 13.0%	44 = 81.5%	3 = 5.6%
	unknown 6; known 54		
1870	2 = 2.4%	64 = 75.3%	17 = 20.0%
	'ind. means' 2 = 2.4%; abroad 11; unknown 4; known UK 85		
1895/1900	6 = 6.7%	58 = 65.2%	20 = 22.5%
	abroad 11; 'gent.' etc. 4 = 5.6%; unknown 4; known 88		

ST PAUL'S

	Land	Professionals	Business
	Fathers		
1840	1=1.6%	48=78.7%	12=19.7%
	known 61		
1870	2 = 2.8%	50 = 70.4%	16 = 22.5%
	'gent.' 3 = 4.2%; unknown 2; known 71		
1895/1900	1 = 1.0%	57 = 57.6%	38 = 38.4%
	'gent.' 3 = 3.0%; unknown 1; known 99		
	Sons		
1840	0 = 0%	39 = 86.7%	1 = 2.2%
	'ind. means' 5 = 11.1%; abroad 2; unknown 14; known 53		
1870	0 = 0%	33 = 62.3%	17 = 32.1%
	'ind. means' 3 = 5.7%; abroad 4; unknown 16; known 53		
1895/1900	0 = 0%	58 = 79.5%	14 = 19.2%
	'ind. means' 1 = 1.4%; abroad 7; unknown 20; known UK 73		

CHELTENHAM

	Land	Professionals	Business

Fathers

	Land	Professionals	Business
1840	7 = 13.2%	36 = 67.9%	2 = 3.8%
	'no occupation', 'gent.', 'esq.' 8 = 15.1%; known 53; unknown 7		
1870	14 = 18.7%	46 = 61.3%	14 = 18.7%
	known 75; unknown 5		
1895/1900	4 = 5.1%	53 = 67.1%	19 = 24.1%
	'esq.', 'gent.' 3 = 3.8%; known 79; unknown 3		

Sons

	Land	Professionals	Business
1840	4 = 8.5%	39 = 83.0%	3 = 6.4%
	abroad 5; known 47; unknown 8		
1870	7 = 11.7%	39 = 65.0%	13 = 21.7%
	'ind. means' 1 = 1.7%; abroad 4; known 60; unknown 18		
1895/1900	4 = 7.8%	35 = 68.6%	10 = 19.6%
	'no occ.' 2 = 3.9%; abroad 3; unknown 20; known 51		

DULWICH (1870 and 1895 only)

	Land	Professionals	Business

Fathers

	Land	Professionals	Business
1870	1 = 1.7%	27 = 45.8%	30 = 50.8%
	'gent.' 1 = 1.7%; unknown 1; known 59		
1895	0 = 0%	36 = 61.0%	19 = 32.2%
	'gent.' 4 = 6.8%; known 59		

Sons

	Land	Professionals	Business
1870	2 = 4.0%	30 = 60%	18 = 36.0%
	abroad 4; unknown 6; known 60		
1895	1 = 2.2%	32 = 69.6%	13 = 28.3%
	abroad 12; unknown 3; known 46		

MILL HILL

	Land	Professionals	Business

Fathers

	Land	Professionals	Business
1840	0 = 0%	19 = 33.9%	36 = 64.3%
	unknown 4; known 56		
1870	2 = 3.6%	21 = 38.2%	29 = 52.7%
	'gent.' 3 = 5.5%; abroad 3; known 55; unknown 2		
1895/1900	1 = 1.8%	11 = 20.0%	42 = 76.4%
	'gent.' 1 = 1.8%; unknown 5; known 55		

Sons

	Land	Professionals	Business
1840	1 = 2.4%	21 = 50.0%	20 = 47.6%
	abroad 7; unknown 11; known 42		
1870	1 = 2.3%	24 = 55.8%	18 = 41.9%
	abroad 10; unknown 7; known 43		
1895/1900	1 = 1.8%	26 = 54.2%	21 = 43.8%
	abroad 9; unknown 3; known 48		

and other sources often – indeed, usually – shows the man to have clearly been a professional such as a solicitor or a businessman.

Turning to Table 3.4, a number of conclusions stand out. Comparatively few businessmen sent their sons to a public school while many more professional men did so. Indeed, it is hardly an exaggeration to say that the nineteenth-century public schools were schools for the sons of the professional middle classes. Professional fathers were in an absolute majority among 12 of the 23 cohorts (compared with 4 cohorts where businessmen comprised the majority of fathers, 3 at Mill Hill), and were the largest single group among 4 others. It is noteworthy that, except at Eton and Harrow, bona fide landowners were remarkable for their rareness, with only a tiny (or non-existent) percentage of entrants at the London day schools drawn from landed families, and even the percentage at Rugby declining to only 2.6 per cent in the 1895/1900 cohort.

It is especially significant that professional fathers are in the majority or clear plurality at Rugby, a school where Thomas Arnold and the changes he effected are often assumed to have been highly attractive for Victorian businessmen in their choice of schooling for their sons. Although some notable Victorian businessmen did indeed send their sons to Rugby – Joseph Chamberlain, for instance, sent both Austen and Neville to Rugby, while the randomly selected Rugby cohorts in this study include Roger Cunliffe, first baron Cunliffe (1855–1920), Governor of the Bank of England in 1913–18 and Sir Herbert Cayzer, first Baron Rotherwick (1881–1958), the shipowner – Rugby's appeal was much more clearly to the professional middle classes of vicars, civil servants, physicians, lawyers, and professional army officers than to businessmen, much as in other leading schools. Among all the cohorts of all the schools examined here, only about 36 per cent of entrants' fathers were businessmen, just over one-third (649 of 1,802). This again supports the conclusion we found from other sources, that the Victorian public schools probably did not attract a sufficiently large proportion of the sons of businessmen to have the intergenerational effects urged by the 'cultural critique', even if its assessment of these effects is accurate. It is also true that, limited in number as entrants from business families appear to have been, not all of these, or even many, came from northern industrial business backgrounds which were most affected by Britain's post-1870 decline, a point we shall discuss in more detail below.

The second evident inference from Table 3.4 is that public school entrants, in their own later careers, regularly followed in their fathers' footsteps: the sons of professional men normally took up a professional career, the sons of businessmen, in the majority of cases, themselves became businessmen. The intergenerational shift from business to the professions was amazingly small, despite all of the anti-business, anti-entrepreneurial influences the public schools are constantly alleged to engender. This very important point is probably insufficiently appreciated – or not appreciated at all – by advocates of the 'cultural critique'. Professor Wiener's *English Culture*, for example, quotes the following extract from Margaret Drabble's novel *The Ice Age* (London, 1977, p. 16) – to be sure, about Cambridge University in the early 1960s, not the Victorian public schools – but the point is exactly the same:

> It must be said that it never once crossed Anthony Keating's mind that he might get a job in industry. Rebel he was, but not to such a degree: so deeply conditioned are some sections of the British nation that some thoughts are deeply inaccessible to them. Despite the fact that major companies were at that time appealing urgently for graduates in any field, despite the fact that the national press was full of seductive offers, the college notice boards plastered with them. Anthony Keating, child of the professional middle classes, reared in an anachronism as an anachronism, did not even see the offers: he walked past them daily, turned over pages daily, with as much indifference as if they had been written in Turkish or Hungarian. He thought himself superior to that kind of thing: that kind of advertisement was aimed at bores and sloggers, not at men of vision like Anthony Keating.

This extract is reproduced in the chapter of Professor Wiener's book entitled 'The Gentrification of the Industrialist', and is evidently cited by him to illustrate the disdainful and atavistic attitude of 'gentrified' Cambridge products toward business life. The point is that he has missed the point (as, perhaps, has Miss Drabble): Anthony Keating, 'a child of the professional middle classes' finds business life incomprehensible not because of snobbery but because, as the son of professional parents, it is an alien world. But would this have been Keating's attitude if his own father had been a businessman?

To be sure, there *was* an intergenerational shift into the professions but it affected only a minority of businessmen's sons: the majority followed in the family pathway. A total of 568 fathers among all the cohorts can be identified as businessmen, while 329 sons were definitely businessmen, or 57.9 per cent.[31] This figure, however, is almost certainly a considerable understatement of the business percentage, for it excludes public school boys who subsequently migrated permanently abroad. At least half of these were probably businessmen in their latter careers – merchants in Melbourne, Australia, large-scale rubber planters in Malaya, and so on – and their inclusion would raise the 'business' percentage by another 10 per cent or more. Furthermore, a significant number of entrants who are classified as 'Professionals' were military officers killed in the First World War and other wars who might well, in many cases, have entered business life had they lived. It is reasonable to suppose that if these two factors are taken into account, the true intergenerational shift away from business life to the professions between fathers and sons is of the order of 25 per cent – a noteworthy figure, but one obviously far removed from the catastrophic effects upon entrepreneurship which the 'cultural critique' suggests. Above all, it seems clear that the effects of public school education on the choice of a career were far less important than family background.

Futhermore, there are several good reasons for viewing even the fairly limited intergenerational decrease in business occupations observed here as an exaggeration of the move away from business life and toward the leisured, parasitical lifestyle of the English 'gentleman'. Many of those who moved from a business family background to the professions, especially to military service in the Empire, were younger sons of businessmen who were simply superfluous to the continuity of the family business – fourth, fifth, and sixth sons whose elder brothers or cousins were intended for eventual business succession and were trained for it from early age. Indeed, the whole notion of a 'haemorrhage of talent' away from business life in Britain may be nothing more than a persistent demographic illusion created by the fact that sons and grandsons of successful businessmen exceeded the number of those who could usefully take over the running of the family firm. It is also possible that, if entrepreneurial success in Britain did decline after 1914–18, this was in part due to the fact that many sons and grandsons who had been trained for business life and intended eventually to succeed to business leadership were killed in the war and were replaced by other sons and grandsons with less business training and experience, or none at all. Of course this suggestion must be speculation in the absence of any real evidence.

It is also the case that as much as representing an intergenerational change in status from businessmen to 'gentlemen', the growth in the number of professionals across the generations was a rational response to the fact that the professions, and professional opportunities, were almost certainly growing more rapidly than the population as a whole. According to W. J. Reader's research on professional occupations in the Census returns, seventeen leading professional groups increased in number from 73,215 in 1841 to 148,302 in 1881 – an increase of 103 per cent – and to 221,729 in 1911, a further increase of 50 per cent, compared with total increases in the population of England and Wales of, respectively, 63 and 39 per cent in these two periods.[32] The professional groups noted here exclude teachers – chiefly the domain of the lower middle class, except for teachers at the public schools – and also military officers. Both the army and the navy rose steadily if not dramatically in size during the nineteenth century as Britain's imperial commitments increased – the army's total, officers and men, increased from about 100,000 in 1845 to 155,000 in 1895 just before the Boer War, the navy from 40,000 to 89,000 in the same period, although there were many fluctuations.[33] Of course the expansion in the professions was certainly not necessarily filled by the public school men alone, whose syllabus, it is clear, did not have the deliberate intention of training its alumni to succeed at pre-professional qualifying exams but to become 'generalists' rooted in the classics.[34] Indeed, this lack of any deliberate training aimed at a career in professional life, despite the traditional status of clergymen, lawyers (barristers at any rate), and doctors as *ipso facto* gentlemen, may have had the unintended effect of keeping public school entrants rooted in their hereditary occupational pathways, rather than driving them from business to professional life. In contrast, American colleges and universities, with their very explicit pre-professional courses of training and undergraduate majors, may well have effected a much more pronounced intergenerational shift away from businessman fathers to professional sons, certainly before the contemporary rise in popularity of the American business school.

In any case, the integenerational shift from business life to the professions among our public school samples should certainly not be viewed as simply exchanging the 'hard' path of industrial or commercial life for the 'soft' path of the professions or, still less, of gentlemanly vegetation as an Empire army officer or a country vicar, but, as much as anything, as a rational response to realistic perceptions of areas of growth in the economy. There is evidence, too, of an increasing willingness by public school boys increasingly to enter 'hard' as well as 'soft' fields, requiring genuine professional or scientific knowledge and professional competition. The change in career choice of entrants among our samples at Rugby, to take one typical example, is indicative of this. Among the 34 entrants classified as professionals in the 1840 sample were 17 Anglican clergymen, 6 Indian civil servants, 5 army officers, 4 barristers, 3 solicitors, 2 civil engineers, and 2 others, a diplomat and (by conversion) a Roman Catholic priest. The 1870 sample, comprising 42 future professionals among the entrants, was divided among 12 military officers, 6 vicars, 4 each among solicitors, barristers, and engineers, 3 physicians, 3 clerks in the civil service, and 1 accountant, artist, local government Inspector of Weights (in Shropshire), and a public school master. Among the 1895/1900 sample, there were now 48 professionals, divided among 14 army officers – possibly an exaggeration, due to the wartime deaths of so many in South Africa, their service as officers listed as their occupation on their death certificates – 10 solicitors, 8 engineers, 3 physicians, 2 barristers, colonial civil servants, land agents, and university tutors. Among the remainder was one scientist but also, significantly, only one vicar. The chief impression here, even at a school like Rugby, is clearly the rise in the number of professional men in areas requiring long and difficult training or subject to market forces, and the *decline* in the popularity of pre-industrial 'gentlemanly' professions, with the exception of military officers, where the figure may well be swollen by wartime deaths cutting short careers that would in due course have gone into very different areas.

In one perhaps surprising way the findings here differ somewhat from other previous studies of public school entrants. These previous studies have found a clear pattern of increase in the percentage of public school graduates who entered business life. Among Wykehamists, studied by Bishop and Wilkinson, the percentage making a career in business rose – according to these researchers – from 6.4 per cent of all Winchester alumni born in 1820–9 to 27.9 per cent born in 1900–9. W. J. Reader's data on Clifton, Marlborough, Merchant Taylors', and Mill Hill found a remarkably similar rise, with similar percentage rises over time at the first three of these schools; at Mill Hill, however, the percentage remained the same (at about 30–5 per cent) from 1837 to 1907. At two other schools studied by him, Sedbergh and Winchester, there was also a rise, but a smaller one (his figures being in disagreement with those of Bishop and Wilkinson); T. W. Bamford, studying Rugby and Harrow in *The Rise of the Public Schools*, again found an increase in the percentage of businessmen alumni almost identical to those found by Bishop and Wilkinson and by Reader.[35] Our data does show a fairly similar increase in entrants who became businessmen at Harrow, Rugby, and Winchester; an increase from 1840 to 1870, followed by a decline from 1870 to 1895/1900, at Eton; but virtually no change at all at Mill Hill and indeed, an actual decline at Dulwich. The differences here can be explained by the far more comprehensive and searching nature of this study, compared with others, which goes well beyond the listing of careers in the school alumni registers employed by previous researchers, although the greater willingness of alumni frankly to state that their careers were as businessmen is, of course, significant. The evolution of each school, too, is also an important factor, with all of the schools, except perhaps Eton and Harrow, probably tending to become more similar to each other, in terms of their clientele, over time. Eton, at one extreme, was an exception to this, with consistently more landowners and fewer businessmen than the other schools; at the other, Mill Hill, the Dissenters' school, attracted many more sons of businessmen who themselves remained in business life, and fewer sons of professionals. The most important pattern we have identified here, however, is the broad similarity of occupations of the fathers of entrants and the entrants themselves, and there can be no doubt whatever that a consistently rising share of the fathers of entrants in our samples were businessmen: at Rugby, the number of businessman fathers rose from 14.5 to 40.3 per cent, at Harrow from 20.8 to 44.6, at Cheltenham from 3.8 to 24.1. At Dulwich there was, however, an actual decline with a concomitant rise in fathers who were professionals: here, in all likelihood, as the re-founded Dulwich was progressively perceived as more prestigious and efficient, it successively attracted a more 'normalized' clientele, similar to the other schools. At Eton, too, the percentage of businessman fathers, always lower than at Harrow or Rugby, also declined slightly from 1870 to 1895/1900, for reasons which are unclear. In sum, however, it is the similarity of professional paths taken by father and son that is the most striking aspect of the data.

There is another point, too, of key importance which ought to be discussed here. Apart from representing a segment of the economy that was demonstrably growing rapidly, and hence one whose choice by a public school graduate was economically rational, the choice of a professional career often represented not so much the achievement of high status and acknowledgment as a gentleman, as proponents of the 'cultural critique' often urge, as the gaining of a secure position, or at least one more secure than the life of a businessman before the large-scale corporation, with its high risk factor and ever-present danger of personal liability for debt. This aspect of career choice – the search for a *secure* position – is surely one of the great unnoticed themes of modern British economic history as it impinges on the evolution of the middle classes. The intergenerational drift away from business life was most pronounced, among the samples here, both in the very highest status schools like Harrow but, more surprisingly, in the lowest status schools like St Paul's, especially in the earliest period when St Paul's took in the sons of the local lower middle class and even artisans of the City of London. There seems little doubt that a safe lifelong career in a salaried profession, preferably with tenure, and certainly in one where lifelong employment could be reasonably expected as a reward for reasonable competence, was the necessary ideal of many, perhaps most from the lower part of the middle class. Once the examination system became ubiquitous in the civil service, the typical administrative civil servant, including most Permanent Under-Secretaries, was commonly drawn from such a background: young men who were extremely hard-working and able scholars in a conventional sense, normally from families with little wealth and no access to privileged positions, often scholarship boys, who had to find something safe as quickly as possible, of which the administrative civil service was the example *par excellence*.[36] *This search for security is regularly confused with the search for status*: to many of those who chose such a career path, status was far less important than security. Among the St Paul's entrants in our 1840 sample (to take the sample where this pattern was perhaps most striking, although there are many examples in every sample except perhaps those from Eton) were many boys from minor business backgrounds for whom the achievement of security in this way was of central importance. For example – to take several such cases of many which could be nominated – there was Samuel Lobb (1832-76), son of a hosier of Cheapside who left £1,500, who worked at the Education Department at the Indian Office and then as an Assistant Master at Highgate School after success as a Cambridge Wrangler; (Rev.) Robert Scott McDowell (1830-1902), son of a printer at Gough Square, who became an Assistant Master at Newark Grammar School and then a vicar in Dorset; and (Rev.) Sherrard Burnaby (1832-1902), son of a banker's clerk with Smith, Payne, and Smith who left £1,250; he served as Vicar of Hampstead for many years after a distinguished academic career as Pauline Exhibitioner at Christ's, Cambridge, and Senior Optime. In such cases – and any of fifty others might have as readily been chosen from our school samples – if there was a 'haemorrhage of talent' away from business life this was, arguably, not because business life had become repellent to the newly acquired value system of the entrants in question, but, at least as importantly, because a career in the Church, the civil service, or in teaching offered the security, with a reasonably high starting salary, which a business career notably lacked, and which the fathers or other close relatives of these entrants were evidently unable to provide. It is important that proponents of the 'cultural critique' understand this crucial distinction, so often misunderstood.

The evident academic excellence and notable school and university success of the entrants we have just considered also suggests that many of those, emerging from business backgrounds, launched highly successful professional careers that in no sense exhibited a 'haemorrhage of talent' in their own careers, but, on the contrary, a working out of their own 'comparative advantage' for which due allowance ought to be made; not every case of intergenerational drift from businesses to the professions represented a loss to the British economy, and even taken strictly on the terms of the argument, a successful career in the professions might well generate as much income for the British economy, or far more, than if that professional man had pursued a business career for which he was unsuited. Kenneth Clark (Lord Clark), the renowned art historian and museum curator, was a scion of the millionaire family which jointly owned Coats & Clark, the giant sewing thread manufacturers at Paisley; his grandfather invented the cotton spool. If Lord Clark had made a career in sewing thread, the world would certainly have lost one of its most distinguished art scholars while, in exchange, gaining perhaps a mediocre businessman; it is at least arguable that Lord Clark did more for British exports by writing *Civilization*, which sold more than one million copies, chiefly in America, to say nothing of overseas royalties on the television series, than he was ever likely to have done as an industrialist.

On a question related to those we have been considering, it is also worth looking in more detail at those entrants in our samples who *emerged from northern industrial family backgrounds* to see if, as a rule, they abandoned business life in their own careers. Here we will consider all such entrants in our samples at Eton, Harrow, and Rugby. The first and most striking point is the very small numbers in this sample, as Table 3.5 makes clear.

Table 3.5 Number of public school entrants' fathers who were industrialists or manufacturers in northern England, Scotland, or Wales (includes East Anglia), 1840–1895/1900

	1840	1870	1895/1900
Eton	1	3	5
Harrow	3	6	14
Rugby	1	6	7

The Eton sample of 1840 apparently includes only one northern manufacturer father from a total of 100. There is some doubt about one of these, no less a personage than Sir Robert Peel, 2nd Bt (1788–1850), the Prime Minister. While his enormous family fortune was certainly earned during the previous generation in cotton manufacturing by the first Sir Robert Peel, there is no evidence that the Prime Minister (a Harrovian and Double First at Oxford) had any business interests in the course of his active life of political service; one wonders, indeed, if he ever saw the inside of a cotton factory. His fourth son, John Floyd Peel (1827–1910), is the entrant in our sample. He was an army officer and minor landowner. In the 1870 Eton family there are three entrants from industrial backgrounds. The first, Charles Robert Chadwick, the son of a Manchester cotton manufacturer, died at the age of only 22. The second, Frederick Lees (1856–1929), was a mining engineer and colliery manager and a director of the cotton manufacturer A. & A. Crompton & Co., and the son of a Lancashire colliery owner. The third, Robert Preston (1855–1908), was a barrister at the Middle Temple; his father was a Liverpool engine manufacturer and civil engineer. Among the 1895/1900 entrants were five such men. Four clearly remained active in business life, despite undergoing years of the imparting of allegedly anti-business 'gentlemanly' values at Britain's most privileged school. Cecil Bickersteth (d. 1918) was a varnish manufacturer at Ripon, just as his father had been; George Crompton Lees-Milne (1880-1949) was Chairman of A. & A. Crompton, the Oldham cotton manufacturers and the family firm; Eric MacKay (1886-1961) was a lifelong director of Palmer & MacKay Ltd., the family woollen cloth manufacturers at Trowbridge, Wiltshire; and, similarly, Arthur Nicholson (b. 1879) was a silk manufacturer at Macclesfield, as was his father. Only one such Etonian in our 1895/ 1900 sample left business life, (Rev.) Hugh Lowthian Bell (1878-1926), an Anglican vicar and the younger son of Sir Thomas Bell, 2nd Bt, of the famous Middlesbrough steel manufacturers whose relatives include Clive Bell, the celebrated Bloomsbury Group art historian, and whose family was clearly notable for their non-business activities in later generations.

The pattern found at Eton is very similar for the other elite schools in our study. At Harrow, two of the three entrants from industrialist backgrounds in the 1840 cohort, at least five and probably all six among the 1870 cohort, and seven of the fourteen in the 1895/1900 sample, remained in business life, almost always in the family business. Of the seven in the last of these cohorts who left business life, four went abroad – at least two being employed in business pursuits in Ceylon and New Zealand – suggesting they were superfluous younger sons. Of the others, one became a journalist, one a vicar, and one, apparently, a professional army officer. At Rugby, the pattern is even more clear-cut, with only two (from the 1870 and 1895/1900 groups) among the fourteen entrants from industrial backgrounds definitely leaving business life, to become a surgeon and a physician.

There is also increasing evidence of the intergenerational shift in occupations running in the other direction, *towards* business life from a different family background, normally in the professions. Examples of this include the 1895 entrant at Harrow, Charles Hamilton Martin (1882-1969), the son of a barrister at Longborough, who was employed as the Managing Director of several local granite companies, while William Armine Bevan (1856-1939), whose father was an Anglican vicar, became Chairman of Newcastle Breweries Ltd. and a director of several other companies. At Rugby Ernest Honey (1856-1939), the son of a London accountant, founded a leading London fabric-printing firm, Honey & Mellersh. Nationally, too – and apart from our public school samples – the late Victorian and Edwardian period saw something of an intergenerational shift back from the professions to business life; possibly the best-known examples of this tendency were the press lords

Lord Northcliffe and his brothers, the sons of a failed Irish barrister, and Lord Beaverbrook, son of a Canadian Free Church of Scotland Minister. There were, however, others almost as notable, for example the Hon. C. S. Rolls, younger son of Lord Llangattock, a Welsh landowner, the Rolls in Rolls-Royce. The two brothers John and Owen Phillips, leading City financiers and shipowners who notoriously sailed close to the wind in their business dealings and who were created, respectively, Viscount St Davids and Baron Kylsant in the early part of this century, were the sons of Rev. Sir James Philipps, 12th Bt, Prebendary of Salisbury and Vicar of Warminster. Indeed, the late Victorian period saw a movement, albeit possibly minor, toward business from other established social groups, possibly for the first time in modern history. By the 1930s, the aristocratic or landowning 'lords on the board', their name adorning the letterhead list of directors of innumerable firms, respectable and dubious, became both a stock-in-trade and a very welcome generator of income as land revenues declined catastrophically.[37] Most of these were public school and university-educated, and it is quite possible that the contacts gained by rubbing shoulders at school with the sons of leading businessmen assisted this process; certainly it did not drive them away. The importance of the 'social web' of future contacts and associates, with the business knowledge and information they engendered, which the public schools and universities provided, has been noted in one recent study of nineteenth-century investment patterns. The author, Ranald C. Michie, has acutely suggested that:

> Public school or university education extended the web of contact for the upper classes away from a purely local environment. Weston Jarvis [an old Harrovian] '. . . made countless friends for life. . .' when at Harrow between 1869 and 1874, and the same was true for a growing number of the wealthy. Through this educational web was exchanged information and suggestions as the former students became involved in various fields of business.[38]

While it seems fairly clear that the public schools did not act as an intergenerational sieve to eliminate future businessmen, it may still be urged that the *quality* of those businessmen who emerged did in fact decline, however this might be measured. Determining the quality of a businessman is, obviously, extremely difficult and there is no clear-cut or obvious test, especially in the twentieth-century era of corporate capitalism where responsibility for profit or loss is seldom an individual matter.

For what it is worth, however, we might look at the broad figures for probate valuation for fathers and sons in our study in both current and

Table 3.6 Median probate valuations, in current and constant terms, of public school entrants and their fathers, 1840–1895/1900

	Current (£)			Constant (£)		
	1840	1870	1895/1900	1840	1870	1895/1900
			FATHERS			
Eton	80,000	88,463	64,184	71,483	103,110	46,377
Harrow	25,000	47,653	41,978	20,833	58,113	23,337
Winchester	37,500	21,317	15,513	32,355	25,669	16,646
Rugby	10,000	30,929	35,291	8,930	31,888	15,862
Cheltenham	7,000	10,000	7,858	6,605	9,755	4,695
St Paul's	1,516	2,000	3,778	1,651	1,903	2,633
Dulwich	–	3,238	5,192	–	4,139	4,104
Mill Hill	5,451	8,234	24,949	5,162	11,071	22,976
Average*	23,781	26,479	23,593	21,003	30,706	17,071
			SONS			
Eton	21,990	19,346	24,076	22,665	12,217	6,369
Harrow	4,386	13,824	12,033	4,527	10,901	4,026
Winchester	2,722	5,854	15,123	2,929	4,099	3,081
Rugby	10,000	5,422	21,891	10,705	2,906	7,641
Cheltenham	9,391	4,592	1,357	6,250	3,536	486
St Paul's	702	675	3,154	500	424	813
Dulwich	–	1,842	2,481	–	1,072	893
Mill Hill	3,000	4,300	5,114	1,304	3,095	2,033
Average*	7,456	6,982	10,654	6,983	4,781	3,168

*The 'Average' value here simply totals the values in each column and divides by the number of schools; it is not weighted for the varying number of persons in each sample.

Table 3.7 Public school entrants' probate valuations as a percentage of their fathers', 1840–1895/1900

	Current			Constant		
	1840	1870	1895/1900	1840	1870	1895/1900
Eton	27.5	21.9	37.5	31.7	11.8	13.7
Harrow	17.5	29.0	28.7	21.7	18.8	17.3
Winchester	7.3	27.5	97.5	9.1	15.7	18.5
Rugby	100.0	17.5	86.6	119.9	9.1	48.4
Cheltenham	134.2	45.9	17.3	94.6	36.2	10.4
St Paul's	46.3	33.8	83.5	30.3	22.3	30.9
Dulwich	–	56.9	47.8	–	33.1	21.8
Mill Hill	55.0	52.2	20.5	25.3	28.0	8.8
Average	55.4	35.5	52.4	47.5	21.9	21.2

constant terms, 'constant' being based upon an average of 1865 and 1885 as 100 compared with inflation or deflation in other years.[39]

Tables 3.6 and 3.7 present the median values, in constant and current terms, of the value of the estates left for probate including the capitalised value of their land, in so far as this could be determined,[40] for fathers of entrants and entrants themselves, together with the median percentage of their fathers' valuations left by the entrants. It will be seen that fathers were much wealthier than sons, both in current and constant terms. Taking this at face value, it appears as if attendance at a public school worked to diminish the likelihood of leaving significant sums of money at death; in so far as this is indicative of an anti-capitalist mentality, it apparently confirms a part of the 'cultural critique' thesis. But it is certainly unreasonable to take these con-clusions at face value. For one thing, most fathers and sons were not businessmen, but professionals, and hence these largely reflect econ-omic aspirations and opportunities in the professions rather than in business life. Rampant inflation, after 1914, was extremely important, while taking these figures at face value omits the major effects of increased taxation and estate duty avoidance in this century – the figures reflecting, it must not be forgotton, probate valuations at the time of death of fathers and sons, not economic conditions at the time our sample cohorts entered school. Thus if the fathers of the 1895/1900 entrants were, on average, 45 years old in 1895, and died at the age of 75, the typical father here would not have died until 1925, when both taxation and estate duties had reached unprecedented levels and much estate duty avoidance was to be expected. An entrant aged 15 in 1895/ 1900, deceased at 75, would have died only in 1955, when levels of estate duty on a millionaire's property had reached 75 per cent and the top marginal rate of income tax in Britain stood at an incredible 83 per cent: clearly, in a great many cases, wealthy people gave their property away before death if they had any to leave. By 1953, after thirteen years of unprecedentedly high taxation, things had reached the point where, according to one Inland Revenue Officer, there were only thirty-six millionaires in Britain, compared with over one thousand in 1939: only thirty-six persons in Britain in 1953 had an after-tax income of £6,000, representing a pre-tax income of £56,000, the approximate return generated by wealth of £1 million![41] Very likely, inflation and unprecedented taxation account for the fact that the median values of *fathers'* estates in these samples declines by half, in constant terms, between the 1870 and 1895/1900 cohorts at the more prestigious schools. Since it is extremely difficult to believe that fathers of entrants at Eton and Harrow were only, respectively, 45 per cent and 40 per cent as wealthy in 1895/1900 – when Britain's late Victorian and Edwardian plutocracy was at its absolute zenith – as in 1870, this must be a statistical illusion created by inflation and the extraordinary levels of income tax and by estate duty avoidance much later. There are other

Table 3.8 Constant values of businessman fathers' probates among the public school samples, and their sons', 1840-1895/1900

	1840	1870	1895/1900
HARROW			
Fathers	27,658	150,427	42,165
Sons	30,799	20,164	5,339
Percentage Sons' to Fathers' valuations	111.4	13.4	12.7
RUGBY			
Fathers	49,587	53,828	58,318
Sons	28,299	2,674	10,875
Percentage	57.1	5.0	18.6
WINCHESTER			
Fathers	74,766	52,025	34,317
Sons	840	6,163	6,489
Percentage	1.1	11.8	18.9

important reasons, too, for the sharp decline in the entrants' probate valuations compared with their fathers: many sons died at a youthful age in the Boer War, the First World War or other imperial conflicts, leaving little or nothing and certainly far less than if they had survived. Estates probated abroad, by public school *emigrés* in our sample, are excluded from these statistics, estates which, in the case of *emigré* businessmen, may well have been substantial. The capitalised value of the land held by landowning fathers is included in their valuations, but excluded in the case of younger sons who failed to inherit the land, just as superfluous younger sons of businessmen who entered the professions would probably have left much less.

If, from all fathers and sons in this sample, one abstracts the fathers who were businessmen, and compares them in the same way with their sons in our sample (*regardless* of the occupation of these entrants), the results (Table 3.8) are broadly similar as for the last set of tables, at least for Harrow, Rugby, and Winchester, for which this exercise has been carried out.

Both businessman fathers and their sons were, generally, wealthier than the median of all fathers and all sons, with the peaks coming in 1870 and then declining slightly, presumably for the variety of reasons, chiefly related to taxation and to demography, just discussed. The estates left by the sons of businessmen consistently totalled only a small fraction of their father's; just as in the case of all fathers of entrants, by about the same percentage.

Some greater substance to the processes suggested by these statistical tables may be adduced by a consideration of the thirteen fathers of entrants in our samples at these three schools (Winchester, Harrow and Rugby) who left £500,000 in *constant* terms and their sons, the entrants.[42] At Harrow there were 9 businessman fathers of entrants in our samples who left £500,000 or more in constant terms, 1 among the 1840 sample, 5 in 1870, and 3 in 1895/1900. Joseph Baxendale (1785–1872), Chairman of Pickfords and of the South-Eastern Railway Company, left £546,875 in constant terms (£700,000 in current). His third son, Salisbury Baxendale (1827–1907), entered Harrow in 1840. He left £44,266 (£42,938 current). He was a barrister and served as High Sheriff of Hertfordshire in 1883; no business career could be traced. Among the five fathers of 1870 Harrow entrants here were Sir Edward Bates, 1st Bt (1816–96), the shipowner and MP, who left (with land) £1,384,000 (£1,011,000 current). His fourth son, Wilfred Bates (1856–86), was killed at the age of 30 by falling from a horse. He left £48,705 (£40,425 current). Again, no business career could be traced. In contrast, Walter Cunliffe, first Baron Cunliffe (1855–1920), an 1870 entrant at both Harrow and Rugby, became Governor of the Bank of England from 1913 to 1918 after serving as a partner in the family bank, Cunliffe Brothers. His father, Roger Cunliffe (1824–95), was also a wealthy City banker who left £1,384,000 (£1,185,000 current). Although the son left an enormous estate in current terms – £905,192 – through inflation its constant value was only £345,494, a pattern which will be found among most entrants deceased after 1918. The third 1870 Harrow entrant, Cecil Wyburn Peters (1856–1936), was the son of William Winpenny Peters, coach builder to the royal family and others, who left £653,000 (£691,000 current). The younger Peters was a major in the Hussars who left £213,728 (£333,415 current). The two remaining 1870 Harrovians, however, were both engaged in business. Herbert Straker (1856–1929), of the prominent Durham colliery family, left £150,796 (£266,909 current). He was a younger son of John Straker (1814–85), a colliery owner who left £1,490,000 (£1,312,000 current, with his land). Robert Sanderson Whitaker (1856–1923), lived most of his life in Sicily, where his family, 'princes under the volcano', were large-scale vintners and wine exporters; he left £19,460 in England (£36,391 current), and was the seventh son of Joseph Whitaker (1802–84) of Sicily and Tickhill, Yorkshire, vintner and wine exporter, who left £674,096 (£604,391 current). Each of the three 1895/1900 Harrow entrants whose businessman fathers left £500,000 or more in current terms also remained in business life. Walter Dunkels (1886–1956), director of the family diamond broking firm and of other South African diamond and other companies, left £416,000 in current terms but only £98,000 in constant pounds; his father, Anton Dunkels (né Dunkelsbuhler, 1856–1911) a Belgium-born Jewish South African

British diamond merchant in London, left £1,557,000 (£1,589,000 current). Hugh Edward Joicey, third Baron Joicey (1881-1966), of the leading colliery family, was also chairman of various shipping and insurance companies. Again, his substantial fortune in current terms £748,000, totalled only £132,305 by the inflation index employed here. His father, Sir James Joicey, first Baron Joicey (1846-1936), the colliery owner, left £974,178 (£1,520,000 constant). Finally, Lionel de Rothschild (1882-1942), a director of the great merchant bank and a Conservative MP, left £685,545 in current terms but only £302,002 in depressed constant terms; his father, Baron Leopold de Rothschild (1845-1917), left £802,139 (£1,500,000 current).

Three entrants (apart from Lord Cunliffe, discussed above) at Rugby in this sample were the sons of businessmen who left £500,000 or more in constant terms. An 1840 entrant, David Ward Chapman (1828-1901), a partner in the banking firm of Overend Gurney & Co., was the eldest son of David Barclay Chapman, a City banker who left £1,293,000 (£1,112,000 current). Although a City banker for many years, the younger Chapman left only £7,552 (£6,495 current), for reasons which are unclear. Among the 1895/1900 entrants was Sir Herbert Cayzer, first Baron Rotherwick (1881-1958), the fifth son of Sir Charles Cayzer, 1st Bt (1843-1916), a leading shipowner and an MP who left £1,460,000 (£2,204,000 current). Rotherwick was Vice-Chairman of Clan Lines and of Cayzer Irvine & Co., and other companies, President of the Chamber of Shipping, 1941-2, and of the Institute of Marine Engineers in 1949-50, and was a Conservative MP for most of the inter-war years. As with others, he left the superficially impressive sum of £637,000 at his death in current terms, but only £140,300 in constant pounds. Finally, Sir Robert Spencer-Nairn, 1st Bt (1880-1960) was Managing Director of M. Nairn & Co., the linoleum manufacturers. He left £319,000 in current terms, £69,500 in constant pounds. He was the second son of Sir Michael Barker Nairn, 1st Bt (1838-1915), a Scottish linoleum manufacturer who left £673,000 (£882,000 current).

It will be seen from this that the majority of public school entrants in this sample from this background of great wealth remained in business life and were at least superficially successful; one of the men in this small sample, Lord Cunliffe, became Governor of the Bank of England, arguably the most important position in British business life. Most managed to combine their business careers, without inconsistency, with the normal lifestyles of those born to wealth and status in modern Britain: Herbert Straker was a Master of the Foxhounds, a Major in the Northumberland Yeomanry, and a JP, while Hugh Joicey served as High Sheriff of Northumberland in 1933. Others combined business life with Tory politics, like Lord Rotherwick and Lionel de Rothschild.

Although they did not necessarily expand their well-established and successful family firms, they did not turn success into failure: once again, the picture is one of the public schools having remarkably little effect on intergenerational performance. The decline in probate valuations between father and son can readily be explained by unprecedented inflation, duty avoidance, and the deeply progressive effects of extraordinarily high taxation, and by the necessity to divide a single fortune among many heirs. Often, this affected the *relative* place of father and son in the wealth hierarchy only marginally, because the same trends influenced all wealthy persons. For instance, the estate of the first Baron Joicey (d. 1936) was one of the half-dozen largest estates left in 1936; the estate of his son, the third Baron Joicey (d. 1966) was, roughly, the fifteenth largest left in 1966, although in constant terms it was worth only 13.6 per cent of his father's. Similarly, although the estate of Leopold de Rothschild (d. 1917) was the third largest left in Britain in that year, his son's (d. 1942) was approximately the twelfth largest of 1942 despite the fact that its value, in constant terms, was only 37.6 per cent of the father's. Most of these apparently sharp declines are probably due to one or another of these factors, or a combination of them, and not to entrepreneurial decline in the strict sense.

It should be noted, too, that there are also many examples of the opposite trend from this, of considerable increases in the size of fortunes left by the entrants in constant terms, compared with their businessman fathers'. Some of the more striking of these intergenerational rises among the three schools included the Derbyshire ironmaster George Henry Strutt (1826–95; Harrow 1840), who left £2,256,000 compared with the estate of ironmaster father Jedediah Strutt (d. 1854), who left £383,248; the Leicester worsted spinner Thomas Fielding Johnson (1856–1931; Rugby 1870), who left £343,573 in constant terms compared with his father, a worsted spinner (d. 1921) who left £74,281; and James Forman (1855–1931; Rugby 1870), a Nottingham newspaper proprietor who left £200,758, compared with his father's (d. 1888) £55,481 earned as a printer and newspaper proprietor. More recently, Paul Speak (1882–1961; Harrow 1895), a Halifax worsted spinner, left £503,219 in current terms, among the twenty largest estates left in Britain in that year (£106,164 in constant pounds), compared with his father's (d. 1914) £88,832, also made as a worsted spinner. These cases – and there are many others – occurred, it will be seen, in northern manufacturing industries. Plainly the obstacles to leaving a large fortune were not invariable.

Enough has probably now been said to allow some conclusions to be drawn, however preliminary in nature these must necessarily be. The public schools simply did not produce a 'haemorrhage of talent' away from business life in the sense continuously suggested by their critics. Too few sons of entrepreneurs attended a public school to make any real difference. Most entrants followed in their father's footsteps, and if large numbers of public school graduates failed to enter business life, it was because their families were never in it in the first place. Public school products who entered finance and commerce did notably well, as did chairmen of large companies; these trends mirrored Britain's true economic evolution over the past century. Those who entered the professions sought security as much as, or far more than, status. While there was a sharp intergenerational decline in probate valuations, there are good reasons, apart from any falling-off in business ability, why this should have been so. The whole thrust of these findings is that the public schools were considerably *less* important to understanding the role of Britain's elites in guiding broad movements in the British economy than is normally urged, certainly less important than the underlying factor of Britain's growing comparative advantage as a commercial/financial power. Far from leading Britain into an economic dead-end, the public schools appear, in so far as they have had much influence at all, to have guided its products into the economically most dynamic areas of the economy.

A further question, not directly related to those we have been addressing, is whether the public schools did actually engender an anti-business, anti-entrepreneurial mood through their education and the atmosphere of the school. Although this presumably is at the heart of the case made by advocates of the 'cultural critique', there is remarkably little *direct* evidence that they did, and, presumably, few businessman fathers would educate their sons at schools preaching an ideology so much at variance with their own; nor perhaps, would headmasters and boards of governors so willingly bite the hands that fed them. There is also the point that *even if* the prevalent *ethos* of the public schools was clearly and demonstrably anti-business, it simply does not follow that the resultant products would decline to enter business life or would be inferior businessmen. The volume of speech, sermon, and official discourse at all public schools aimed at discouraging vice, immorality, and onanism most certainly exceeded that relating to business life by many orders of magnitude, yet its alumni do seem to have included a certain component of confirmed and accomplished amoralists. In his pioneering study *The Prefects: British Leadership and the Public School Tradition*, Rupert Wilkinson's *only* example of the existence of such a bias is taken from a biography of Lord Lugard, the colonial administrator, who was the son of a poor clergyman. He attended Rossall and was offered a job in 'the business of his elder half-sister's husband'.[43] Lugard declined, entering the Army instead, giving as his reason that 'the Lugards have been in the Army and in the Church, good servants of *God* or the *Queen*, but few have been tradesmen.'[44] But Wilkinson produces no evidence whatever that education at Rossall was in any way responsible for this decision, which seems, on the contrary, clearly to have been an example of following in the footsteps of one's ancestors, a pattern which, as we have seen, was ubiquitous and in no way inconsistent with the sons of 'tradesmen' doing the same.

There is, in fact, a good deal of scattered evidence that public school boys were, normally, always impressed by big money and by the wealthy parents of their classmates, regardless of how this money was made, and that there was no prejudice, even an unofficial one, against trade or business. Sir Alwyne Ogden (1889–1981), who was later Consul-General in Shanghai, was quoted in one recent history of Dulwich College, which he attended from 1902 to 1908, as saying:

> I remember when I first went to the college that there were traces of a snobbish prejudice against people who were 'in trade': it was silly and quite unreasonable, because our property depended on our world-wide trade. *I don't think we boys ever took this view at all* – on the contrary, I think we found it rather intriguing to be rubbing shoulders with sons of well-known manufacturers such as Epps (cocoa), Johnston ('Bovril'), and above all Brock (fireworks).[45]

This is the picture which emerges from an accurate examination of the products of some leading public schools and their family backgrounds down to those who were in senior positions after the Second World War: it is clearly considerably brighter than most similar studies. Nevertheless, all very recent studies of the public schools during the past twenty years or so are agreed that they have changed dramatically in recent decades, discarding most obsolete remnants of Britain's imperial era and adapting to the age of computers and neo-*laissez-faire*, although without sacrificing their specific historical traditions. The studies of twenty-five leading public schools in James McConnell's *English Public Schools* (London, 1985) illustrate these changes: the 'acquisition of high grades', in terms of O and A levels 'is now so essential as a qualification for Higher Education and also for employment that parents demand good results'.[46] Academic performance – at least as measured by test results and university entry – has now become quite the fetish that games and sport were ninety years ago. The decline of Empire and of many traditional professional areas of employment have led, it would seem, to a marked shift by public school graduates into business and less traditional professions. A survey of 2,035 Old Etonians leaving between 1967 and 1977 showed that the largest segment, 450 in all, were in accountancy, stock-broking, insurance, or some form of banking; only seven had become Anglican clergymen.[47] In 1983 Oundle opened a Microelectronics Centre, 'the first such centre in any school', with a computer room, a computer systems room, and an electronics room.[48] Presumably every fee-paying school in Britain has something similar by now. Although this may simply be imitative faddism, and although parents demand such training, one must presume that this, too, is a rational response to broader economic movements, or at least to changing expectations.

The alleged effects and defects of the universities have never quite formed part of the indictment of the 'cultural critique' in quite the same way as the public schools. If few sons of successful businessmen attended a public school until surprisingly recently, it is likely that even fewer attended a university. Many more university students were scholarship men. Honours at university have always, at least since the early nineteenth century, depended upon intellectual ability, and those who criticise the anti-scientific bias of Britain's Establishment customarily fail to remember the central role of mathematics at Cambridge, as well, indeed, as the fact that the honours system is based strictly and objectively upon perceived merit. Even more than the public schools, there was a clear and explicit nexus between the older universities and the professions, with nearly 60 per cent of graduates entering the Anglican clergy until after the 1860s and another significant portion entering the bar. While everyone in the middle classes had to attend a school of some sort – or else receive private tuition – post-secondary education was widely regarded until this century as superfluous and certainly exotic. For many business families, there was no *point* to a grown man spending three unnecessary years luxuriating in the classics and dissipation if he could be helping out in the business to which he would eventually succeed; he learned nothing of obvious value and was prey to unholy temptations of every sort. For these reasons, there existed the paradoxical situation that although the universities preached both reason and intellectual merit rather than muscular Christianity, heartiness, and sport, few businessmen sent their sons there until this century; certainly far too few to have produced a 'haemorrhage of talent'. While 66 per cent of the 460 company chairmen holding office from 1905 to 1970, examined by Stanworth and Giddens in their study of leading company chairmen in this period, attended a public school, only 46 per cent attended a university, and only 41 per cent attended Oxbridge.[49] As with public school attendance, the percentage of university-educated bankers was the highest of any occupational group in their study, the percentage of notable retailers the lowest, although with a considerable decline in rates of attendance among all groups in their study compared with attendance at a public school.[50] With the much greater degree of professional training required among leading businessmen in the recent past, this gap may be narrowing: of the 18 Directors of the Bank of England in 1983, 15 attended a recognized public school (5 attended Eton), but 17 attended a University (Oxford, 7; Cambridge, 9; London, 1).[51] As with the public schools, such superficial evidence as exists on the social background and career patterns of university students indicates a very considerable increase in recent times in the numbers of fathers of entrants in business and entrants who subsequently pursued a business career. A study of the fathers of all Cambridge entrants from 1752 to 1886 showed that only 9.4 per cent of their fathers were businessmen (compared with 32.7 per cent described – accurately or not – as 'nobles' or 'gentry', and 32.6 per cent who were clergymen), while 3.9 per cent of entrants became businessmen. Among the under-graduates at Cambridge in 1937/8, 32.5 per cent of their fathers were in 'commerce' (clergymen had declined to 8.3 per cent; there is no separate listing for 'nobles' or 'gentry'), while, by 1952, 17.8 per cent of the undergraduates were engaged in 'commerce' as a career.[52] Interest-ingly, the percentages of fathers and sons in the same occupation or profession among the 1937/8 undergraduates were always fairly similar: for instance, 7.0 per cent of fathers and 8.4 per cent of sons were in the military, 8.1 per cent and 11.2 per cent were, respectively, in medicine, and the other professions showed similar figures.[53] The intergenerational decline among businessmen here does appear to be both particularly sharp and more marked than among our public school cohorts; assuming these figures are accurate, they would, presumably, be a product of the special, professional, and career education received at a university; indeed it is perhaps surprising that the intergeneratio-nal decline was not sharper, given the obvious linkages between university education and the range of professional careers and those associated with the intelligentsia, and the paucity of direct linkages with industry. At Gonville and Caius College, Cambridge, where detailed information on the fathers of entrants is available for the whole period from 1886 to 1971, the percentage of fathers who were businessmen doubled in this period, from 11.0 per cent of under-graduates entering in 1886–90 to 22.0 per cent in 1967–71. Clergymen of all denominations declined from 11.2 per cent to 0.8 per cent in this period, while engineers rose from 1.4 to 13.0 per cent.[54] The percentage of Gonville and Caius entrants pursuing a business career in later life rose even more rapidly, from 3.6 per cent of those entering in 1886–90 to 20.6 per cent of the entrants in 1951–5, the final years in this study.[55] As with everything else we have considered in this chapter, there is nothing whatever in this statistical picture to lend weight to the notion of a 'haemorrhage of talent'. Moreover, we are here considering Cambridge entrants, one of the universally acknowledged peaks of English classical education. Recent research on non-Oxbridge higher education has shown the strong linkage between, on one hand, the 'redbrick', Scottish, and non-university tertiary institutions, and, on the other, science, technology, engineering, and applied research, ever since the foundation of London University in the 1830s and the 'redbricks' in the late Victorian period (and the Scottish universities long before).[56] The current revisionist view is, in fact, that German university science and technology in the 1870–1933 period has been significantly overrated, being notably lacking in flexibility or innovation, while German middle-class education, perhaps even more than its English equivalent, focused excessively on the classics; by the inter-war period there was a growing nexus at all levels between British higher education and British industry, providing some confirmation for the view advanced here that the positivistic and rationalistic elements in British culture became notably stronger over the past century. Beyond everything else, on closer inspection and when relevant and searching evidence is adduced, the 'cultural critique' appears plainly to evaporate as an explanation of long-term trends in the British economy.

4

Elites and the evolution of the British economy

In Chapter 1, a view of the general nature of the British economy since the mid-eighteenth century was outlined, one that views Britain as having always been essentially a financial and commercial power, even during the zenith of the industrial revolution. It is now necessary to look in more detail at the evolution of Britain's elite structure in light of this argument.

In the opinion of this author it is probably best and most fruitful to view Britain's elites, down to the Second World War at least, as consisting of three rival elite groups whose interaction with each other, and with the majority of the population, constituted the substance of modern British history – the landed elite, the commercial-based London elite, with those professionals and administrators based in London, and the northern manufacturing elite.[1] In this chapter, the interaction of these groups will be examined for the light they throw on the British economy and on the contentions of the 'cultural critique' as they affect the arguments of this book. If these three separate elites have indeed been properly identified and distinguished, the chronology and evolution of their interrelationship is highly significant, in my view, for understanding the nexus between Britain's elites and the country's economic performance. Chronologically one can distinguish four separate broad periods during the past 200 years, in terms of the interrelationship of these elites and their interaction with the rest of society. The first, probably lasting from before 1780 to 1832, saw the three elites essentially unified – with of course, the manufacturing and industrial elite relatively insignificant compared with the landowners and the London-based commercial magnates. This unity was rooted in the fact that the unreformed parliamentary system, and successive British governments, at once accommodated, represented, and furthered the interest of the two most important elements in the ruling group, of the landed elite and the old mercantile and financial elite, dominant in the first British Empire and controlling the old mercantile system. Contrary to widespread belief, the pre-1832 British elite, in Parliament or outside, certainly did not consist simply of the landed aristocracy, nor till 1832 represent the replacement of rule by the middle classes for rule by the landowners. Such a contention is not merely false but egregious: in all likelihood the middle classes were more directly a part of the ruling elite before 1832 than afterwards, for the pre-Reform Establishment also included, most definitely and certainly, the old professions – the law, the Church, the universities, much of the medical profession – besides the merchants and financiers of London, Liverpool, Bristol, and even many of the first generation of manufacturers like Sir Robert Peel, 1st Bt, who were Anglicans and worked within the constraints of the system. The middle classes were, almost certainly, as well represented in the House of Commons, via many borough seats and the occasional county seat, before 1832 as afterwards; what changed in 1832 was that the larger towns, especially the newer industrial towns, came to have a greater representation in Parliament and more and more chose local men, local captains of industry, to represent their town and their interests in Parliament. According to the much neglected research of Gerrit P. Judd, in no House of Commons elected from 1802 to 1831 were there ever fewer than 150 businessmen, a figure which might rise further with more detailed research. In the Parliament elected in 1812, for instance, there were 160 businessmen MPs; in 1826 there were 179; in 1830, 186; in 1831, 185.[2] To this number must be added an average of 100 lawyers in every Parliament, several physicians, and 80–100 career army and navy officers.[3] Of course many of these military officers – but not all, by any means – and some of the lawyers were landed aristocrats or gentry, or their close relatives, but on some interpretations very nearly one-half of the pre-Reform Parliament elected under Lord Liverpool and his successors were, consistently, middle-class men in middle-class trades and professions. This figure, moreover, necessarily excludes clergymen of the Church of England, legally debarred from election to the Commons, although at all times represented by twenty-six archbishops and bishops in the House of Lords. It is difficult to identify a precisely similar figure for the post-1832 Parliaments, since the only study of this question, undertaken by J. A. Thomas as long ago as 1939, provides the numbers of economic interests among MPs in each Parliament by party, but evidently double counts those with multiple interests.[4] In the House of Commons elected in 1832, the Whig-Liberal party consisted of 321 landowners, 168 MPs with business interests of all kinds, 46 lawyers, 59 in the army and navy, and 14 other professionals. Among the Tory-Conservative MPs, there were 123 landowners, 47 businessmen of all kinds, 8 lawyers, 32 army officers, and one other professional. Although these figures are not strictly comparable to those provided by Judd, it seems fairly clear that the percentage of middle-class MPs did not rise materially as an immediate result of the Reform Bill, and may well actually have declined.[5] Historians of this subject have perhaps missed the point that although the Great Reform Bill created 65 new English borough seats in the large towns, as well as 60 English county seats and 18 new seats in Wales, Scotland, and Ireland, it also disfranchised 143 small borough seats which, often before 1832, went to the highest bidder, the money of the middle class being as good as anyone else's. Sir Lewis Namier noted the tendency for London merchants, when in search of parliamentary seats, not to 'go to populous expensive constituencies where they were strangers; they preferred to buy them outright in pocket boroughs, or to cultivate an "interest" in some small manageable corporation'.[6] In 1832 this possibility vanished or was comprehensively changed in nature.

In economic terms the pre-1832 elite was based in a close and harmonious connection between mercantile wealth, especially that based in the old Empire, City finance, land, the professions, and the government as contractor, loan-agent, and originator of 'Old Corruption', the extraordinary system of lucrative perquisites which came to fortunate aristocrats, government employees, and their relatives. The British government itself acted as the central matrix of this system, directly through contracts and perquisite, indirectly by maintaining British control of the seas, the Empire, and the balance of power. The key role of the British government in the pre-1832 elite structure was understood many years ago by historians like Sir Lewis Namier, although it has been more or less lost sight of in recent years. In 1929 Namier noted that

> Professor Werner Sombart, in his brilliant studies on the origins of modern capitalism, points to luxury trades and Government contracts as the two factors responsible for its growth prior to the industrial revolution. . . .
>
> By means of taxation and Government loans, agglomerations of capital were effected such as could not easily have arisen in private trade. The Paymasters of the Forces, of the Navy, and the Ordnance, held balances which were of the first importance in the money market; remittances of subsidies to allied countries or of money for the use of troops on foreign or colonial service were among the most coveted plums of finance; even receiverships of the land-tax were much more sought after by provincial merchants and bankers as providing them with the deposits of public money, when private deposits and savings were as yet insignificant. On the other hand, the underwriting of Government loans was the chief financial transaction in an age when

142

joint-stock companies were few and 'Government stock' was the main object of speculation in the Alley.[7]

This nexus of London–mercantile wealth–government patronage–land was extraordinarily lucrative and left its mark on Britain's elite structure for generations to come. Among the 905 persons leaving £100,000 or more in personalty in Britain between 1809 and 1839, 43.2 per cent were chiefly engaged in commerce or finance, 19.8 per cent in the professions and public administration, with 22.3 per cent being landowners leaving fortunes of this size in personal property. Only 9.8 per cent were manufacturers. Fully 72.3 per cent of this group who could be assigned to a specific business or professional venue earned their fortunes in London. Only 5.5. per cent made their money in Lancashire or Yorkshire.[8]

This pre-1832 elite was also distinguished by its fierce Anglicanism and its loyal patriotism to Britain and the British heritage. J. C. D. Clark has performed a most important historical service in restoring Anglicanism and religious conformity, as well as loyalty to the throne and Britain's history, to the centrality these values plainly had for most of the pre-1832 elite.[9] The overwhelming impression made by a realistic assessment of this elite is that it functioned as the head of a unified national system – united, or virtually united, in venue, religion, purpose, and values in a way in which no successive ruling elite could accurately be described, although the elite of the period 1886–1964, especially in its earlier phase, demonstrated many of these features. It is of crucial importance here to note that virtually all of the salient components of Britain's upper and upper-middle classes were then closely allied and aligned: the aristocracy, the Church, the City, the professions, the universities. In political and economic terms, too, it was remarkably successful: Britain's industrial revolution, its unprecedented population explosion, and the dominant political position it reached after Waterloo, were products of this period and occurred under this ruling group. In many respects no succeeding elite was quite as successful, while the perpetual *leitmotif* in all of Britain's further economic evolution, the dominance of its commercial and financial sector, although it began earlier, became of central significance at this time, as did the ambience of the rather misnamed 'gentlemanly capitalism' as it has come to be known among recent economic historians.[10] It also should be evident from this examination how utterly misleading and simply inaccurate is the widely held belief that Britain passed from being a rural society in which the landed aristocracy was dominant to an urban, industrial society headed by a middle-class manufacturing and industrial elite.

Were any groups excluded from this relatively unified elite? A number of groups, marked by their wealth, economic activity, or potential leadership ability as possibly equal to other components of the ruling elite can be distinguished, but only a few – chiefly: from time to time the Whig aristocracy, voluntarily ghettoised beyond the Pitt–Liverpool consensus; Dissenters, legally barred from participation in government but still enormously influential, especially at the local level; and perhaps the intellectual radicals although they were obviously of little importance at most times. More significant was the growth of a new manufacturing class, often (though not always) of Nonconformist background, who perhaps alone could potentially combine the wealth, geographical base, and adversarial ideological stance to provide some measure of a challenge to the old order, although their numbers were surprisingly small until surprisingly late. The 1832 Reform Bill both caused and mirrored the first fundamental transformation in the elite structure of Britain and the reformulation of its elites into the form they took until the late nineteenth century (1886 is a convenient and significant date to mark the end of this period). The *national*, consensual unified complex of essential qualities which constituted perhaps the primary feature of the old elite (and of the British 'ancient regime' generally) was destroyed by the Reform Bill and the reforms which either preceded it or the consequential reforms which flowed from it. Removal of the disabilities suffered by Dissenters and Catholics, as well as reform by the state of the Anglican Church, led to a crisis of conscience among many intellectuals, such as Gladstone and Newman, when the Church of England seemed to forfeit its role as the national church. The unity of the three old socio-economic elites was ended by the Reform Bill, with the landed elite, the emergent northern manufacturing elite, and London's commercial elite functioning separately rather than as a single system. This was, of course, the period in which Britain's manufacturing and industrial prowess reached its zenith and England became the 'workshop of the world'. As we noted in Chapter 1, however, the north never broke through to overtake London and the south as the chief venue of middle-class incomes, nor did manufacturing and industry in the broadest sense ever employ more than a fraction of the population, while factories, coal mines, and other products of the new technology in industry employed even smaller proportions. The reputation Britain's economy enjoyed as one based upon industry and manufacturing is largely a result of the fact that its artefacts and products were more traumatic, novel, frightening, and disruptive than other sections of the economy, while subsequent radical critics of capitalism have always viewed class conflict, factory- and industry-based, as central to history's very evolution to a higher stage – something we today can recognise for the sheer fantasy it is.

Yet it was in this period that the northern manufacturing elite came into its own as a separate, powerful ruling group. The Municipal Corporations Act of 1835, which gave the vote in borough elections to all ratepayers who had lived in that borough for three years, electing borough councillors who in turn elected mayors and aldermen, set the stage for domination of the major cities and towns of England by the local business elite of the day untrammelled either by the pre-industrial revolution elite previously dominant in the old closed boroughs or by working-class populist pressures.[11] As a rule, the composition of borough councils mirrored the economic activity of that town fairly well. In Sheffield, to take one example, about 15–25 per cent of the Town Council in the mid-Victorian period were steel manufacturers, with over 50 per cent being other manufacturers and merchants. In Salford, an average of 46 per cent of the Council between 1846 and 1890 were manufacturers or merchants. The range in other industrial towns was similar.[12] There was apparently a growing tendency for big businessmen to take part in local political life in place of small businessmen and tradesmen.[13] The northern manufacturing elite and its ideologues are often seen as responsible for the most famous economic Act of Parliament of the nineteenth century, the Repeal of the Corn Laws, and by the 1860s or 1870s had evolved a separate distinctive provincial civic culture whose monuments and aspirations may be found, literally and figuratively, in the municipal buildings of most large provincial cities and towns.[14]

The factory working classes of the factory towns often, to a remarkable extent, demonstrated electoral loyalties which mirrored those of their employers and demonstrated a quasi-feudal loyalty to the factory owners – for example, at coming-of-age parties for the eldest son of the factory master – which was utterly at variance with the notion of an adversarial working class; working-class discontent seems clearly to have declined markedly after 1850, a state of affairs which continued until the Edwardian period or even later.[15]

Nevertheless, there is universal agreement among historians of the bourgeoisie of the nineteenth-century cities that something crucial was missing in all this. The middle classes, especially the industrial middle classes, were virtually unrepresented at the highest levels of British politics. John Bright, virtually the only manufacturer to serve in a mid-Victorian Cabinet, and one of the most famous men in Britain, remained 'essentially an outsider' even at the end of his career, his career in essence 'a failure', according to one recent historian.[16] Bright's proposal for a separate middle-class party came to nothing.[17] Several theories have been put forward to account for this notable middle-class failure, including the advanced age at which most manufacturer MPs entered Parliament, their inability to speak persuasively in the House of

Commons style or to master it, the limited number of parliamentary seats in industrial towns until after the 1884 Reform Act, and their preoccupation with local affairs.[18] There were other reasons for this failure as well. Middle-class magnates and political notables in the northern towns had little or nothing in common, either in political or sociological terms, apart from their success. John Foster and other recent historians of the northern bourgeoisie have noted a fundamental split between an older, more conservative sector, chiefly Anglican and often intermarried with or a part of the landed gentry, and a newer segment, chiefly Nonconformist, pro-Liberal, or radical in politics and 'self-made' at one or two generations' remove.[19] The elite structure of each city and town was quite different, in overt or subtle ways, from one another. In cities like Liverpool and Newcastle-upon-Tyne it was chiefly or entirely Anglican and mainly Tory; in Birmingham the celebrated late Victorian elite of Chamberlains and Kenricks were Liberal (subsequently Liberal Unionists) and Noncon-formists, as the town notables tended to be in most new manufacturing towns. Given these differences, no comprehensive and exclusivist political co-operation was possible among the northern middle classes once the most basic goals were achieved.

Another important reason for the failure of the middle classes to achieve political dominance at this time was the fundamental split between London and the north. Industrial and manufacturing Britain has arisen, as is well known, with few salient connections to London. London did not finance the factories and mines of the north; its economic leaders and notables were socially and sociologically far removed from those of the north; the self-conscious civic culture of the northern cities most notably affected London little or not at all, local governance of London being either non-existent or unreformed. London's own economic base, as always, led to the outside world, to finance and commerce abroad and overseas. Its other chief functions, as the centre of Britain's government, its professions, the press, entertainment, and as an urban home for the rich and the upper-middle classes, also had little to do with the north and built on a pre-industrial base. Poverty, too, was essentially different in London from that in the northern cities, being chronic and founded in a population far in excess of the industries to employ the labour at hand, while in the northern cities it was cyclical and based in the trade cycle. Within the elite of the City of London, too, one can discern something of a sharp dichotomy between, on the one hand, the enormously wealthy financial magnates of the merchant banks and clearing banks, the Stock Exchange, big insurance companies, and so on, and, on the other, the traditional civic notabilities of the City livery companies who, as a general rule, represented second-ranking local businesses which were far less successful than the more celebrated City banks and other financial and commercial enterprises, whose chiefs as a rule had little or nothing to do with the City livery companies.[20] This dichotomy also echoed one between financiers and merchants who traded with the whole world – both with areas within the Empire and outside of it – and the remnants of those who benefited from the old colonial system, the East India Company, and the old West Indies interest. As with the northern elite, too, the post-1832 Parliamentary system was weighted against the direct representation of London, the City returning only four MPs and the rest of London fewer than twenty. MPs with financial or banking interests were always well represented in the Commons – in 1832 there were 64 MPs with traceable financial interests on Thomas's figures, in 1859 there were 55, in 1885 nearly 200 – but the number of large-scale City magnates among them was probably much smaller.[21] As is well known, also, many City financiers and bankers were, socially and sociologically, much closer to the traditional landed aristocracy than were northern manufacturers, attending a public school and university earlier and far more frequently, and often marrying among the aristocracy.[22] The London middle classes also perhaps saw themselves as potentially threatened by Chartism, Fenianism, working-class militancy, and the potential of revolution to an even greater extent than did northern manufacturers, lacking an interface with (and hence, direct knowledge of) operatives, labourers, and workers apart from their servants and hired menials; as inhabitants of the capital, Londoners could expect to see the bloody face of any revolutionary situation just as directly as did the inhabitants of Paris, Vienna, and Berlin. For a variety of reasons, middle-class London switched decisively from Liberalism to Toryism earlier than much of the north, despite the continuing liberal, cosmopolitan inclinations of the City, with the City constituency returning chiefly Conservative MPs from 1874, and only Conservative MPs from 1885.

In the absence of a strong or united challenge from the middle classes during the period 1832–86 (and beyond, to 1905), this time in British history saw the apogee of the landed aristocracy as a governing class. There had been, perhaps, a slightly higher proportion of landed aristocrats as a rule in the Cabinets from Walpole to Wellington, but the extraordinary domination by the landed aristocracy of all ministries in this period occurred in the context of a phenomenally larger and wealthier middle class, a class which was self-differentiated from the aristocracy and politically successful in other respects. Moreover, the landed aristocracy as it existed in the mid-nineteenth century appears to have been significantly more closed to newcomers than its predecessor fifty or one hundred years before, with only a handful of peerage creations from the new business classes; new men of wealth seldom purchased land on a truly significant scale, as will be discussed.[23] Landowners and their close relatives comprised a remarkable proportion of the House of Commons: 444 MPs (by identifiable interest) in 1832, 394 in 1865, 194 even in 1885.[24] By another method of counting, 31 per cent of the House of Commons in 1865 consisted of aristocrats (baronets, Irish peers, sons of baronets and United Kingdom peers), with a further 45 per cent consisting of members of the landed gentry: fully 76 per cent of the House of Commons when Britain was at its zenith as the 'workshop of the world'.[25] Large-territorial peers and their sons comprised 56 out of all 103 Cabinet ministers serving between 1830 and 1868, with a further 12 drawn from gentry ranks; among 150 Cabinet ministers serving between 1868 and 1896, 76 were aristocrats or their close relatives.[26] From the late 1830s until about 1880, the wealth of Britain's landowners grew significantly with agricultural improvements, the growth of its cities, and profits from minerals. After 1880, much purely agricultural land declined in value, although landowners with significant urban property or mineral deposits continued to rank among the very richest men in the country well into this century; some, of course, still do.

Nevertheless, there are some important respects in which the 'golden age' of the aristocracy in the mid-Victorian period differed significantly from the previous period. In the years before 1832, our argument is that the British elite was consensual and unified; for the next half-century it was neither, with the bulk of lesser landowners constituting the backbone of the Tory party, a party still closely allied with the Church of England, the older professions, the universities, and some businessmen from the old commercial trades, but, especially after 1846, a pale, attenuated shadow of the truly national party it had been before 1832, while the Whig-Liberal party consisted of an increasingly uneasy alliance between Whig grandees, northern (often dissenting) businessmen, newer City magnates and many London professionals. Neither party grouping, in other words, embodied the majority of the 'Establishment' or of the wealthy, the middle classes, and opinion-leaders, and indeed, high politics in this period more or less consisted of unsuccessful attempts to create a new national party and a new national consensus: first by the Whigs under Grey, then by the Tories under Peel, then, with perhaps the nearest approach to success, by the Whig-Peelite coalition under Palmerston and Gladstone. But each foundered on the stubborn fact that very significant elements in the Establishment remained blindly loyal to the opposition Tories, especially the majority of landowners, the Church, and the universities, while the Whig axis always included many of the larger landowners and most 'newer' businessmen.

Eventually, when a new national consensus was reached it would be formed and headed not by the Liberals but by the Conservatives, the familiar Establishment as it has become known in this century. Probably the central event in the formation of the Establishment – and the next stage in the reorientation of the elites we have been examining – was the Liberal Unionist split of 1886, which brought the residual Whig aristocracy, many (perhaps most) Liberal financiers and merchants in London, some intellectuals, and Chamberlainite manufacturers into a permanent alliance with the resurgent Conservative party under Lord Salisbury. The Tories, embracing even at their lowest ebb most landowners, the Church of England, and the universities, had benefited even before 1886 by an inevitable drift to the right among the wealthy and the established, especially among former Whig landowners.[27] By 1900, for the first time since before 1832, nearly all of the major elements in the British upper and upper-middle classes were politically united, the major exception being the northern manufacturers, chiefly of dissenting origin. Apart from these, however, the pre-1832 ruling elite had essentially been reconstructed in modern dress, from the Church of England, the landowners, the public schools, universities, and most of the London middle class to the City and beyond them to many manufacturers. This alliance also brought with it a revivified and transcendentally appealing concept of Empire, imperial service, and a special British mission in the world. The Unionist Party successfully came to terms with the new democratic policy by creating a formidable political machine and securing the support of most of the press.[28] The Liberals at this stage were reduced to a rump of Celts, radicals, and Nonconformists, conceivably doomed to permanent opposition. It is important to note that Disraelian social reform and the policy of 'dishing the Whigs' with Tory democracy was far less significant in this successful consensual alliance than Salisbury's wooing of the middle classes.[29] A disastrous combination of internal Tory bickering, Nonconformist discontent, trade union pressure, and A. J. Balfour's inept leadership of the Unionist party after Salisbury's retirement, meant, however, that Edwardian Britain would be governed after 1905 by the Liberals rather than the Tories, with Imperial Preference – seemingly the logical capstone of this revival of neo-mercantilism – rejected again and again at the polls. In practice, and despite Lloyd George's attempts to hijack the Liberal government for the left to meet the labour and socialist challenge, the Liberal government proved little different in practice from the Tories. It rearmed and entered the war in 1914, guarded the Empire just as vigorously as its Tory predecessors, and was no more anti-business than any Conservative government.

The profound effects of the First World War on every aspect of British life perhaps affected the essential nature of Britain's elite structure less than most other elements in British society and less than many historians had supposed. Indeed, from the viewpoint being advanced here, the chief effect of the war was greatly to *enhance* the process under way since 1886. The collapse of the Liberal party as the alternative party of government meant that the middle-class elements still loyal to the Liberals – chiefly Nonconformists and industrialists in the north and Celtic areas – in general joined the Conservative party, now more than ever the normal party of the Establishment, the wealthy, and the middle classes, strongly based in London but now also strong almost everywhere, and dominant over an Empire (as is often forgotten) now mightier than ever, having extended the Union Jack for the first time to places as different as Jerusalem and Dar-es-Salaam, Baghdad and Rabaul as a result of the war. As before, a major segment of the upper middle classes was engaged in administering and policing the Empire, in general benignly, and always with the aim of increasing the political and economic strength of the vast but in theory cohesive system of the British Empire. When the Empire did collapse, this was due to two causes, the fact that the self-governing Dominions increasingly had their own agendas and regarded links to the 'Mother Country' as anachronistic, and more importantly of course, the inherent impossibility of situating the colonial nationalist movements, and the non-European peoples these represented, into any concept of Empire in which Britain remained hegemonic.

The term 'system' to describe Britain and its Empire down to 1939 or even later is highly significant, for, as with the British polity before 1832, Britain did function very much as a system in this period, at least so far as its elites and middle classes are concerned. The landed aristocracy, formerly by definition pre-eminent in the social and political hierarchy, had now diminished greatly in status, wealth, and certainly in power, a process as discernible at the highest levels of the Conservative party as in the country at large.[30] While some scions of the old aristocracy, including Curzon, Churchill, Eden, and Salisbury, continued to reach the most senior levels of political leadership, in general power and visibility had passed to the business and professional middle classes, who, with the administrative civil service, London-based professionals, and more arguably the press, constituted the Establishment of this period.

It was also the case that the First World War effectively diminished, or at least altered significantly, the nature of the provincial industrial elite. Effectively, the self-conscious, assertive, ideologically distinctive provincial elite disappeared in the First World War, together with its vision of a liberal, meritocratic provincial civic culture not dissimilar to that which emerged in nineteenth-century America. This process has never really been analysed in the detail it deserves, so far as I am aware, but it is not unreasonable to view it as the product of two underlying causes. The first was the rise of Labour at the local level, which severed the vertical linkages along the occupational/geographical lines that existed in the nineteenth century, replacing them with antagonistic and hostile class loyalties. The second was the failure of much of the northern manufacturing elite to produce successful and assertive successors after the First World War, in the context of an economy whose comparative advantage increasingly favoured commerce and industry. The economic underpinnings of the old system were disappearing at a time when the provincial entrepreneurial elite of the old centres of British staple industry were apparently losing their vigour. Yet it would be wrong in my view to see this as evidence of an 'anti-industrial culture' in Britain. The decline of the old staple industries was a world-wide phenomenon of the inter-war period caused by a world-wide decline in the demand for these goods; second and more importantly, the inter-war period was one, it is now generally agreed, of vigorous new growth in newer manufacturing industries (and services), especially consumer durables, *geographically situated elsewhere*, especially in London and the West Midlands rather than in the north and Celtic areas. The alleged evils of Britain's anti-industrial culture did not work adversely, from 1918 to 1939, in Birmingham, Coventry, the Great West Road in West London, or 'semi-detached London' in the north-west of the Metropolis. It might well be asked why a Lord Nuffield appeared in and operated from Oxford rather than Jarrow or Paisley. But this query is, at best, an indictment of the old industrial areas rather than of British culture as a whole, which continued to produce its full share of Nuffields.

The great challenge to the hegemony of this Establishment and to the Conservative party's almost unbroken rule now came, of course, from the Labour party, on paper committed to socialism and far-reaching economic change, though in office, as we have seen, not greatly different from the Conservatives. From the perspective being advanced here, the Labour party and the trade union and other elements in its leadership and mass base are rather difficult to situate, being extremely varied in social origin, ideology and perspective. Many trade union leaders were (notoriously, to some) working-class Tories, men who would have been pillars of the Establishment had they been born higher up the social scale, instinctive patriots and imperialists. For many men of this type, the trade union hierarchy and the Labour party were simply a realistic way of achieving upward social mobility, attaining power and status unavailable by other means. On the other hand, many working-class Labourites were genuinely radicals, intent on achieving social reform and social justice, sometimes from a Nonconformist background and perspective, sometimes from one of secular radicalism. Often, as in the case of Ramsay MacDonald himself, this radicalism became vaguer, rather than more concrete, when its details were required to be spelled out. Middle-class Labour leaders were, generally, often more radical than their working-class colleagues, although their radicalism embraced any number of highly disparate elements, from the elitist quasi-fascism of the Webbs to the liberal Keynesianism of Hugh Dalton to the practical radicalism, with its roots in local government, of Clement Attlee, to the radical democratic socialism of Nye Bevan. The overwhelming impression made by the Labour party from 1918 to 1940 is that it did not have the slightest idea what it was about, what it represented, or what policies it intended to pursue if given the chance. When the chance came, in 1945, it showed a preference for strict regulation of the economy in the interests of efficiency, Keynesianism, social reform, at once far-reaching and restricted in nature, and maintenance of Britain's traditional foreign policy and military role in the context of withdrawal from India and other areas – a programme still confused enough.

It is therefore especially difficult, too, to know when the long period which began around 1886 came to an end.[31] Harold Macmillan's 'one nation' rhetoric and ideology clearly is a post-imperial, post-Keynesian echo of the traditional Conservative effort to achieve a genuine national consensus of all Establishment groups and the majority of all segments of the population, including the working class. It is, however, abundantly clear that at some date in the relatively recent past this long era did come to an end. The economic assumption underlying it, that Britain could remain a great power by trading in large part as the leader of an Empire bloc, clearly became obsolete, as did, of course, the Empire itself, and most of Britain's great power aspirations altogether. Just as significantly, the sociological assumption on which this system rested, that the London-based Establishment, amounting to perhaps 3–5 per cent of the population at most, could live in a manner very different from most of the rest, different in education, income, and standard of living, also came to an end, as did many accoutrements of this system, from the *raison d'être* of public schools as training grounds for this elite to the imperial administrative class itself. Suez marked a crucial psychological turning-point, but it is probably more accurate still to fix the date when the Tory-Imperial Establishment finally expired in October 1964, when the Wilson government came to power at a time when unprecedented social change was becoming manifest.

This break in the 1960s also coincided with many essential changes in Britain's social structure. There was a significant growth in the size and level of affluence of the middle classes – an inevitable concomitant of 'Petty's Law' discussed in Chapter 1, the increase in all advanced economies of the size of the tertiary sector. There was, unquestionably, a sharp rise in the affluence of the working class. The secondary- and tertiary-educated sector of the population also rose enormously in size.[32] Married women entered the work-force in ever-increasing numbers. These were genuine, endogenous changes in the social structure which had no real precedent in British history, creating a new, articulate constituency for political and economic policy different from any of the previous systems. One important facet of the previous system, the general role of the public schools in identifying a 'candidate class' for leadership, was overtaken by the sheer weight of well-educated and upwardly mobile persons without precedent in number.

It was also absolutely clear by the 1960s that one of the major props of most of the previous systems, the Empire connection, was gone, never to return. The familiar post-war British dilemma, whether to align itself with the remnants of the Commonwealth, with the United States, or with Europe, remained unresolved for many decades and still is so, in the sense that the apparent solution of the dilemma, to cast Britain's lot unequivocally with Europe, was probably the least popular option despite its overwhelming approval in the 1975 Referendum. By the 1970s, too, unemployment mounted disastrously, heavily centred in the old northern manufacturing cities and other former industrial areas and in the 'inner cities', especially London, with their racially diverse *lumpenproletariat*. The north–south split, papered over by full employment from 1940 to 1965, re-emerged with a vengeance as an apparently intractable condition of British life.[33] The gap between the south-east and the rest of Britain probably grew to unprecedented proportions, although, as noted in Chapter 1, the standard of living throughout Britain also rose enormously. The older industrial areas, in particular, have been consistently unable to seize upon and develop manufacturing industries as potentially lucrative as those of the industrial revolution, while service industries grew more strongly in their traditional home in London and the south-east.

The crisis of the 1970s in the British psyche also coincided with a deep and perhaps unprecedented cynicism among British intellectuals, coinciding with the removal of almost all traditional restraints on comment and depiction in the media, and, in the 1960s and 1970s, with a well-publicised 'generation gap'. It also took place in an international context in which, first, European powers like West Germany and Italy and, second, countries on the rim of east Asia experienced 'economic miracles', Britain apparently being virtually the only exception to this pattern of world-wide economic growth. Facts on the other side were consistently ignored or misunderstood – that Britain's growth area in the service sector was not as well measured by the normal macroeconomic statistics, as they have emerged in the Keynesian era, as are manufacturing industries and national economies which have experienced significant growth in this area; that unemployment in Britain in the 1970s and 1980s was no higher than in France, Italy, or even West Germany, nations with whose economies Britain is invariably compared adversely; that the standard of living in Britain grew as rapidly as that in any other comparable country and was virtually identical to that in any other comparable country; that realistic measurements of social mobility – for instance the percentage of the population attending a university – rose at unprecedented rates. Since the 1960s this concurrent series of events and perceptions became the central focus of virtually all political and electoral debate in Britain. Since 1945, too, virtually every politically feasible approach to the perceived problems of the British economy have been tried and, by the criteria of most commentators, failed, from (by British standards) the rigid central control of the Attlee government to the 'Selsdon man' policies of Edward Heath. It is in this context that 'Thatcherism' should be viewed.

Although Thatcherism is sometimes viewed as the opposite side of the coin of the successful drive by the Labour party's left wing from the early 1970s to the late 1980s to control that party and to set its agenda, there are salient differences, albeit also the obvious similarity that both represented ideological positions previously assumed to be beyond the boundaries of mainstream politics.[34] Thatcherism at its heart *was* simply the admission, as the centre-piece of governmental policy, that Britain's comparative advantage in the international economic sphere lay in the services, finance, and commerce, and that deliberate attempts by the government to focus economic policy on the fostering of a truly revivified manufacturing sector were likely to be quixotic and counterproductive. In so far as Britain could remain a leading industrial power – the reasoning of Thatcherism went – this depended crucially upon building up a strong service sector which would generate demand in the manufacturing sector. By the mid-late 1980s, the evidence is that this strategy was succeeding very well; only in the late 1980s did it become relatively unstuck because of re-emergent inflationary pressures and the international effects of the 1987 Stock Market crash. The *OECD Economic Survey: United Kingdom* for 1987/8, reflective on the period when Thatcherism appeared to be at its most successful, summarised the previous year by noting that

> The United Kingdom's economic performance continues to compare favourably with that of most other Member countries. Over the past two years output growth has exceeded the OECD average by a wide margin. Inflation has remained low. . . . With buoyant tax revenues, the budget has swung into surplus. . . . [T]he Government has been able to repay debt for the first time in thirty years.

– and so on in a glowing report.[35] By 1991, the fact that 'the U.K.

economy entered a period of severe overheating in early 1987' was the keynote of the OECD's annual report, although the remarkable achievement of the Thatcher government in closing the gap in labour productivity between Britain and comparable countries was noted, together with its achievements in tax reform and other areas.[36] The well-known close correlation between real wage rigidities and unemployment, together with relative unit labour costs – areas in which Britain had long been notoriously bad – showed that, if anything, Mrs Thatcher's reforms did not go far enough in freeing up the British labour market.[37]

From the viewpoint of our analysis of changing elite structures in modern British history, the post-1964 period seems very different – indeed, categorically different – from any in the past. It is possible to view the Thatcher experiment in simplistic terms, simply as an attempt by the rich and by businessmen to be rid of socialism and collectivism. Such a view begs more questions than it answers. A more sophisticated assessment would see the elite structure of Britain during the recent past as bifurcated into one grouping consisting of the rich and middle classes employed by private industry on the one hand, and, on the other, a grouping of the highly educated middle class employed by the state (especially local government), left-leaning intellectuals, non-profit-making interest groups, especially the welfare lobby, together with the traditional trade union leadership element.[38] If this view is accurate, political debate and division is likely to revolve increasingly around social rather than economic issues, with a moderately 'tough-minded' private enterprise elite opposed by a 'tender-minded' elite from the public sector. Nevertheless, it is the nature of the Thatcherite Conservative party which presents the most problems to the observer. The Thatcher Cabinets have been markedly less elitist in their social backgrounds than any Conservative Cabinets in history, and deliberately so. After shedding its 'wets' in the early 1980s, Mrs Thatcher's Cabinets contained only a small minority of members from the old governing classes, with only one or two Etonians. Douglas Hurd was the only Etonian in the Cabinet when Mrs Thatcher resigned at the end of 1990. As recently as 1963, Sir Alec Douglas-Home's Cabinet contained no fewer than 11 old Etonians out of 21 members. In 1990 the Thatcher Cabinet did not contain a single member of the traditional landed aristocracy or gentry, being drawn almost exclusively from what might simply be described as the middle class – not necessarily the 'solid' middle class, or the lower middle class, as in the case of Mrs Thatcher herself and her successor John Major. The social composition of Mrs Thatcher's Cabinets was similar to that of the '1922 Committee' of backbenchers which had long been drawn from a lower social cachet than had the Tory ministry.[39] The views of the 1922 Committee (as with its equivalent among the backbench groups in the Labour party) have long been regarded as more extreme than those of the post-war Tory front bench: they would, in all likelihood, have ditched 'Butskellism' and consensus politics far earlier, and held notably more 'tough-minded' views on crime, immigration, and other social questions. Nevertheless, the social origins of the Thatcher government appear to represent something quite new, a product of the genuine widening of the 'candidate class' from which the Conservative leadership can be drawn. The wider social basis of Conservative leadership also reflected the much larger size of the middle classes *per se*, as well as the vastly greater opportunities for social mobility through education than had ever previously existed.

This social broadening in the contemporary Tory leadership can also be seen as an important reason for the sharp movement away from the concept of 'one nation' Conservatism, so important a *leitmotif* of the Tory approach to national leadership from the late nineteenth century until the 1960s. The new leaders of the Conservative party, who had made their own way up (in their eyes) by sheer talent, were unlikely to look kindly on either *noblesse oblige* or the coddling of the allegedly disadvantaged. Nevertheless, rightly or wrongly, the new Toryism was also free of the fundamental illusion of all recent governments, that Britain could be restored to her former position as 'workshop of the world' by direct and purposeful intervention in manufacturing industry. Realists to the end, they saw that this was to fight against history, to make water run uphill. By keeping a lockhold on the plurality of the population resident in the south-east of England, the Conservatives fashioned a mighty political machine (based upon a steady 43 per cent of the total electorate, with the Opposition split among Labour and the Liberal Democrats), fashioned by Mrs Thatcher, which unexpectedly gave her successor John Major a fourth consecutive Tory victory in 1992. This successful electoral machine rivalled or surpassed the three other successful Tory electoral juggernauts of the past, those led by Liverpool, Salisbury, and Baldwin, although its social bases and ideological assumptions were categorically different.

If this account of the evolution of Britain's elites over the past two hundred years be accurate, we are now in a better position to situate Britain's elites, and their cultural underpinnings, into this history. The important changes in Britain's elite structure described here have coincided with a number of features of equally impressive durability. Perhaps the most important of these has been the perpetually central role of London, which has *always* comprised the axis of Britain's elite structure, standing to the rest of the country, including the elites of the provinces, in a manner very reminiscent of the sun in our solar system. This central role of London is perhaps not fully understood. London's central role both preceded Britain's industrialisation and yet continued while Britain was the world's major industrial power, and still continues in, if anything, an enhanced position today. It was and is constant, not a characteristic of an earlier, less developed stage. London's role is, in itself, good and telling evidence for the view of Britain's economy as always, essentially, a commercial and financial one that we have argued for here.

London's continuing central role also made for the existence of a fundamentally important urban bourgeoisie that, in size, almost certainly far exceeded the former bourgeoisie which opted for rural gentry status and total withdrawal from the middle classes. It is most important to keep this in mind, for the postulation of the 'gentrification' of the business bourgeoisie, whatever else this term might mean, certainly did not imply the actual purchase of rural acres and the abandonment of urban life. Among other things, such a view simply fails to take the reality of London into account. London was *simultaneously* the centre of Britain's business life, the chief residence of its middle class, and the main area of middle-class leisure. There was no hard-and-fast division between these functions, and contemporaries recognised no real dichotomy. Francis Wey (1812–82), a Frenchman who visited London in the 1850s, astutely noted:

From St. Paul's to the Tower of London you go through a labyrinth of narrow little streets, clean and flagged like a church and lined with small brick houses, hermetically closed. These are the premises of trading companies, warehouses, offices, private banks, etc. The district which looks like a monastery belonging to the canons of the Exchange and Bank is as alive and busy as the inside of a beehive. Each door, carefully painted, has a shining brass knocker, a peep-hole and a metal plate inscribed with the name of the firm. There is no outward sign to attract the eye, for these small counting-houses of the city, where millions change hands, have customers with whom they have traded for centuries. The sons of millionaires succeed fathers richer than nabobs and the heirs of these dynasties no more dream of giving up the trade of their forefathers than the eldest son of a peer would dream of giving up his title. Up to five o'clock this district buzzes with activity but after that it is utterly deserted for no one lives here.

The day's work over, these modest fatherly-looking business men go back to their mansions in Portland Place, Regent Street, Burlington Terrace or Grosvenor Square – some even go off to magnificent suburban villas – only to reappear next morning with their unassuming air of small City merchants. While in France prosperity flaunts itself, here it tries to hide in the general mediocrity. This type of hypocrisy has its maniacs. I am told that there are wealthy bankers who go in person to the butcher's shop every morning to buy the mutton chops, which they carry ostentatiously to some tavern in Fleet Street or Cheapside, where they insist on grilling them themselves. They then buy a threepenny loaf of brown bread and devour this Spartan meal in public, while they have their first business talks of the day.

As one strolls about this neighbourhood one is struck by the confidence which governs all transactions. There are no sentries guarding the Bank, no troops anywhere about. All doors are open, one can penetrate anywhere without question. The iron cages in which in our counting-houses we imprison our cashiers with their funds are unknown here. There are low tables, accessible to all, with no gratings or metal trellises. Gold is weighed out and handled in small shovels, exactly like those used in our country by grocers and just as though salt or cloves were being ladled out.[40]

London's place in the structure of British life was and perhaps still is unique among comparable countries: perhaps nowhere else is the size, function, and centrality of the Metropolis equal to that of London, a fact which has been true since Elizabethan times.[41] In many other countries, among them the United States, Canada, Australia, Russia before 1917, and West Germany until reunification, the administrative capital of the country was placed elsewhere than in its foremost urban centre, normally as a matter of deliberate choice. Perhaps nowhere else was the chief city as relatively populous as London was (and is) compared with the rest of the country. In 1801, Greater London had a population of 1,117,000 in a total British population (England, Wales, and Scotland) of 10,686,000, or 9.6 per cent. In 1861 these figures were 3,227,000 and 23,188,000 (13.9 per cent), and in 1911, 7,256,000 and 40,887,000 (17.7 per cent). At its peak just before the Second World War, Greater London probably contained 20 per cent of the British population. By the 1980s, Greater London's share had declined somewhat – in 1987 its population was estimated at 6,775,000 in a total British population of 55,300,000 (12.3 per cent) – but was still vastly larger than any other British city. The contrast here with other major European cities is very illuminating: in 1911, the population of Paris was 2,888,000, or about 7 per cent of France's total population of 40 million. At this time, Paris was considerably larger than any other city in Europe, with only four other cities containing more than one million people: Berlin with 2,071,000; Vienna with 2,031,000; St Petersburg with 1,908,000; and Moscow with 1,481,000. The populations of Germany, Austria-Hungary, and of course Russia were very much larger than Britain's, and the percentage of the population dwelling in their leading city or cities accordingly very much smaller. Even in the United States, and even after recalling that New York was never (since 1790) the seat of American government, Greater New York peaked in its percentage of the total American population around 1940–50, when no more than about 6.7 per cent of the people of the United States lived there (perhaps 10 million of 150 million). Since then its share has declined consistently, and is now only around 5.5 per cent.

While London was always unequivocally the capital of Britain in every sense, in most other comparable societies the chief city never enjoyed the unrivalled status of London. In the German-speaking areas of Europe, Berlin and Vienna fought a lengthy contest for supremacy until Bismarck's time: even after Berlin won this battle, it never (except during the Nazi period) was the capital of a unitary state and always looked nervously to Germany's growing Rhine–Ruhr industrial district and to more cosmopolitan ports like Hamburg. Moscow and St Petersburg/Leningrad have similarly contested supremacy as rivals. Even in the United States, 'gilded age' America saw Chicago emerge as a possible commercial rival to New York, while since the 1950s Los Angeles has grown to rival New York in virtually every sense. Perhaps only the situation of Paris as the capital of France is even remotely comparable to London; yet Paris (until very recently) was much smaller and largely owed its position to France's relative lack of urbanisation, whereas London has plenty of rapidly growing urban competitors within Britain. Even more significantly, London's position as the capital and headquarters of so much in so many different fields – its financial and commercial life, the governmental and administrative centre of the nation and the Empire, its press, its professions including the whole of the bar and medical specialists, retailing, entertainment, the arts, Society and the rich – almost certainly was without parallel anywhere.[42] This continuing and astonishing combination of leading roles gave London a status *sui generis*, with each of these roles reinforcing the others.

The essentially urban nature of Britain's entrepreneurial elite, centred especially in London, is also the main reason for the notable failure of Britain's business elite to purchase land on a scale in keeping with their ability, via their wealth, to enter the landed gentry at an unprecedented rate. There can now simply be no doubt that only a small minority of new-rich businessmen purchased land in more than very limited amounts, while it seems clear that those who did were the very richest nineteenth-century businessmen who, even after their land purchase, retained the largest amounts in non-landed farms of wealth and investment.[43] According to one very detailed study of leading Lancashire cotton manufacturers in mid-Victorian times, an amount equal to only 4 per cent of the total of capital invested in the cotton industry was used to purchase land, while only 3.7 per cent of these 351 cotton manufacturers owned as much as 3,000 acres of land.[44] These figures appear highly typical of the affluent business classes as a whole. No doubt most manufacturers and businessmen aspired to all forms of social prestige, but significant land purchase simply was not a reality for most of them, even those who were, financially, able to afford it. For many the West End became an urban substitute for landed gentry status, with the other milestones of social acceptability, like education at a public school and university, also creating an urbanised world of status neither traditionally gentry nor wholly removed from the old facets of the status system, yet intimately connected with Britain's most dynamic economic growth area. The failure of a self-conscious, articulate, genuinely dissenting provincial industrial elite to become a permanent facet of Britain's elite structure after the end of the nineteenth century has many causes, but in essence its failure lay with economic and political changes unfavourable to its continued existence in its old form.

Britain's elites as they emerged into this century thus bear some resemblance – but only some – to the elites in other industrialised countries where sophisticated research on this subject has appeared. At the centre of our understanding of Britain's elites is a curious paradox. Although it has long been imagined that Britain's business elites effectively 'merged' with the landed aristocracy much more effectively than in the continental countries which had industrialised by 1900, detailed research will almost always show that the degree of merger, as assessed by salient quantitative measurements, was actually less in many respects in Britain than elsewhere, and was certainly not greater. The matter of landowning has been mentioned. Another area is the granting of titles of nobility in Europe. While it is commonly imagined that reactionary governments like those in Prussia or Russia erected insurmountable barriers aimed at preventing all but the very richest or luckiest *nouveaux riches* businessmen from entering the titled elite, actually this impression appears quite false: literally hundreds, perhaps thousands, of successful businessmen were ennobled by the monarchies of Europe down to 1918 (and even beyond, in the case of countries like Hungary which retained a titled nobility), vastly more than received peerages in Britain. In Prussia, a sample of 700 titles of nobility conferred between 1819 and 1900 included at least 582 which went to businessmen.[45] Of this number, 62 were Jews, despite the pervasiveness of German high society anti-semitism. The number of Prussian manufacturers given titles rose from 30 in the period 1861–72 to 146 in the years 1890–1900.[46] Another study of the wealthiest businessmen in late Imperial Germany found that about 23.3 per cent had been ennobled, around 17.4 per cent since 1870.[47] This total was probably as high as in Britain, or higher. In Austria–Hungary, literally thousands of middle-class men and families were ennobled by the Emperor Francis-Ferdinand. One study of Jewish creations of nobility under the Hapsburgs found that between 1750 and 1918, 326 Jewish families had been ennobled in Austria and 350 in Hungary, again in a land where anti-semitism permeated every pore of society and nurtured the young Adolf Hitler.[48] In Russia, ennoblement came automatically, by the so-called 'Table of Ranks', to many thousands of middle-class men in the permanent civil service and other branches of official society: Lenin's father had been ennobled by this process.[49] Between 1825 and 1896 over 50,000 men of non-noble origin had been ennobled.[50]

In Britain, although the middle classes were certainly more powerful – and always had been – than anywhere else, until the twentieth century the granting of a peerage to a businessman was extremely rare. Until the mid-1880s not more than half a dozen businessmen had been ennobled, among them two members of the Baring family in 1835 and 1866 and Edward Strutt, the cotton manufacturer, ennobled as Lord Belper in 1856. Only in the 1880s did the ennoblement of businessmen become something more than a rarity. In that decade, 15 out of 60 non-royal peerage creations went to businessmen, or 25 per cent. This rose to 34 per cent in the decade 1890–9, (22 of 65), 41 per cent in 1900 (27 of 66), and 39 per cent in 1910–19 (45 of 117).[51] Nearly all of these, however, had previously been MPs and many had only tenuous links with active business life. Only in the decades of 1920–9 and 1930–9 did the percentage of new peerages awarded to businessmen exceed 50 per cent, and then only marginally (50.0 and 51.4 per cent, respectively), the others being awards to professional men, Empire administrators, soldiers, and some Labour figures.[52] Thereafter, the percentage of new peers who were businessmen actually declined. Among peerage creations in 1960–70, only 24 per cent were businessmen (56 of 236), and only a minority of these were ennobled *because* of their business activities, as opposed to service in Parliament, chairmanship of a major committee, or other forms of public service.[53] The intolerable feature of the so-called Lloyd George honours scandal was not that rich men bought titles – such has been the case at all times in British history – but that those who did performed no other form of public service of any kind.[54]

Quite conceivably, an investigation of slightly lower ranks on the honours list – baronetcies and knighthoods – would reveal a much greater propensity toward honours for businessmen, and certainly a great many very wealthy businessmen received (in particular) baronetcies, but only after about 1880.[55] Lord Mayors of London were normally offered a baronetcy as a matter of course from about 1860, while prominent Lord Mayors of the larger provincial cities were often

– though not always – offered baronetcies or knighthoods from about 1880. Non-hereditary knighthoods, however, seem to have been chiefly reserved for leading public servants, especially in the Empire and the military, until just before the First World War.[56] Only after the First World War was it really common for a leading businessman or millionaire to receive a title, by which time no real comparison with post-monarchical Europe is possible.

In a variety of ways Britain, in fact, appears to be at one extreme of a common European pattern in terms of the interpenetration of the old and new elites, whatever other differences there obviously were in this matter. On the other hand, Britain differed from the other major European countries as well as from America and most other states in having always possessed a Metropolis unique in its size, importance, and true centrality. In many other ways, too, Britain was unique, and the failure of subsequent historians fully to understand the dimensions of this uniqueness, above all in the application of thoroughly inappropriate ways of examining Britain's recent economic performance, especially by the procrustean bed of industrial and manufacturing output, have caused so many to view this humane, rational, and successful society much more adversely than is warranted by the facts.

Notes

1 The British economy since industrialisation and the 'cultural critique'

1 An important exception to this was Sir John Clapham (1873–1946), author of the classic *An Economic History of Modern Britain* (London, 3 vols, 1926–38), who argued for the slow and gradual nature of the British industrial revolution and its haphazard effects.

2 Carlo M. Cipolla, 'Introduction', *The Fontana Economic History of Europe*, vol. 3, *The Industrial Revolution* (Glasgow, 1973), p. 7.

3 Harold Perkin, *The Origins of Modern English Society, 1780–1880* (London, 1969), pp. 3–4.

4 A vast literature critical of Britain's post-1850 economic performance, especially in the years 1870–1914, includes David S. Landes, *The Unbound Prometheus* (Cambridge, 1972), especially pp. 231–358; A. L. Levine, *Industrial Retardation in Britain, 1880–1914* (New York, 1967); P. L. Payne, *British Entrepreneurship in the Nineteenth Century* (London, 1974); A. R. Hall (ed.), *The Export of Capital from Britain, 1870–1914* (London, 1968); William R. Kennedy, *Industrial Structure, Capital Markets, and the Origins of British Economic Decline* (Cambridge, 1987). Two other works by historians far less critical of Britain's economic performance in this period (indeed, concerned specifically to 'redeem' its good name) should also be read in conjunction: David N. McCloskey, *Enterprise and Trade in Victorian Britain* (London, 1981), and Sidney Pollard, *Britain's Prime and Britain's Decline: The British Economy 1870–1914* (London, 1989).

5 Alan Maddison, *Phases of Capitalist Development* (Oxford, 1982), pp. 8, 161.

6 C. H. Lee, *The British Economy Since 1700* (Cambridge, 1986), p. 5, Table 1.1. On the very low rates of British economic growth during its industrial 'take off,' see N. F. R. Crafts, *British Economic Growth During the Industrial Revolution* (Oxford, 1985).

7 Pollard, op. cit., pp. 13, 15.

8 A useful summary of many of these critiques can be found in David Coates and John Hilliard (eds), *The Economic Decline of Modern Britain: The Debate between Left and Right* (Brighton, 1986).

9 See especially Donald N. McCloskey and Lars G. Sandberg, ' "From Damnation to Redemption": Judgements on the Late Victorian Entrepreneur', in McCloskey, op. cit.; (on textiles) L. G. Sandberg, *Lancashire in Decline: A Study in Entrepreneurship, Technology and International Trade* (Columbus, Ohio, 1874);

(on machine tools) R. C. Floyd, *The British Machine Tool Industry, 1850–1914* (Cambridge, 1976).

10 J. H. Porter, 'Cotton and Wool Textiles', in Neil K. Buxton and Derek H. Aldcroft (eds), *British Industry between the Wars* (London, 1979), Table 1, p. 26.

11 ibid., Tables 2 (p. 27) and 3 (p. 29).

12 J. R. Parkinson, 'Shipbuilding' in ibid., Table 2 (p. 82). The tonnage of all ships built in the United Kingdom for British citizens and companies declined from 975,000 in 1913 to 502,000 in 1922 and to only 84,000 in 1933; in 1937 this figure rose to 518,000 (B. R. Mitchell and Phyllis Deane, *Abstract of British Historical Statistics* (Cambridge, 1931), p. 222).

13 Mitchell and Deane, op. cit., p. 130.

14 David Butler and Gareth Butler, *British Political Facts, 1900–1985* (6th edn, London, 1986), p. 372.

15 ibid., p. 372.

16 Alan A. Jackson, *Semi-Detached London* (London, 1973).

17 Butler and Butler, op. cit., p. 332. The highest six-year total of new homes built by private builders in the post-war period, from 1964 to 1969, was 1,264,000 (ibid., p. 333).

18 Statistics in B. R. Mitchell (ed.), *European Historical Statistics 1750–1975* (2nd edn, London, 1980); Barry Eichengreen, 'The Australian Recovery of the 1930s in International Comparative Perspective', in R. G. Gregory and N. G. Butler, *Recovery from the Depression: Australia and the World Economy in the 1930s* (Cambridge, 1988), which contains much useful comparative data.

19 A point worth bearing in mind is that production figures for the totalitarian regimes given here – Soviet Russia and Nazi Germany – are likely to have been doctored upward for propaganda purposes, especially by the Stalinist regime in the Soviet Union. Britain's (and America's) are, in contrast, presumably accurate.

20 Sidney Pollard, *The Wasting of the British Economy; British Economic Policy, 1945 to the Present* (New York, 1982), p. 2.

21 Apart from the works which have already been mentioned, see P. L. Payne, *British Entrepreneurship in the Nineteenth Century* (London, 1974); and D. H. Aldcroft, 'The Entrepreneur and the British Economy, 1870–1914', *Economic History Review*, 2nd ser., XVII (1964). D. C. Coleman's 'Gentlemen and Players', ibid., XXVI (1973), with its critique of the amateur entrepreneur in the family firm, anticipates Wiener and Barnett but is much more sensible and subtle.

22 Anthony Sampson, *The Changing Anatomy of Britain* (London, 1983), pp. xix–xxi.

23 Corelli Barnett, *The Audit of War: The Illusion and Reality of Britain as a Great Nation* (London, 1986), p. 152.

24 ibid., p. 215.

25 For instance, aircraft production in Britain rose from 7,940 in 1939 to 26,243 in 1943; in Germany the equivalent figures were 8,295 and 24,807. Total armaments production (in 1944 American dollars) rose in Britain from $3.5 billion in 1940 to $11.1 billion in 1943; the German equivalents were $6.0 billion and $13.8 billion. (Cited in Paul Kennedy, *The Rise and Fall of the Great Powers* (London, 1988, pp. 455, 458.)

26 Barnett, op. cit., pp. 259–60.

27 Martin J. Wiener, *English Culture and the Decline of the Industrial Spirit, 1850–1980* (Harmondsworth, 1981), p. 3. It evidently did not occur to Wiener to ask

why, until barely a decade before his book appeared, British success seemed so much more obvious than British failure.

28 ibid., p. 5.
29 ibid.
30 ibid., p. 10.
31 ibid., p. 16. As we shall see in our discussion of education and elsewhere, Wiener is quite wrong in literally every statement in this quotation.
32 ibid., p. 154.
33 See, especially, C. H. Lee, *The British Economy Since 1700: A Macroeconomic Perspective* (Cambridge, 1986); P. J. Cain and A. G. Hopkins, 'Gentlemanly Capitalism and British Expansion Overseas', *Economic History Review*, 2nd ser., XXXIX (November 1986) and XL (February 1987); N. F. R. Crafts, *British Economic Growth Through the Industrial Revolution* (Oxford, 1985); W. D. Rubinstein, *Men of Property: The Very Wealthy in Britain Since the Industrial Revolution* (London, 1981).
34 P. J. Cain and A. G. Hopkins, 'Summary' of 'Gentlemanly Capitalism . . .', op. cit. (November 1986), p. ii.
35 See my 'The Geographical Distribution of Middle Class Income in Britain, 1800–1914', in W. D. Rubinstein, *Elites and the Wealthy in Modern British History* (Brighton, 1987), for more details.
36 Complete county-by-county breakdowns at five-year intervals from 1806 to 1911/12 are given in ibid., 92–6.
37 Stana Nenadic, 'Businessmen, the Urban Middle Classes, and the "Dominance" of Manufacturers in Nineteenth-Century Britain', *Economic History Review*, XLIV, February, 1991.
38 That is, Figure 1.1 records only incomes assessed under Schedules D and E of the nineteenth-century income tax, excluding Schedule A (rental incomes).
39 Rubinstein, *Men of Property*.
40 P. P. 1861 (90) L. 785–90. On this Return and its implications, see W. D. Rubinstein, 'The Size and Distribution of the English Middle Classes in 1860', *Historical Research* 61 (no. 144), February 1988.
41 Harold Perkin, *The Rise of Professional Society: England Since 1880* (London, 1989) p. 80. These figures are taken from the Censuses and are, therefore, based solely on occupational self-definitions provided by respondents. They tell us nothing about the incomes enjoyed by men employed in these groups, or their career success-rates, only about Census figures.
42 Quoted in Harold Perkin, *The Origins of Modern English Society, 1780–1880* (London, 1969), p. 124. Although Professor Perkin most astutely notes the accuracy of this observation, he does not, I fear, see its evident implications for the development of the British economy.
43 Phyllis Deane, *The First Industrial Revolution* (Cambridge, 1965).
44 Youssef Cassis, 'British Finance: Success and Controversy', in J. J. Van Helten and Y. Cassis (eds), *Capitalism in a Mature Economy: Financial Institutions, Capital Exports and British Industry, 1870–1939* (Aldershot, Hants., 1990), p. 2.
45 J. Coakley and L. Harris, *The City of Capital* (Oxford, 1983), p. 4.
46 ibid., p. 5.
47 See, e.g., Geoffrey Ingham, *Capitalism Divided? The City and Industry in British Social Development* (London, 1984).
48 Douglas Jay, *Change and Fortune: A Political Record* (London 1980).
49 R. C. Michie, *The London and New York Stock Exchanges, 1850–1914* (London, 1987).

50 ibid., p. 275.
51 See, for instance, Luther A. Harr, *Branch Banking in England* (Philadelphia, 1929), for a history of banking amalgamation through the 1920s.
52 *American Banker*, 1991, cited in *World Almanac for 1992* (New York, 1991), p. 157.
53 'Why London?' *Economist*, 4 May 1991.
54 One recent work of value on the City, outlining these trends, is David Liston and Nigel Reeves, *The Invisible Economy: A Profile of Britain's Invisible Exports* (London, 1988). See also Hamish McRae and Frances Cairncross, *Capital City: London as a Financial Centre* (London, 1985) and William M. Clarke, *Inside the City: A Guide to London as a Financial Centre* (London, 1983).
55 Especially W. D. Rubinstein, *Men of Property* and *Elites and the Wealthy in Modern British History*.
56 Lee, op. cit., p. 140.
57 For a brief popular summary of these views see Gareth Stedman Jones, 'The Changing Face of 19th Century Britain', *History Today*, May 1991. Some leading economic historians would go even further, questioning whether Britain experienced a 'take-off' into self-sustained economic growth, at least before the railway age. See, e.g., N. F. R. Crafts, *British Economic Growth through the Industrial Revolution* (Oxford, 1985).
58 Phyllis Deane, *The First Industrial Revolution*.
59 See, for instance, Perkin, *Origins*, p. 18.
60 Allison Lockwood, *Passionate Pilgrim: The American Traveler in Great Britain, 1800–1914* (East Brunswick, NJ, 1981), especially pp. 227–49.
61 Peter Laslett, *The World We Have Lost* (London, 1965); W. D. Rubinstein, *Wealth and Inequality in Britain* (London, 1986), pp. 55–72.
62 Derek H. Aldcroft, *The British Economy Between the Wars* (Oxford 1983); John Stevenson, *British Society, 1914–45* (Harmondsworth, 1984).
63 *Statistical Abstract of the United States, 1982–1983*, p. 762.
64 This observation, moreover, takes no account of the relatively high quality of public services in ritain, with a health system, educational system, and (certainly) a public transport network probably still far superior to that in the United States and possibly elsewhere.
65 *Statistical Abstract of the United States*, ibid.

2 British culture and economic performance

1 Martin J. Wiener, *English Culture and the Decline of the Industrial Spirit, 1850–1980* (Harmondsworth, 1981), p. 13.
2 ibid., p. 5.
3 ibid., p. 7.
4 ibid., p. 55.
5 ibid., p. 81.
6 ibid., p. 90.
7 ibid., p. 96.
8 ibid., p. 96.
9 Corelli Barnett, *The Audit of War: The Illusion and Reality of Britain as a Great Nation* (London, 1986), p. 12.
10 Anthony Sampson, *Anatomy of Britain* (London, 1962), pp. 620, 622.
11 See in particular James Raven, 'Viewpoint: British History and the Enter-

prise Culture', *Past and Present*, 123 (May 1989), which summarises the debate at length.

12 Peter F. Drucker, *The Future of Industrial Man: A Conservative Approach* (London, 1943), p. 8.

13 Nikolau Pevsner, *The Englishness of English Art* (London, 1956), p. 15.

14 ibid.

15 Fritz Stern, 'Capitalism and the Cultural Historians' in *Dreams and Delusions: The Drama of Germany History* (New York, 1987), pp. 282–3. See also the interesting essays in F. A. Hayek (ed.), *Capitalism and the Historians* (London, 1954), highlighting the anti-capitalist tradition among economic and cultural historians in Britain, America, and Europe.

16 Fritz Stern, *The Politics of Cultural Despair: A Study of the Rise of the Germanic Ideology* (Berkeley, California, 1961), pp. 65–6.

17 Paul Johnson, 'Berthold Brecht' in *The Intellectuals* (London, 1988), pp. 173–96.

18 Martin Seymour-Smith, *Guide to Modern World Literature* (London, 1975), vol. 2, p. 231.

19 The transformation of Soames's persona begins in an obscure short story by Galsworthy, 'Soames and the Flag', which was not included in the celebrated television series, based on the novels alone. This story concerns Soames's hostility to the populist patriotic anarchy of Mafeking Night during the Boer War, and depicts him sympathetically as a decent old-fashioned liberal.

20 Harold James, 'The German Experience and the Myth of British Cultural Exceptionalism', in Bruce Collins and Keith Robbins (eds), *British Culture and Economic Decline* (London, 1990), pp. 91–128. This essay was written especially for a collection of essays examining the 'cultural critique' of Britain's economy, and in the light of Wiener's book.

21 ibid., p. 104. See also Charles E. McClelland and Steven P. Scher (eds), *Postwar German Culture: An Anthology* (New York, 1974).

22 Neil McKendrick 'Gentlemen and Players Revisited', in Neil McKendrick and R. B. Outhwaite (eds), *Business Life and Public Policy: Essays in Honour of D. C. Coleman* (Cambridge, 1986), pp. 126–7.

23 Alexander Gerschenkron, *Economic Backwardness in Historial Perspective* (Cambridge, Mass., 1962).

24 Cited in A. Milward and S. B. Saul, *The Development of the Economies of Continental Europe, 1850–1914* (London, 1977), Table 1, p. 19.

25 Dolores L. Augustine-Perez, 'Very Wealthy Businessmen in Imperial Germany', *Journal of Modern History*, vol. 22 (1988), Table 1, p. 305. The largest single category among wealth-holders, however, were bankers at 27.1 per cent (136 of 502 persons).

26 British statistics are either those for probate, recording wealth at death, possibly many years after peak economic activity, and the income tax statistics, which are anonymous. These German figures, in contrast, are those for the wealthiest German entrepreneurs at the time, by name.

27 W. D. Rubinstein, 'Entrepreneurial Effort and Entrepreneurial Success: Peak Wealth-holding in Three Societies, 1850–1939', in W. D. Rubinstein, *Elites and the Wealthy in Modern British History* (Brighton, 1987) p. 122; Ronald Hoffman, *et al.* (eds), *The Economy of Early America: The Revolutionary Period, 1763–1790* (Charlottesville, VA, 1988); Carole Shammas, Marylynn Salmon, and Michael Dahlin, *Inheritance in America from Colonial Times to the Present* (New Brunswick, NJ, 1987).

28 Gerald Graff, 'American Criticism Left and Right', in Sacvan Bercovitch and Myra Jehlen, *Ideology and Classic American Literature* (Cambridge, 1986), pp. 96–7.
29 George Nash, *The Conservative Intellectual Movement in America: Since 1945* (New York, 1976), p. 140.
30 Seymour Martin Lipset and Everett Carll Ladd, Jr, 'Jewish Academics in the United States: Their Achievements, Culture and Politics', *American Jewish Yearbook 1971* (New York, 1971), p. 120, reworking of data. The chief purpose of this article was to report on the number and beliefs of Jewish tertiary academics, but for this purpose an enormous sample of 60,028 academics of all religious backgrounds was surveyed, only 8.7 per cent of whom were Jewish. The data in the text refers to all academics in the humanities and social sciences at 'elite' universities.
31 ibid., p. 115.
32 ibid.
33 Hiroshi Minami, *Psychology of the Japanese People* (Toronto, 1971).
34 Robert Guillain, *The Japanese Challenge* (London, 1970), p. 79.
35 On pre-1939 Japan see, for instance, Paul Kennedy, *The Rise and Fall of the Great Powers* (London, 1988), pp. 385–8; G. S. Allen, *A Short Economic History of Modern Japan* (London, 1981).
36 The perhaps cryptic remarks here on Britain are discussed at greater length in Chapter 4.
37 Some of these points are made in Bill Emmott, *The Sun Also Sets: Why Japan Will Not Be Number One* (London, 1989).
38 Mollin Charuka, 'In Defence of Nose Brigades' (*sic*), *Moto* (Gweru, Zimbabwe), March 1991.
39 Geoffrey Gorer, *Exploring English Character* (London, 1955), p. 13–17; Harold Perkin, *Origins of Modern English Society* (London, 1969), p. 169. The essays in the collection edited by Robert Colls and Philip Dodd, *Englishness: Politics and Culture, 1880–1920* (London, 1986) generally suffer from their Marxist approach in viewing 'Englishness' as the deliberately manipulated outcome of a small elite. See also Robert Blake (ed.), *The English World: History, Character and People* (London, 1982); J. B. Priestley, *The English* (London, 1973); Ernest Barker, *National Character and the Factors in its Formation* (London, 1927); and Salvador De Madariaga, *Frenchmen, Englishmen, Spaniards* (Oxford, 1929). A most interesting collection, which should be read by anyone interested in the evolution of British national character, is Francesca M. Wilson (ed.), *Strange Island: Britain Through Foreign Eyes, 1395–1940* (London, 1955).
40 Wiener, op. cit., pp. 27–30, 137–40, etc.
41 D. J. O'Connor (ed.), *A Critical History of Western Philosophy* (New York, 1964), pp. 204–19, 236–74, 341–64.
42 W. D. Rubinstein, *Men of Property* (London, 1981), pp. 145–63.
43 ibid., pp. 150–1. On Germany's Jewish business elite see W. E. Mosse, *Jews in the German Economy: The German-Jewish Economic Elite 1820–1935* (Oxford, 1967).
44 Raymond Williams, 'The Social History of English Writers', in *The Long Revolution* (New York 1961), pp. 236–9.
45 Alan W. Swingewood, 'Intellectuals and the Construction of Consensus in Post-war England', in Alain G. Gagnon, *Intellectuals in Liberal Democracies: Political Influence and Social Involvement* (New York, 1987), p. 87.
46 Perry Anderson, 'Origins of the Present Crisis', *New Left Review*, 23 (1964).
47 Wiener, op. cit., pp. 98–111.

48 Paul Smith, *Disraelian Conservatism and Social Reform* (London, 1962).
49 Mathew Fforde, *Conservatism and Collectivism 1886–1914*, (Edinburgh, 1990), p. 153.
50 Quintin Hogg, *The Case for Conservatism* (London, 1947), Table of Contents, p. 5. These are all chapter titles. Cf. Wiener, op. cit., pp. 110–11, for a very misleading view of Hogg's book.
51 Hogg, op. cit., p. 104.
52 Simon Haxey, *Tory M.P.* (London, 1939), pp. 43–5.
53 See N. Soldon, 'Laissez-faire as Dogma: The Liberty and Property Defence League 1882–1914' and Kenneth D. Brown, 'The Anti-Socialist Union, 1908–1949', both in Kenneth D. Brown (ed.), *Essays in Anti-Labour History: Responses to the Rise of Labour in Britain* (London, 1974).
54 Cited in David Cannadine, *The Decline and Fall of the British Aristocracy* (New Haven, 1990), pp. 221, 222.
55 John Ramsden, *The Age of Balfour and Baldwin, 1902–1940* (London, 1978), p. 361.
56 Weiner, op. cit., p. 48.
57 ibid., p. 100.
58 Fforde, op. cit., p. 153.
59 ibid.
60 From the Constitution of the Labour Party adopted in February 1918; the last three words were added in 1928. The wording is usually attributed to Sidney Webb. See also Maurice Cowling, *The Impact of Labour* (Cambridge, 1971), pp. 15–44.
61 Paul Foot, *The Politics of Harold Wilson* (Harmondsworth, 1968), p. 51.
62 David Coates, *The Labour Party and the Struggle for Socialism* (Cambridge, 1975), p. 52.
63 Cited in Henry Pelling, *The Labour Governments, 1945–51* (London, 1984), p. 215.
64 Coates, op. cit., p. 45.
65 ibid.
66 David Butler and Gareth Butler, *British Political Facts, 1900–1985* (London, 1986), p. 361.
67 Cited in Coates, op. cit., p. 53.
68 Cited in Foot, op. cit., p. 58.
69 See Foot, op cit. Alan Doig, *Westminster Babylon: Sex, Money and Scandal in British Politics* (London, 1990), pp. 201–14, 241–60. When Wilson was elected leader of the Labour party in 1963 on the death of Hugh Gaitskell, Richard Crossman is supposed to have said 'At last we have got a leader who can lie.'
70 See, e.g., Christopher Johnson, *The Economy Under Mrs. Thatcher, 1979–1990* (Harmondsworth, 1991), pp. 27–9.
71 Ralph Miliband, *Parliamentary Socialism* (London, 1973).
72 Wiener, op. cit., p. 20.
73 P. E. Hart, *Studies of Profit, Business Savings and Investment in the United Kingdom, 1920–1962* (London, 1965); W. A. Thomas, *The Finance of British Industry, 1918–1976* (London, 1978); G. D. N. Worswick and D. G. Tipping, *Profits in the British Economy, 1909–1938* (Oxford, 1967).
74 Worswick and Tipping, op. cit., pp. 109–11.
75 ibid.
76 Cited in E. Varga and L. Mendelsohn, *New Data for V. I. Lenin's Imperialism, The Highest Stage of Capitalism* (Sydney, c. 1939), p. 57.

77 Andrew Glyn and Bob Sutcliffe, *British Capitalism, Workers and the Profits Squeeze* (Harmondsworth, 1972), p. 58.

78 ibid.

79 D. C. Coleman, 'Gentlemen and Players', *Economic History Review*, 2nd ser., XXXVI (1973), p. 116. The date here, 1962, coincides with the end of the annual Gentlemen vs. Players cricket match at Lords.

80 Johnson, op. cit., p. 200.

81 ibid.

82 ibid.

83 Some explanations are required here for those unfamiliar with railway terminology. The 'up' Perth sleeping car express was a London-bound train; a 'double-headed' train is one pulled by two locomotives; 'Quintinshill' refers to the terrible crash at Quintinshill, near Gretna in Scotland, in 1915, in which 227 people, mainly soldiers, were killed.

84 H. W. Fowler and F. G. Fowler, *The King's English* (3rd edn, Oxford 1931), p. 4. The older brother, Francis George Fowler, also a Cambridge graduate, died in 1918 of tuberculosis contracted in the First World War.

85 ibid., p. 11.

86 S. N. Eisenstadt (ed.), *The Protestant Ethic and Modernization* (New York, 1968).

87 Significantly in my view Ross McWhirter (1925–75) was an outspoken right-wing activist who was assassinated by the IRA after campaigning vigorously against terrorism, while Guinness is of course one of the largest private companies in Britain.

88 Britain has a flourishing cottage industry in the occult as well; at the present time about half of the bookshops in Bloomsbury appear to be devoted to 'New Age' books and paraphernalia, but there are subtle differences. England seems to stress the studied and benign control of these 'powers', to be altogether more rational and to be lacking in the *National Enquirer* type of repellent tabloid *demi-monde*, all features of American occultery.

89 George Orwell, 'Politics and the English Language', in *Inside the Whale and Other Essays* (Harmondsworth, 1962), p. 145.

90 Sidney Pollard, *Britain's Prime and Britain's Decline: The British Economy 1870–1914* (London, 1989), pp. 115–213. See also Michael Sanderson's *The Universities and British Industry* (London, 1972).

91 Pollard, op. cit., pp. 194–204.

92 In 1980, 57.1 per cent of the population of England and Wales had been baptised into the Church of England, but only 18.5 per cent of the population aged 13 or more had been confirmed and only 5.2 per cent were members of a parochial electoral role. In 1921, the first year for which there are similar statistics, these respective percentages were 62.2, 30.1, and 14.0 (*British Political Facts*, p. 512). Membership in the Baptist Union has declined from 419,000 in 1910 to 222,000 in 1983, of the Congregationalist Union from 494,000 in 1910 to 165,000 in 1971, and of the Methodist Church from 823,000 in 1940 to 459,000 in 1984. (ibid., pp. 514–15). The percentage of marriages in England and Wales performed in a secular ceremony has risen from 15.8 per cent in 1901 to 29.6 per cent in 1962, to 49.0 per cent in 1981, although many of these would presumably be between divorced persons forbidden to marry in a church (ibid., p. 518).

93 Rubinstein, *Men of Property*, pp. 145–62.

94 From Karel Capek, *Letters from England* (1923), cited in Wilson (ed.), *Strange Island*, p. 248.

3 Education, the 'gentleman', and British entrepreneurship

1 Martin J. Wiener, *English Culture and the Decline of the Industrial Spirit, 1850–1980* (Harmondsworth, 1981), pp. 16, 17, 20.

2 Corelli Barnett, *The Collapse of British Power* (London, 1972), pp. 32, 36.

3 Anthony Sampson, *Anatomy of Britain* (London, 1962), p. 180–1.

4 Jonathan Gathorne-Hardy, *The Old School Tie* (New York, 1978), p. 62.

5 ibid.

6 ibid., p. 63. This kind of treatment survived, of course, in modified form for many generations. When Bishop Wilson of Singapore was taken for torturing by the Japanese guards at Changi, he said to himself as the beatings began, 'Well, thank heaven I went to St John's, Leatherhead' – a minor public school for the sons of clergymen, renowned for its severe discipline. (Adrian Hastings, *A History of English Christianity 1920–1985* (London, 1986), p. 385.

7 On the public schools, three books (from a great many) are especially useful: Brian Gardner, *The Public Schools* (London, 1973), a Baedeker-like guide to all public schools, including lists of the most prominent alumni of each; J. R. DeS. Honey's *Tom Brown's Universe* (London, 1977), and Jonathan Gathorne-Hardy, *The Old School Tie* (New York, 1978) are the two best scholarly histories. T. J. H. Bishop and Rupert Wilkinson, *Winchester and the Public School Elite* (London, 1967) is the most interesting study of a particular school. James McConnell, *English Public Schools* (London, 1985) is an interesting up-to-date guide to the history and current situation of twenty-three leading schools.

8 David Ward, 'The Public Schools and Industry in Britain after 1870', *Journal of Contemporary History*, II (July 1967), p. 52.

9 My research assistant in London, Dr Carole Taylor, traced most of the probate valuations for me and obtained birth, marriage, and death certificates for me. I am most grateful for her help. Occasionally, slightly more than 100 entrants were selected due to counting error; all of these were included in the study. The final sample, 1895/1900, generally consisted of two-thirds chosen from 1895 entrants and one-third from 1900 entrants; some alumni books cease in 1899 and only 1895 entrants were used.

10 The 'Clarendon Schools' are the nine leading public schools studied by the Public Schools Commission, established by Parliament in 1861 and headed by Lord Clarendon. The nine schools are Eton, Harrow, Winchester, Rugby, Westminster, Shrewsbury, Charterhouse, Merchant Taylors', and St Paul's. It should be noted that these were of widely differing prestige, with the non-boarding schools, particularly St Paul's and Merchant Taylors', not really schools for the elite.

11 David Butler and Gareth Butler, *British Political Facts, 1900–1985* (London, 1986), p. 83.

12 W. L. Guttsman, *The British Political Elite* (London, 1963), pp. 41, 90.

13 ibid., p. 99.

14 Gardner, op. cit., pp. 161–2.

15 ibid., pp. 43–8.

16 ibid., pp. 128–30.

17 See my article on this question, 'Education and the Social Origins of British Elites 1880–1970', *Past and Present* 112 (August 1986), reprinted in my book of essays, *Elites and the Wealthy in Modern British History* (Brighton, 1987).

18 Bishop and Wilkinson, op. cit., esp. pp. 63–70 and 103–9. See also Edward A. Allen, 'Public School Elites in Early-Victorian England: The Boys at Harrow

and Merchant Taylors' Schools from 1825 to 1850', *Journal of British Studies*, XXI, no. 2 (1982), which attempts this comparison for Harrow and Merchant Taylors' but is much less valuable; being wholly reliant on the very inadequate alumni directories of these schools for its conclusions it may well be misleading. A number of other studies of this subject, by W. J. Reader and T. W. Bamford, will be discussed below.

19 Bishop and Wilkinson, op. cit., pp. 69, 108.

20 ibid., p. 109. Curiously, and most disturbingly, Professor Wiener cites Bishop and Wilkinson's work as the *only* source in support of his statement that 'However many businessmen's sons entered [the public schools], few future businessmen emerged from these schools', despite the fact that Bishop and Wilkinson's research, taken at face value, shows the precise opposite to be true. (Wiener, op. cit., p. 20 and footnote 36.) Neither Barnett nor Sampson provide any statistical evidence of this kind to support their conclusions.

21 Honey, op. cit., p. 297.

22 Cited in Gathorne-Hardy, op. cit., p. 102.

23 B. R. Mitchell and Phyllis Deane, *Abstract of British Historical Statistics* (Cambridge, 1971), pp. 29–31. These figures exclude Ireland, while a good many public school entrants would certainly have been born abroad, e.g. to Indian army officers' families and missionaries.

24 Hartmut Berghoff, 'Public Schools and the Decline of the British Economy 1870–1914', *Past and Present*, 129 (November 1990).

25 ibid., pp. 6–7. Dr Berghoff might be criticised here for not systematically checking these missing 574 businessmen in the alumni registers of the leading public schools. These are readily available at the Institute of Historical Research and the Society of Genealogists in London.

26 ibid., p. 156.

27 ibid., footnote 19.

28 ibid.

29 Philip Stanworth and Anthony Giddens, 'An Economic Elite: Company Chairmen', in P. Stanworth and A. Giddens (eds), *Elites and Power in British Society* (Cambridge, 1974), p. 92.

30 They are not classified with the 'landowners' unless it was clear they owned sufficient land to derive the bulk of their income from that source. Categorising such men as 'gentry' and hence as landowners is a capital mistake in such studies, unless of course it can be demonstrated that they actually owned land. 'Landowners' include farmers. 'Professionals' include full-time military officers.

31 Many more entrants proved impossible to trace than their fathers; their subsequent careers are unknown even to their schools. It seems probable that many of these migrated abroad or were killed in a war. Comprehensive information on these unknown entrants would probably raise the 'business' percentage again.

32 W. J. Reader, *Professional Men: The Rise of the Professional Classes in Nineteenth Century England* (London, 1966), p. 211.

33 Chris Cook and Brendan Keith, *British Historical Facts, 1830–1900* (London, 1975), p. 185.

34 Reader, op. cit., pp. 100–15.

35 Bishop and Wilkinson, op. cit., pp. 64–9; Reader op. cit., Appendix 2, pp. 212–13; T. W. Bamford, *Rise of the Public Schools* (London, 1967), p. 214.

36 See the discussion in my 'Education and the Social Origins of British Elites, 1880–1970'.
37 David Cannadine, *The Decline and Fall of the British Aristocracy* (New Haven and London, 1990), pp. 393–420.
38 Ranald C. Michie, 'The Social Web of Investment in the Nineteenth Century', *Revue Internationale d'Histoire de la Banque*, 18 (1979), p. 169.
39 As with Table 3.2 above, the retail price indexes from which constant values are derived are the Rousseaux Index as given in B. R. Mitchell and Phyllis Deane, *Abstract of British Historical Statistics* (Cambridge, 1971), pp. 471–3, which covers the period 1800–1913, and post-1913 figures from David Butler and Gareth Butler, *British Political Facts, 1900–1985* (London, 1986), pp. 380–2, column 5.
40 Land was excluded entirely from the probate valuations until 1898 and settled realty (i.e. which a person held by pre-existing settlement) until 1926.
41 'Vanishing Race of Millionaires', Melbourne (Australia), *Age*, 15 May 1954.
42 A good many other fathers left £500,000 or more in current terms, both at these schools and the others, especially Eton: many of these were not businessmen but landowners. Hence the probate valuations here are in terms of the average of 1865 and 1885. One entrant in this study, Roger Cunliffe, first Baron Cunliffe (1855–1920) briefly attended Rugby before being transferred to Harrow, and appears in this study as an entrant at both schools.
43 Rupert Wilkinson, *The Prefects: British Leadership and the Public School Tradition* (Oxford University Press, 1964), p. 18. This example has been cited in at least three other studies of this question, including Wiener's book.
44 ibid.
45 Sheila Hodges, *God's Gift: A Living History of Dulwich College* (London, 1981), p. 89. (My italics in text.)
46 James McConnell, *English Public Schools* (London, 1985) pp. 9–10.
47 ibid., pp. 212–13.
48 ibid., p. 74.
49 Philip Stanworth and Anthony Giddens, 'An Economic Elite: A Demographic Profile of Company Chairmen', in Stanworth and Giddens, eds., *Elites and Power in British Society* (Cambridge, 1973), Tables 4 and 5, p. 85.
50 ibid.
51 Anthony Sampson, *The Changing Anatomy of Britain* (London, 1983), p. 300.
52 John Twigg, *A History of Queen's College, Cambridge* (Woodbridge, Suffolk, 1987), Appendix 16, p. 462.
53 ibid.
54 Christopher Brooke, *A History of Gonville and Caius College* (Woodbridge, Suffolk, 1985), pp. 312–13.
55 ibid., pp. 314–15.
56 See, for instance, Michael Sanderson, *The Universities and British Industry, 1850–1970* (London, 1972) and Sidney Pollard, *Britain's Prime and Britain's Decline: The British Economy, 1870–1914* (London, 1989), especially Chapter 3, 'Education, Science and Technology', pp. 115–213.

4 Elites and the evolution of the British economy

1 My views on this subject were first put in 'Wealth, Elites, and the Class Structure of Modern Britain', *Past and Present* 76 (August 1977). the views examined here also have an obvious affinity with those of P. J. Cain and A. G. Hopkins, 'Gentlemanly Capitalism and British Expansion Overseas',

Economic History Review, 2nd ser., XXXIX (1986) and XL (1987), while differing on a number of points. Cain and Hopkins, too, are chiefly examining British imperialism and overseas trade, not the domestic political process.

2 Gerrit P. Judd IV, *Members of Parliament 1734-1832* (originally New Haven, 1955, reprinted Hamden, Conn., 1972), p. 89. See also the 'Introductory Survey' in R. G. Thorne, *The House of Commons 1790-1820* (History of Parliament Trust, London, 1986), esp. pp. 288-92, 297-9, and 300-26, for an interesting discussion of the economic interests of MPs at this time. According to the History of Parliament's research, there were, on average, 111 'merchants, industrialists, and bankers' in Parliaments between 1790 and 1818 – about one-sixth of all MPs – with a high of 125 (of whom 62 were bankers) in 1807 (ibid., p. 318). These figures presumably exclude some types of businessmen, as well as professionals.

3 ibid., p. 88.

4 J. A. Thomas, *The House of Commons 1832-1901: A Study of Its Economic and Functional Character* (Cardiff, 1939). In the 1832 Parliament, for instance, Thomas identifies a total of 608 Whig-Liberal MPs by economic interest, 211 Tory-Conservatives, 64 Radicals, and 51 'Repealers', as he terms the 'Irish Party' (ibid., pp. 3-7). At that election, a total of 479 Whig-Liberals and 179 Tory-Conservatives were elected. See also Gwen Whale, 'The Influence of the Industrial Revolution (1760-1790) on the Demand for Parliamentary Reform', *Transactions of the Royal Historical Society*, 4th ser., 5 (1922), which long ago demonstrated the 'slight influence' (p. 130) that the industrial revolution had on the movement for parlimentary reform.

5 According to John Garrard (citing W. L. Guttsman), the 'combined proportions of bankers, merchants and manufacturers in the House of Commons [in 1831] stood at 24 per cent. In 1865 it was only 23 per cent and in 1874, 24 per cent. Only by 1885 had there been a perceptible rise in the representation of this group – to 38 per cent.' (John Garrard, 'The Middle Classes and Nineteenth Century National and Local Politics', in John Garrard *et al.* (eds), *The Middle Class in Politics* (Farnborough, Hants., c.1979), p. 35).

6 L. B. Namier, *The Structure of Politics at the Accession of George III*, vol. I (London, 1929), p. 106.

7 ibid., pp. 57-8. See also John Cannon, *Aristocratic Century: The Peerage of Eighteenth-Century England* (Cambridge, 1984).

8 W. D. Rubinstein, 'The Structure of Wealth-holding in Britain, 1809-39: A Preliminary Anatomy', *Historical Research*, February 1992.

9 J. C. D. Clark, *English Society 1688-1832* (Cambridge, 1985).

10 Cain and Hopkins, op. cit. Anyone familiar with the rapine and slaughter associated with Britain's economic activities overseas at this time must assume that the authors are being ironical.

11 John Foster, *Class Struggle and the Industrial Revolution* (London, 1974), p. 59. Many large towns were incorporated after 1835.

12 Dennis Smith, *Conflict and Compromise: Class Formation in English Society, 1830-1914* (London, 1982), p. 172; Garrard, op. cit., and his *Leadership and Power in Victorian Industrial Towns 1830-80* (Manchester, 1983); J. Wolff and J. Seed (eds), *The Culture of Capital: Art, Power and the Nineteenth Century Middle Class* (Manchester, 1988). Before 1832 the old Tory regime increasingly turned to free trade, in part because of the influence of businessmen, in part because of the conversion of the Cabinet to *laissez-faire* ideas. See, for instance, William D. Grampp, 'How Britain Turned to Free Trade', *Business History Review*, 61 (1987), which reviews previous research.

13 Smith, op. cit., p.173.
14 Asa Briggs, *Victorian Cities* (London, 1963).
15 Patrick Joyce, *Work, Society, and Politics: The Culture of the Factory in Later Victorian England* (London, 1982); John Foster, op. cit., p. 205.
16 Keith Robbins, 'John Bright and the Middle Class in Politics', in Garrard *et al.* (eds.), op.cit., p. 32.
17 ibid.
18 James P. Cornford, 'The Parliamentary Foundations of the Hotel Cecil', in R. Robson (ed.), *Ideas and Institutions of Victorian Britain* (London, 1867); Garrard, op. cit.
19 Foster, op. cit., pp. 161–93.
20 I. G. Doolittle,. *The City of London and Its Livery Companies* (Dorchester, 1982); Y. Cassis, *Les Banquiers de la City à l'Epoque Edouardienne* (Geneva, 1984). The statement here about the failure of genuinely wealthy city financiers to be represented among the City's civic elite is based upon an as yet unpublished study by the author (W. D. Rubinstein) of Lord Mayors of London, 1832–1914.
21 J. A. Thomas, op. cit., pp. 6, 14.
22 Cassis, op. cit.
23 R. A. Pumphrey, 'The Introduction of Industrialists into the British Peerage: A Study in the Adaptation of a Social Institution', *American Historical Review*, LXV (1959–60); F. M. L. Thompson, *English Landed Society* (London, 1963); W. D. Rubinstein, 'The Evolution of the British Honours System Since the Mid-Nineteenth Century', in *Elites and the Wealthy in Modern British History* (Brighton, 1987).
24 Thomas, op. cit.
25 W. L. Guttsman, *The British Political Elite* (London, 1963), p. 41.
26 ibid., pp. 38, 79.
27 Harold Perkin, *The Rise of Professional Society: England Since 1880* (New York, 1989), pp. 40–5.
28 Peter Marsh, *The Discipline of Popular Government* (Hassocks, 1978); Eric Akers-Douglas, Viscount Chilston, *Chief Whip: The Political Life and Times of Aretas Akers-Douglas, 1st Viscount Chilston* (London, 1961); Kenneth D. Wald, *Crosses on the Ballot: Pattern of British Voter Alignment Since 1885* (Princeton, 1983); Henry Pelling, *Social Geography of British Elections 1885–1910* (New York, 1967).
29 Paul Smith, *Disraelian Democracy and Social Reform* (London, 1967).
30 David Cannadine, *The Decline and Fall of the British Aristocracy* (New Haven, Conn., 1990).
31 Assuming, as I now believe, that the First World War did not mark a *fundamental* break in the chronology. For a very important and useful series of essays making the point that British power did not decline significantly until after the Second World War, see the four articles in the *International History Review*, XIII, no. 4 (November 1991): Gordon Martel, 'The Meaning of Power: Rethinking the Decline and Fall of Great Britain'; Keith Nelson, '"Greatly Exaggerated": The Myth of the Decline of Great Britain Before 1914'; John R. Ferris, '"Greatest Power on Earth": Great Britain in the 1920s'; and B. J. C. McKercher, '"Our Most Dangerous Enemy": Britain Pre-eminent in the 1930s'.
32 The percentage of 14-year-olds enrolled in secondary school rose from only 38 per cent in 1938 to 100 per cent in 1962, the percentage of 17-year-olds from 4 per cent (*sic*) in 1938 to 15 per cent in 1962 and 26 per cent in 1970, and of 19-year-olds from 2 per cent in 1938 to 7 per cent in 1962 and 13 per

cent in 1970. University students rose in numbers from 20,000 in 1900/1 to 50,000 in 1938/9 to 118,000 in 1962/3 and to 235,000 in 1970/1. David Butler and Gareth Butler, *British Political Facts, 1900–1985* (London, 1986), p. 342.

33 S. Fothegill and G. Gudgin, *Unequal Growth: Urban and Regional Employment Change in the U.K.* (London, 1982); C. M. Law, *British Regional Development Since World War I* (Newton Abbot, 1980); Wayne Parsons, *The Political Economy of British Regional Policy* (London, 1988); David Smith, *North and South: Britain's Growing Divide* (London, 1989).

34 See, for instance, Perkin, *Rise of Professional Society*, pp. 472–519.

35 *1987/88 OECD Economic Surveys: United Kingdom* (Paris, 1988).

36 *1990/91 OECD Economic Surveys: United Kingdom* (Paris, 1991), pp. 11, 80–8.

37 ibid., pp. 66, 105.

38 This is suggested, in effect, by Harold Perkin in *The Rise of Professional Society*, pp. 516–19, although his further suggestion that this corresponds with the contemporary south vs. north divide seems more dubious, since the roof bodies of most of the professional elites are also in London, as are many of their members.

39 Guttsman, op. cit., p. 313. In 1957–8 the twenty-seven members of the '1922 Committee' included 22 per cent who had attended Eton and Harrow and 22 per cent who had attended another top public school. In 1961 among the Tory ministry of thirty-six, the respective percentages here were 35 and 32. The 1922 Committee also included far more businessmen, self-made men, and, interestingly, women (ibid).

40 Francis Wey, *Les Anglais Chez Eux* (1856), in Francesca M. Wilson (ed.), *Strange Island: Britain Through Foreign Eyes, 1395–1940* (London, 1955), p. 214.

41 E. A. Wrigley, 'A Simple Model of London's Importance in Changing English Society and Economy, 1650–1750', *Past and Present*, 37 (1967).

42 In fields where London did not actually contain the physical centre of activity, these too were often near by – for instance the two old universities and the major naval ports. *Only* manufacturing industry genuinely developed elsewhere, and then only for a time.

43 This view is advanced simultaneously in my 'New Men of Wealth and the Purchase of Land in Nineteenth-Century Britain', *Past and Present*, 92 (1981), and in Lawrence Stone and Jeanne C. Fawtier Stone, *An Open Elite? England 1540–1880* (Oxford, 1984). These findings have generated an enormous volume of debate, for instance by F. M. L. Thompson, 'Life After Death: How Successful Nineteenth-Century Businessmen Disposed of Their Fortunes', *Economic History Review*, 2nd ser., XLIII (1990) and his 'Desirable Properties: The Town and Country Connection in British Society Since the Late Eighteenth Century', *Historical Research*, LXIV (1991), and Martin Daunton, 'Gentlemanly Capitalism and British Industry, 1820–1914', *Past and Present*, 122 (1989), to which I have responded, *inter alia*, in 'Cutting Up Rich: A Response to F. M. L. Thompson', *Economic History Review*, 1992, and 'Businessmen into Landowners: The Question Revisited', in R. Quinalt and N. Harte (eds), *Land and Society* (Manchester, 1992).

44 Anthony Howe, *The Cotton Masters 1830–1860* (Oxford, 1984), pp. 32, 29–30. On the other hand, see Richard Trainor, 'The Gentrification of Victorian and Edwardian Industrialists' in A. L. Beier, David Cannadine, and James M. Rosenheim (eds), *The First Modern Society: Essays in Honour of Lawrence Stone* (Cambridge 1989), for an interesting defence of the notion of the 'partial gentrification' (p. 195) of late Victorian industrialists.

45 W. E. Mosse, *Jews in the German Economy: The German-Jewish Economic Elite 1820–1935* (Oxford, 1987), p. 83.

46 ibid, p. 85.

47 Dolores L. Augustine-Perez, 'Very Wealthy Businessmen in Imperial Germany', *Journal of Modern History*, 22 (1988), pp. 303–4. The data is derived from the famous *Yearbook of Millionaires*, published in 1912–13 by Richard Martin, based upon 1911 taxation data. Many prominent German businessmen declined ennoblement, including Albert Ballin and Carl Fürstenberg.

48 William O. McCagg, 'Austria's Jewish Nobles, 1740–1918', *Leo Baeck Yearbook XXXIV* (London, 1989), p. 163.

49 Jerome Blum, 'Russia' in David Spring (ed.), *European Landed Elites in the Nineteenth Century* (Baltimore, 1977).

50 ibid. p. 71.

51 W. D. Rubinstein, 'The Evolution of the British Honours System Since the Mid-Nineteenth Century', in Rubinstein, *Elites and the Wealthy*, op. cit., p. 236.

52 ibid.

53 ibid.

54 ibid. pp. 243–4.

55 ibid., p. 238.

56 John Scott, *The Upper Classes: Property and Privilege in Britain* (London, 1982), p. 110, citing F. M. L. Thompson, 'Britain' in David Spring (ed.), *European Landed Elites in the Nineteenth Century* (Baltimore, 1977).

INDEX

Webb, Sidney 71
Weber, Max 92
Wey, Francis 157
Whitehall 19
Wilkinson, Rupert 112, 123, 135
Wilson government 83-4, 152

Wiener, Martin J. 16, 21-4, 45-6, 48, 56-7, 72, 77, 79, 85, 102, 120
Winchester (school) 105-34

Yorkshire: industry in 36; middle classes of 25-32